A. H. Hermann

A HISTORY OF
The Czechs

ALLEN LANE

Copyright © A. H. Hermann 1975

First published in 1975

Allen Lane
Penguin Books Ltd
17 Grosvenor Gardens, London SW1

ISBN 0 7139 0486 0

Printed in Great Britain by
Richard Clay (The Chaucer Press) Ltd
Bungay, Suffolk
Set in Linotype Plantin

1

Contents

ACKNOWLEDGEMENTS

I would like to dedicate this book to the memory of Dr Tomáš Voldřich, Headmaster of Reálka in Prague VII, who taught me to view historical events as results of economic and political forces not very different from those which confront us today. I am also greatly obliged to my wife who has much helped me by sharing my interest in history though not always my views, and without whose criticism, expressed or merely anticipated by me, the book would have many more shortcomings. She has also contributed to it by compiling the index. My thanks are also due to the *Financial Times*, who very generously gave me freedom to arrange the timing of my work for them so that this book could be completed.

It was Mr Peter Carson of Allen Lane who persuaded me to attempt a complete history instead of writing only about events which I myself have witnessed, and as a patient and understanding editor encouraged and helped me in a task which I found somewhat overwhelming but greatly enjoyed. Finally, I would like to acknowledge gratefully the assistance received from Mrs Lois Warner who volunteered to type the manuscript of the first two parts in its early stages and helped to solve some of the language problems which it presented.

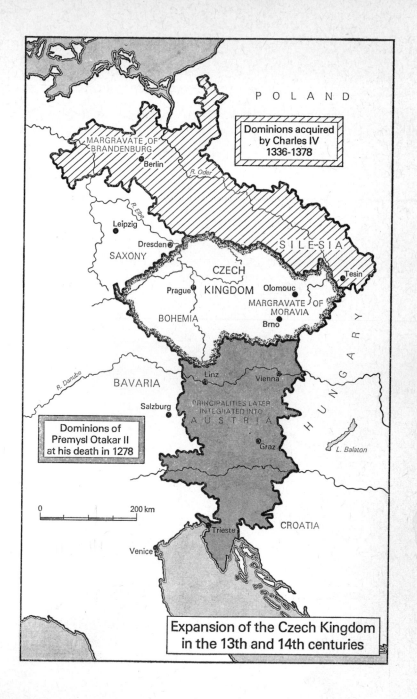

POLAND

Dominions acquired
by Charles IV
1336-1378

MARGRAVATE OF
BRANDENBURG

Berlin

R. Oder

R. Elbe

Leipzig

Dresden

SAXONY

CZECH

KINGDOM

Prague

BOHEMIA

S I L E S I A

Tesin

Olomouc

MARGRAVATE OF
MORAVIA

Brno

R. Danube

BAVARIA

Linz

Vienna

H U N G A R Y

Salzburg

PRINCIPALITIES LATER
INTEGRATED INTO
A U S T R I A

Graz

L. Balaton

Dominions of
Přemysl Otakar II
at his death in 1278

0   200 km

Trieste

CROATIA

Venice

Expansion of the Czech Kingdom
in the 13th and 14th centuries

Habsburg lands about 1786

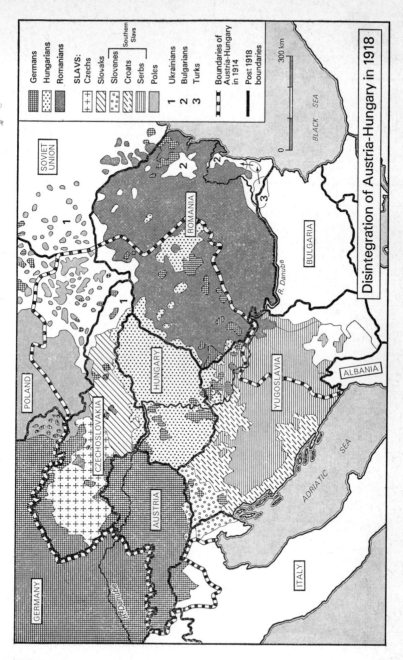

Disintegration of Austria-Hungary in 1918

Germans
Hungarians
Romanians

SLAVS:
Czechs
Slovaks
Slovenes ⎱ Southern
Croats ⎰ Slavs
Serbs
Poles

1 Ukrainians
2 Bulgarians
3 Turks

Boundaries of Austria-Hungary in 1914

Post 1918 boundaries

0 ——— 300 km

SOVIET UNION

POLAND

CZECHOSLOVAKIA

GERMANY

AUSTRIA

HUNGARY

ROMANIA

YUGOSLAVIA

BULGARIA

ALBANIA

ITALY

BLACK SEA

ADRIATIC SEA

R. Danube

R. Danube

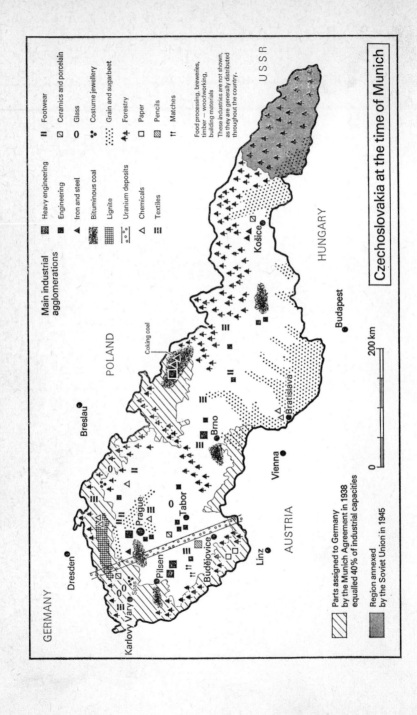

Czechoslovakia at the time of Munich

Main industrial agglomerations

▨ Heavy engineering	‖ Footwear
▨ Engineering	▨ Ceramics and porcelain
▲ Iron and steel	○ Glass
▓ Bituminous coal	•: Costume jewellery
▦ Lignite	∴ Grain and sugarbeet
○°° Uranium deposits	⋏ Forestry
△ Chemicals	☐ Paper
▦ Textiles	▨ Pencils
	↑↑ Matches

Food processing, breweries, timber — woodworking, building materials

These industries are not shown, as they are generally distributed throughout the country.

Parts assigned to Germany by the Munich Agreement in 1938 equalled 40% of industrial capacities

Region annexed by the Soviet Union in 1945

0   200 km

GERMANY
Dresden
Breslau
POLAND
Karlovy Vary
Spas
Pilsen
Prague
Tabor
Budějovice
Coking coal
Brno
Linz
Vienna
Bratislava
AUSTRIA
Košice
HUNGARY
Budapest
USSR

Introduction

When Europe has been under severe stress, the cracks have invariably shown first in what is now Czechoslovakia. Such was the case in 1418 when the Czechs revolted against the Roman Church; in 1618 when they revolted against the Habsburgs and started the Thirty Years War; in 1938 when France betrayed its alliance in a vain attempt at making peace with Hitler; in 1948 when the Communists took over in Prague – the first move in the Cold War; and finally in 1968.

The Czechoslovak Republic straddles a line which has divided Europe into a West and an East since prehistoric times: the ice cap stretching from the North Pole and the ice cap covering the Alps met in Moravia, separating Bohemia in the west from Slovakia in the east. The different varieties of plants and animals which evolved on either side of this ice barrier are still in evidence.

Right up to the end of the nineteenth century the quadrangle of forest-covered mountains enclosing Bohemia made it a fortress. Whoever controlled this natural fortress – whether they were chiefs, Czech kings or foreign conquerors – had a privileged position in Central Europe. For this reason a Central European confederation focused on Bohemia existed in various forms long before the Habsburgs came to the Czech throne in 1526. After the defeat and disintegration of the Habsburg Empire in 1918, the new republic became the unfortunate buffer between the polarized powers of East and West Europe, for even in the twentieth century, the age of rapid communications and nuclear disarmament, geographical factors are not insignificant.

Czechoslovakia has felt more than the usual amount of stress in the present century. Since 1948 its politics have been dictated from the East, while its economic structure and cultural traditions are those of the West and its political clock has long been about 100 years ahead of Moscow's; the country's early industrial development produced a well-organized working class in the second half of the nineteenth century.

In the period between the two world wars the Communist Party was illegal in Poland, Hungary, Romania, Bulgaria and after 1933, in Germany and after 1945 Communist governments in these countries could be formed only out of small conspiratorial groups completely relying on the support of the Soviet Army. By contrast, the Czechoslovak Communists had behind them many years of parliamentary experience and many followers among the intellectuals. As a result the Kremlin found things both easier and more difficult in Czechoslovakia after 1945: easier because it found there a Communist Party existing in its own right and a population which had no grudge against the Russians and was appreciative of the Soviet contribution to the defeat of Nazi Germany; more difficult because this Communist Party and population had strong democratic traditions of their own and had to be purged and terrorized much more severely into toeing the Moscow line.

By 1968 Czechoslovakia had become a test case for the potential of Communism in an advanced industrial country with liberal traditions. The outcome indicates that attempts to adjust Communism to fit the conditions of an advanced country are not allowed by the Soviet Union. The country was forced to accept a regime dispensed from Moscow, a regime which seems to be getting much too repressive even for Soviet Communists.

In relation to the West, the Soviet invasion of 1968 was the first consequence of the then newly gained certainty that the West would not be the first to use nuclear weapons and that any further increase in Soviet conventional forces in Central Europe would oblige Western European countries either to go to the expense of making up the deficiencies in their forces or to try to buy a Soviet withdrawal with political and economic concessions. The Soviet willingness to talk disarmament if the U.S. will talk business has been clearly spelled out during Mr Brezhnev's visit to President Nixon in 1973. Moscow anticipates, perhaps, that the defence of Western Europe will be borne increasingly by the European partners of N.A.T.O., who will therefore be more amenable to the adoption of a Soviet-linked European policy. But it is still uncertain whether it will be possible to construct a stable security system without a neutral zone in Central Europe.

If the dissolution of Austria–Hungary left the Czechs exposed to the power of Germany or Russia, the sharing of Czechoslovakia with the Slovaks added internal tensions to their troubles. The difference between these two ethnically close groups could not be greater as regards economy, political aims or way of life. The Czechs as a nation had passed through the mill of Central European history and in modern times reached a high level of industrialization and a cultural identity before they regained the independence lost three hundred years earlier. Quality of life became their supreme consideration, more important than ideologies or national sovereignty. Seen from Prague, there was little difference between Hitler and Stalin and the merger between the State and the big business seemed dehumanizing regardless of the way it was achieved. Slovaks had a different set of values and different needs.

While geographic conditions speeded up the formation of the Czech state in the eleventh century and contributed to its key role in European politics in the fourteenth century, their effect on Slovakia was quite the opposite. The Slovaks never had a state of their own. Most of Slovakia is covered by the Carpathian mountains: the east–west chain is steepest in the north, separating Slovaks from the ethnically related Poles; the White Carpathians reach almost to the Danube along Slovakia's western frontier thus separating it from the Czechs. The country slopes southward into Hungary, and for the greater part of its history was simply a source of cheap labour and timber for the rich Hungarian plain.

Thus in 1918 Slovakia was still an underdeveloped region. It had a thin layer of Slovak intelligentsia, who were ambitious and nationalistic but infected with the Gentlemen and Players mentality and sharp divisiveness of Hungarian society. There could be no greater contrast to the bureaucratically sober mentality of the Czechs.

This psychological difference stemmed from different social structures combined with a different historical experience and made the two regions divide completely when Hitler invaded Czechoslovakia in 1939. The nationalists among the Slovak politicians readily gave up Czechoslovakia and started to collaborate with Hitler for the price of a separate puppet state of their own.

In spite of considerable industrialization of Slovakia, the same forces remained thirty years later, and the Czechs and Slovaks adopted greatly different sets of priorities in the spring of 1968. In 1968, the Slovak leaders, though Communists, were no less separatists. Federalization of the country and the creation of a separate Slovak republic were for them the foremost aim of the reforms. For the Czechs, however, the emphasis lay elsewhere: for them reforms were to bring about a greater economic efficiency, a better life and greater personal freedom. But their aspirations were all doomed. In the absence of a Central European power the decision was with the two Superpowers. The Soviet Union and the West agreed that Czechoslovakia should remain east of the line dividing the two parts of Europe.

PART I

400 B.C.—1620

Early Slav states in Central Europe

Gaelic, German and Slav settlers

Present-day Czechoslovakia consists of three geographically well defined regions. Bohemia in the west and Moravia in the centre are inhabited by Czechs; Slovakia, in the east, is inhabited by Slovaks. Czechs and Slovaks, who now consider themselves ethnically separate, speak two Slavonic languages between which there is very little difference. Anyone who knows the one will easily understand the other.

The names used in the Western world for the three regions, the Gaelic 'Bohemia' on the one hand and the Slavonic 'Moravia' and 'Slovakia' on the other, indicate that these regions entered European history at different times. 'Bohemia' has no equivalent in the Czech language, in which the region is called 'Čechy'. Around 1800 some Czech political writers used the term 'Bohemians' to embrace both the Czech-speaking and the German-speaking population of the kingdom, but the term never caught on. The term 'Czech republic', introduced after federalization in 1968, covers the western part inhabited by Czechs in Bohemia, Moravia and Silesia.

The name 'Bohemia' is derived from the original Gaelic inhabitants, called 'Boii' by the Romans, who settled there after 400 B.C. The Latin name for their country, 'Boiohemum', was transformed later into the German 'Böhmen' and the English 'Bohemia'. The Gaelic tribes remained in Bohemia for some 400 years, though when and how they vanished is no more certain than when and how they arrived. Until recently the only signs of their occupation were the Gaelic names of the country and of a few mountains and rivers. Now, as excavators and bulldozers used in constructing motorways, river dams and tower blocks uncover deeper layers of earth, new

evidence of their culture is coming to light – furnaces for the smelting of metal, metal tools, beautiful jewellery, and ceramic and glass
beads. Finds of coins minted by the Boii indicate that they had a
fairly advanced civilization with some degree of market economy or
at least external trade.

How this Gaelic population was subjugated, absorbed, killed off
or chased out of the country by the Germanic tribes moving into
Central Europe is not known. We can only conclude that the superior Gaelic civilization, with a more advanced economy, was unable
to resist being taken over by the more primitive, but probably also
more bellicose, new arrivals. Around the beginning of our era two
Germanic tribes gained complete control of the territory: the
Marcomans in Bohemia and the Kvades further east in Moravia and
in part of Slovakia.

In this period Germanic tribes began massing all along the northern frontiers of the Roman Empire, first attracted by its wealth and
later encouraged by its inner weakness. Several attempts were
made to unite them under leaders controlling a larger territory. In
Bohemia, a state-like organization was established in the first
century by a Marcoman ruler called Marobud whose seat was in the
southern part of the country, of which the town of Budějovice is now
the centre. At about the same time a similar organization was established in Moravia and the western part of present Slovakia by the
Kvades and their ruler Vannia. Both Marcomans and Kvades fought
the Romans and between wars had some relations with Rome, probably through Vindobona, the present Vienna. Marobud's son spent a
number of years at Augustus's court in Rome – one can think of
him as hostage and student at the same time. This indicates that
their contacts with the Romans were not restricted to commanders
of the Danube garrisons. The Marcomans and the Kvades are
believed to have perished (at least those of them who could carry
arms) in the 'Battle of Nations' at Châlons-sur-Marne around
450.

The Slav tribes had started to drift westwards into the region
between Visla and Dnieper almost a thousand years before the Germanic invaders wrecked the Roman Empire. When the German
tribes had settled, the Slavs were slowly moving further west, and,
though it can hardly be imagined that this migration was entirely
peaceful, pottery and arms of Germanic and Slav origin found side

by side indicate that, in some places at least, the newcomers lived peacefully with the old settlers.

In the territory of present-day Czechoslovakia the Slav tribes became the dominant population at some time in the fifth century. It is uncertain whether they arrived as an agricultural people, pushed out of their settlements in the east by some population explosion, or whether they took to agriculture only after they had settled on the land prepared for them by their Gaelic and German predecessors.

Czech children are told in primary school the old saga of Čech, the chieftain who brought his people to Bohemia; surveying the country from the mountain of Říp, a bell-shaped volcanic hill some forty miles north of Prague, he said: 'This is the country overflowing with milk, butter and honey, this is where we shall stay.' Echoes of this, mostly ironical, can frequently be encountered in modern Czech literature and conversation.

Samo's Empire, Great Moravia and the separation of Czechs and Slovaks

The First Čech who could be blamed for settling his people in such an exposed spot is, of course, only a legendary figure. In those times the Czechs were one of many Slav tribes moving into Bohemia and many centuries passed before they attained nationhood. But even before they did, the now familiar patterns of Central European politics had begun to take shape in a rudimentary form. Already the tribes of Central Europe could live in relative freedom only by forming a confederation. They could survive without it, but only in those short and transitional periods when both the eastern and western powers of Europe were simultaneously in an internal crisis. At all other times these big powers whatever different names they assumed in the course of the last 1,500 years, tended to advance towards each other, bringing the little countries of Central Europe under their sway until they met and let the iron curtain fall between them.

In the seventh century, the early Slav period of Central Europe, the line dividing Europe into east and west was pushed far to the east. A shortlived merchant empire organized by Samo, a Frankish trader, extended to the fertile plains of Pannonia, including present-day Slovakia and Hungary. This 'empire' could hardly have been more than a series of agreements with local headmen, agreements designed to protect trading routes and depots, but it gained historical importance because it established the first system of communication between the previously isolated Slav tribes and enabled them to join forces in defending their settlements against the invasion of the Avars – after the Huns the second Mongol invasion that penetrated deep into Europe. The Avars turned back and disappeared without trace. Only the Czech word 'obr' for 'giant' suggests that they were of bigger stature than the Slavs – unless it was fear that made them seem so big.

The fear of Mongolian invaders led to the creation by Charlemagne of a military zone on the eastern border of his empire, the East Mark on the Danube, today's Austria. A little later the first Slav empire was formed on what had been Samo's territory. Constantine Porphyrogenitus, the contemporary ruler of Byzantium, called it Great Moravia.

Driving from Vienna to Brno, capital of modern Moravia, and turning east before reaching the township of Mikulov, one arrives at the village of Mikulčice, which in the ninth century was a city crowded into an extraordinary assembly of stone churches and palaces; their foundations have only recently been excavated. Apart from the River Danube and its tributary the Morava to the south and west, and the low range of the White Carpathian mountains to the east, no defence lines can be seen in the immediate vicinity. This must have been the site of a city or at least of a large settlement. It is believed that contemporary French sources referring to a 'fantastic fortress', more populous than contemporary Paris, were in fact describing this settlement. From this centre, not far from Vindobona (Vienna), Great Moravia spread eastwards to embrace present-day Slovakia, Hungary and western Poland and westwards to take in Lusatia and Bohemia, and thence northwards to the area of modern Berlin. Great Moravia must have been a rather loose empire, transitional in character, like the one made by the Western Goths 500 years earlier. Nevertheless it produced a dynasty whose horizon included both Byzantium and Rome, and a strong ruler, Svatopluk, who achieved recognition of his empire from the Frankish emperors.

To avert the influence of the Bavarian episcopate from Great Moravia, its rulers asked for Christian missionaries first from Rome and then from Byzantium. Brothers Cyril and Methodius, the two missionaries sent by the Eastern Church, brought in not only religion but also a script derived from Greek for the use of Slav tribes in the Balkans. With some modification this script is still used by Russians, Serbs and Bulgarians today. Old Slavonic, the language from which the modern Slavonic languages are derived, is no longer spoken but has survived in the Orthodox Churches' liturgy.

The introduction of the Slavonic liturgy in Great Moravia was opposed by Rome as an infringement of its zone of interest in which Latin was to be the only international language: Cyril was taken to Rome and detained there till the end of his life. A long diplomatic struggle with Rome reflected the alternating fortunes in the power contest between Great Moravia and the Eastern Franks. The Pope later approved the Slavonic liturgy and appointed Methodius as Archbishop of Pannonia in 869 and of Moravia in 880. But after Methodius death in 885, shortly after Svatopluk had made peace with Emperor Charles III, Roman priests, and with them the Bavarian episcopate, got the upper hand.

Both Samo's merchant empire and Great Moravia were essentially Central European powers. The first had links with Western Europe and functioned as a defensive organization against the Avars; the second was looking to the east for cultural support and trade, but not exclusively. Great Moravia was soon weakened by its great territorial expanse – and by peace. The productivity of its economy was so low that a permanent military establishment could be maintained only on the spoils of war. This first Slav empire crumbled before the next invasion from the east, by the Magyars who occupied Pannonia (present-day Slovakia and Hungary) at the beginning of the tenth century and ruled over the Slovaks – apart from a brief period at the beginning of the eleventh century – until 1918.

Though the final blow came from the east, by 900 Great Moravia must also have been weakened by the gradual integration of the Slav tribes of Bohemia. One of these, the Czechs (originally only the name of the ruling class of the tribe) settled on the River Vltava and produced a dynasty which ruled central Bohemia from Vyšehrad, a rocky fortress in the southern part of modern Prague. While the Moravian rulers looked to Byzantium, the Czechs established their first international link with the Western Church: fourteen Czech chiefs were baptized in Regensburg in 845. The political integration of Bohemia (sheltered as it was against interference from east and west by its rectangle of forest-covered mountains) by the Czechs then proceeded rapidly through conquest and often wholesale slaughter of other tribal groups.

The centralization of power in the hands of an emerging Czech dynasty, the Premyslids, became an important factor when the Germans developed an interest in the western region of Great Moravia – at a time when the Magyars were over-running its eastern wing. The Czech Prince Václav, the patron saint of the Czechs, (Good King Wenceslas to the English) could already negotiate from a position of relative strength. He bought his peace with the Germans, called by the Czechs 'Němci' i.e. dumb people, by agreeing to pay a small annual tribute of 200 oxen and 30 lots of silver, now proverbial among the Czechs. Another faction, led by his brother Boleslav, felt that even this concession was not necessary and had Václav murdered, in about 935.

Václav was probably a ruthless and intelligent tribal chief who appreciated the advantages of being associated with a Christian civilization. He also appears to have made an efficient use of the time he bought from the Eastern Franks to complete the subjugation of the other Slav tribes in Bohemia. This, of course, is no more than a plausible hypothesis. Because so little is known, legends abound, and Václav became an object of political mythology. Yet the picture of the appeasement-seeking Václav succeeded by the belligerent Boleslav fits well with what is known about the change in Germany. Václav could only remain passive when Henry, ruler of the Saxon Othonian empire, having secured his western flank by establishing friendly relations with Burgundy and Anglo-Saxon England, turned his offensive power eastwards. After making Václav agree to the annual tribute, he captured Brenabor (Brandenburg) from the Western Slavs on the River Elbe in 929 and defeated the Magyars at the River Unstrub in 933.

Under Henry's successor, Otto I, the tide changed. Otto was at war with France and the pressure emanating from Byzantium into the Balkans and Central Europe neutralized German supremacy, so that Boleslav could well afford a stiffer attitude and, while fighting Otto, reach out for the leading role in the zone contested by east and west. Central European integration must have appeared all the more necessary after the Byzantine conquest of the Bulgarian Balkan empire, in order to prevent further Byzantine advance into the former Great Moravia and Russia. The Magyars had their expansion directed westwards and repeatedly raided Czech and German territory, causing them to link their forces. In 955, however, the combined armies of the Czechs, Bavarians, Swabians and Franks, led by Otto I, defeated the Magyars at the Lech. This important victory was followed by a reconstitution of the Ostmark (Austria) and the establishment of the kingdom of Hungary. The two-pronged German drive eastwards – through Austria in the south and across the Elbe in the north – dates from this time: Otto I intended Magdeburg to be a German Rome linking Germany with Eastern Europe.

The equestrian statue which dominates Wenceslas Square in Prague (and which became the focal point of anti-Soviet demonstrations after the Russian occupation in August 1968) presents the image of a patron saint and a warrior prince whose aim was peace. An old choral hymn recalled in time of danger opens with the incantation, 'St Václav, preserve us and those who come after us.' As the first Czech prince who embraced Christianity of western origin, St Václav also stands in Czech political symbolism for Western influence – even for collaboration with the Germans. In the context of Czech politics Saint or Prince Václav has thus many different connotations; but never the jolly image of the 'Good King Wenceslas' of the English carol.

The Czech quest for Central European power

From the time the Czech state emerged on the threshold of history the double danger from east and west was the threat to its existence. At the beginning of the thirteenth century, 300 years after the Magyars settled on the Danube, the Tartars invaded Europe, and in another 300 years the Turkish empire threatened Central Europe. For almost 300 years the Turks held the 'soft underbelly' of Europe until they were pushed out by the Russian empire which then became the expansionist power in the east and finally advanced into Central Europe in 1945.

From the west, the independence of the Czechs and the Poles was always threatened by the Germans. Václav made his peace with the Germans and was assassinated. His brother Boleslav attempted another solution: the establishment of a larger Central European state including Bohemia, Moravia, Poland and Hungary. This confederation was to be reconstructed several times in the course of history under Czech, Polish or Hungarian kings. From 1526 to 1918 it was known as the Habsburg Empire.

Boleslav I's rule extended from Prague to the Polish Krakow and his son, Boleslav II, claimed control of territory reaching to the frontiers of the Ukraine, ruled by the Russian princes from Kiev. If we realize how sparsely populated Europe was at that time and how small were the military forces involved in such wide-ranging conquests, we are probably justified in taking these claims with a pinch of salt. The Czech princes could hardly have controlled much more than the trade route between Central Europe and Kiev – though this, of course, was of some importance. Ibrahim ben Jakob, member of a Spanish mission visiting Central Europe in the 960s, described the Prague of his time as a meeting place of merchants arriving from Russia, the Balkans and the Middle East. The Czech exports of that time were horses and slaves: their home economy was based on subsistence farming. The silver dinars minted by Boleslav and his son confirm the existence of an international business centre in Prague where the south–north and east–west trade routes crossed – and perhaps also some international aspirations of the Prague princes.

After the death of Boleslav II the struggle for succession among the various members of the Premyslid dynasty greatly weakened the military potential of the Czechs and leadership in the Central European arena passed to the Poles. A Polish prince, Boleslaw Chrabry (the Courageous), gained control of Krakow, Slovakia, Moravia and finally in 1003 of Bohemia as well, but he failed in his attempts to include in his realm the Slav tribes on the lower reaches of the River Elbe. The Czech princes joined Henry II, successor of Otto I, and by fighting from 1003 to 1018, forced Boleslaw to give up Bohemia and Moravia around 1020. Slovakia was retaken by the Hungarians and remained under their rule until 1918, but Moravia remained in a political union with Bohemia and these two regions and Silesia were later called the Czech crown lands.

A place in the Holy Roman Empire

After they had defeated the Polish attempt at controlling the Slav part of the Central European bloc, the rulers of Bohemia and Moravia adopted a policy of cooperation with the Holy Roman Empire, and, except for brief intervals, upheld it until the Czech wars of reformation began in 1418. The development of this link was greatly assisted by the 'soft line' adopted by Emperor Otto II towards his eastern neighbours. In contrast with Otto I, who tried to move the empire's centre of gravity eastwards, Otto II was attracted by the rich regions of Italy and northwestern Europe. Rome and Aachen were his two focal points, rather than Augsburg and Magdeburg. In line with these ambitions he tried to secure his eastern frontiers by alliances.

In 1000 Otto made a political pilgrimage to the grave of his martyred friend St Vojtěch (Adalbert), the only surviving member of the clan of Slavnikovci who had ruled eastern Bohemia before they were exterminated by the Premyslids. The grave was in Poland where St Vojtěch had perished on a mission to the Slav tribe of Prussians. Otto concluded an alliance with the Polish prince Boleslaw Chrabry, calling him 'friend and confederate of the Roman people', and founded an archbishopric in Poznan, designed to minimize the interference of the German hierarchy in Polish domestic affairs. The same policy was applied to Hungary, where the first archbishop, Anastasius, a German sent by Otto, crowned King Stephen I with a crown sent by the Pope.

Otto, who acknowledged Rome as the 'capital of the world' and saw himself as the head of an empire consisting of 'Rome, Gallia, Germania and Slavinia', evidently aspired to reunite eastern and western Christendom. He wanted to marry a Byzantine princess but before he could do so he died, aged only 21. The friendship with the Poles did not last long: Henry II, his successor, joined with the Czechs to fight the Poles.

For the greater part of the eleventh and twelfth centuries the Czech state was weakened by the struggle for succession between the Premyslids and this provided the Emperor with frequent pretexts for intervention in Czech affairs: either he was asked to help by one of the factions or he could at least pretend he had been asked. The rulers of Bohemia and Moravia accepted that their countries were part of the Holy Roman Empire but did not hesitate to take arms against the Emperor's attempts to interfere in Czech internal affairs. They also claimed recognition of the unity of the Czech lands under the Prague rulers. Attempts to treat Moravia as '*Reichsunmittelbar*' – directly subject to the Emperor – were firmly rejected.

Throughout the twelfth century the power and independence of the Prague princes grew. In 1126 Soběslav I still had to fight in the border mountains to prevent German emperors intervening in Czech domestic affairs; in 1158 Prince Vratislav II was made king by the Emperor in return for his support in Italy: and finally, at the beginning of the thirteenth century, Přemysl Otakar I played his hand in the politics of the Empire so ably that he obtained confirmation of the Czech kings as Electors and Cup-Bearers to the Emperors and as sovereigns in their own kingdom.

In the wider framework of the contest between the Guolfs and the Hohenstaufen for the imperial throne, Přemysl Otakar I obtained promises from all candidates shifting his support from one to the other as their chances changed. Přemysl could afford to play this game only because after two centuries of faction he was undisputed ruler in Prague. The consolidation of the Czech kingdom's status in the Empire was finally recognized by the Golden Bull of Sicily in 1212, a papal document confirming the Czech kings as sovereigns in their kingdom; their obligations were limited to providing a company of riders for the Emperor's coronation procession.

The newly acquired power of the Czech kingdom soon proved of great value to the security of Western Europe: in the first half of the thirteenth century, when the Tartars, after conquering Kiev, the seat of the Russian princes, turned into Central Europe and moved westwards from Slovakia which they plundered and devastated, Přemysl's son (Václav I), defeated them in Moravia. This, as well as the Golden Horde's internal problems, possibly saved Central Europe from the fate of Russia, which for 200 years was excluded from European development by Tartar occupation. In its turn, the Tartar danger revived the need for a strong central power in Europe and enhanced the importance of the Czech kings.

Economic and cultural growth

The strong international position of the Czech kings was further fortified by an economic boom. Settlers invited from Germany turned forests into agricultural land; mines were opened and towns built. There was a silver and gold rush, and in the course of the next hundred years the Czech Kingdom became the richest gold and silver mining country of Europe. Mining was the king's prerogative and its development increased revenue and introduced new technical skills; both helped to strengthen and equip the king's army. The king began to mint the silver groš of Prague in 1300 and fifty years later issued the Czech florin, the first gold coin of Central Europe.

Slavonic liturgy survived longest in the Sázava monastery founded in 1030, which provides the sparse evidence of early literary efforts in ancient Slavonic. However, after a period of bilingualism, Latin took over. Of the Latin schools of the period, that supported by the Prague bishops was the most important. Foreign priests were gradually being replaced by Czechs who, in their turn, started to study abroad and, as one of them, Kosmas, wrote, returned home 'after having tasted the delicious meals at the table of Philosophy and drawn from all the treasures of France'.

It was this Kosmas who later, as Dean of the Chapter, lived at Prague Castle, observed its politics, and when an old man wrote *The Chronicle of the Czechs*, mixing myth and history with the transparent intention of identifying the ruling class of his day as the nation of the Czechs descended from the First Czech. According to Kosmas, the Czechs took possession of an empty land and lived in the golden era of freedom and equality before they voluntarily, foolishly and irrevocably called Přemysl to rule over them. This *contrat social*, allegiance to the ruling prince rather than language, was for Kosmas the distinguishing mark of the Czechs. It is a political concept dear to all ideologists serving a ruler – even now in Prague one can read banners stating, 'The test of a socialist is his attitude to the Soviet Union.'

2 Links with Western Europe

The first confrontation with the Habsburgs

Přemysl Otakar II who came to the throne in 1253, married the widow of the last of the Battenbergs and thus became Duke of Austria, controlling a territory reaching to the Adriatic Sea in the south.

He extended the zone of Czech influence to the north by allying himself with the Order of Teutonic Knights, taking part in the 1255 and 1267 expeditions against the Prussians (then Slavs and pagan). To fortify the conquered territory he founded the town of Královec ('*Král*' being the Czech word for 'king'), later called Königsberg and now Kaliningrad. A grandson of Philip of Swabia, the Iron and Golden King, claimed to be 'the Hohenstauf' after that dynasty became extinct.

When the time came for the election of a new Emperor, Přemysl pressed his claim, as a protagonist of the Hohenstaufen political faction, as the ruler of a fast expanding kingdom, and as certainly the richest of the Electors. Rome, however, preferred a less powerful and more manageable candidate, Rudolph of Habsburg, who was elected Emperor in 1273. Přemysl did not recognize Rudolph and the military conflict which ensued was only resolved on the Moravian Field (near the confluence of the rivers Morava and Danube) by Přemysl's defeat and death in 1278.

The victory was of greater consequence to the Habsburgs than the defeat was to the Czechs. The Habsburgs were at that time a relatively poor family with small possessions in Switzerland, centred on Habichtsburg between the rivers Hare and Reuss. The imperial throne provided them with an opportunity to consolidate their political influence and to amass the wealth which made them into

Europe's greatest dynasty. For the Czechs the defeat brought only a temporary setback in their involvement in German affairs.

The conflict between the Czech king, then at the pinnacle of his power, and the Habsburgs newly entered into the arena of big power politics, indicates a new dimension in European politics which found full expression only after another 400 years. Since Roman times most conflicts in Europe had had an east-west direction, but in the battle of the Moravian Field in 1278 there was the first hint of a north–south split: Poles, Silesians and Germans fought on the Czech side, while the Habsburg army was drawn from Switzerland, Austria and Hungary.

It is of some significance that the Czech battle-cry was 'Praha' while that of the Habsburgs was 'Rome'. The Habsburgs remained the 'Roman' party till the end, and Prague became the focal point of reform and resistance to the Roman Church first in the fifteenth and again in the seventeenth century.

The defeat and death of Přemysl Otakar II while his son Václav II was still a child gave the Lords of the Rose (Páni z Růže, Rosenbergs) the long awaited chance of reaching out for supreme power. Over the centuries the Premyslids had succeeded in exterminating most of the other ruling families in Bohemia. The only important exception were the Vítkovci, later called Lords of the Rose, after their heraldic emblem. In the thirteenth century this powerful clan controlled a major part of southern Bohemia and was in a position to provide the country with an alternative government. After the defeat of 1278, the Lords of the Rose reached a compromise with the Premyslids, and Záviš, the head of the clan, married Přemysl's widow Kunhuta and became regent during the minority of her son Václav II. Five years later Václav took his stepfather as hostage and forced all but one of the Rosenberg castles to surrender by threatening to have Záviš beheaded under their walls. The last stronghold, the impregnable Zvíkov, resisted and Václav carried out his threat. The central power of the Premyslids was restored, but the Lords of the Rose survived as the family ruling southern Bohemia. In another hundred years, when the reign of Charles IV was drawing to a close, they had more than recovered their former strength.

Relying on the same factors of politics and economics as his defeated father, Václav II succeeded in consolidating the Czech kingdom once more and in 1300 mounted the Polish throne, joining the two countries for the second time. Soon he gained the Hungarian throne for his son, Václav III, thereby uniting three kingdoms.

These last Premyslid rulers continued the policy of colonizing royal forests on the Czech borders with settlers invited from Germany. They gave them privileges and encouragement to build new towns. This urbanization improved the country's defences, swelled the income of the Crown, and promoted the development of trade and arts and crafts. But the extensive colonization by Germans of the border regions also laid the foundation for political strife between Czechs and Germans. In this period Bohemia had the highest density of towns in Central Europe and the Czech kingdom was the leading Central European power. The international relations of the Premyslids were, however, confined to Central Europe and the Holy Roman Empire. The Czech kingdom entered on the wider European scene only after the succession of the Luxembourgs.

The Luxembourg Dynasty makes Prague the centre of the Empire

The assassination of Václav III in 1306 ended the rule of the Premyslid dynasty, for he had no children. The throne was offered to John of Luxembourg, husband of his sister Eliška (Elizabeth). The Luxembourgs were now dramatically to extend the Czechs' international horizon westwards, beyond the Rhine.

The tiny principality of Luxembourg provided little experience for the administration of the rich and relatively large kingdom which John evidently viewed as an expendable asset. Leaving behind him no flattering record in Luxembourg, John was a Czech king only in name. He lived the life of an errant knight fighting other people's battles, returning home only to harry the Jews and extort more money. The barons ruled the country for the absentee king, and despised him. John, by then completely blind, fought on the French side at Crécy in 1345 and found there a stylish end: the three black feathers in the arms of the Prince of Wales are those taken by the Black Prince from the dead king's helmet. At the time of his death he was no longer of any importance in Prague, where his son by Eliška was by then firmly established as regent. This second Luxembourg on the Czech throne became a great ruler, the Emperor

Charles (Karel) IV: 'Father of the Country' and 'the most European of emperors'.

This Luxembourg prince had been given the traditional Premyslid name Václav, but adopted the name by which he is now known after he was taken in 1323 to the court of Charles IV of France. There his education was supervised by Peter Roger, then Abbot of Fécamp, who later became Pope Clement VI. When after two further years spent in Italy, Charles returned to Prague he spoke French, Italian, German and Latin; but he had to relearn his Czech. He is also the only Czech king with literary work to his credit, writing the Legend of St Václav and his own autobiography. This was intended as a guide to his successors and as such was held in great esteem by the Habsburgs who were presented with it by the Czech Parliament after the election of Ferdinand I to the Czech throne in 1526, and handed it down from one generation to the next.

Charles found all the royal estates and castles mortgaged and Prague Castle in such a dilapidated state that he had to take a house in the town. In a relatively short time he succeeded in re-establishing a strong central government and economic prosperity. By four successive marriages Charles added to the Czech crown lands Lusatia and a large part of Silesia and Brandenburg, a region including the present Berlin, and became King of Burgundy. He established a strong central European power and in alliance with the French and the Pope (against the Bavarian Wittelsbachs supported by Edward III of England) succeeded where Přemysl II had failed, attaining the imperial crown in 1355. In 1356 as Emperor, he confirmed (by the Golden Bull of Charles) the special status of the Czech kingdom in the multinational organization of the Empire. His son and successor on the Czech throne, Václav IV, was elected King of the Romans during his father's lifetime and his other son, Sigismund, ascended the Hungarian throne in 1387. By 1400 the Luxembourg dynasty, like the Premyslids a hundred years earlier, was at the peak of its power in Europe.

The establishment of the Luxembourgs on the Czech throne was not an isolated fourteenth century case of a western dynasty successfully planted in Central Europe: on the Hungarian throne the Premyslids were succeeded by another western prince allied to the Pope, Charles Robert of Anjou who was elected King of Hungary soon after Václav III's death in 1306. Among the Hungarian barons who took his side was the powerful Matias Čák who from his seat in Trenčín ruled western Slovakia. Charles Robert reigned in Hungary until 1342, a near contemporary of John of Luxembourg (r. 1310–46). His son Louis I proved to be one of the greatest rulers of Hungary. He did much to improve the economy and administration of his country, and glorified the Crown of St Stephen as John's son Charles IV did that of St Václav. He expanded the Hungarian crown lands by adding to them the Slav countries of the Balkan peninsula. Finally in 1370 Louis was elected King of Poland.

Both the Luxembourgs and the Anjous grew more powerful through their alliance with the Pope. The series of successes papal diplomacy had in central Europe in the fourteenth century was accompanied by a tremendous increase in the wealth and power of the Church in those parts and this in its turn led the Czech Kingdom to the first European revolt against the Roman Church.

As an Emperor with the basis of his power in the Czech kingdom, Charles necessarily had to subscribe to the multinational concept of the Empire. The constitution which he gave it in 1356 by his Golden Bull presented the Holy Roman Empire as a league of sovereign nations and defined it as a commonwealth of nations which could prosper only if the laws, ways of life and languages of its peoples were respected. By shifting the centre of the Empire eastwards and northwards while strengthening its links with France and claiming the political heritage of Charlemagne, Charles IV was a precursor of the Vienna-based Habsburgs and their strong western links with Spain. This affinity was not purely conceptual: in 1364 a succession treaty was concluded between Charles and the Habsburgs Rudolph IV and Albert IV, who married his two daughters. On the basis of this treaty the Habsburgs succeeded to the Czech and Hungarian thrones after the death of Charles's second son, Sigismund, who had married the eldest daughter of the King of Hungary.

The Agricultural Revolution – boom and depression

As regent, Charles had found the country in a state of anarchy, with only robber-knights safe in their little rock fortresses along the highways. The treasury had no money as a result of the understandable reluctance to collect revenue for a king who spent it abroad. Nevertheless, there was a sound basis for economic prosperity in the growing wealth of the towns; the forests too were being exploited and gradually turned into arable land by German and Czech settlers. Two hundred years before the discovery of the riches of the New World a flourishing gold and silver mining industry provided the Czech kingdom with the resources for becoming the leading economic power of Europe. The country lacked only good management and a strong central rule. Charles provided both.

He turned the military skill and organization which his father John had used in foreign wars against the robber-knights. Roads safe for commerce opened a new economic boom for the towns: the trade routes established by Charles connected Prague with Venice, Hamburg and Bruges – Charles himself visited Lübeck in 1375 and showed a great appreciation of Nuremburg's situation on the Prague – Paris route.

In 1348 he founded in Prague the Charles University, the first university in Central Europe. His alliance with the Pope in international affairs was reflected at home by the establishment of an archbishopric in Prague. Arnošt of Pardubic, the first archbishop, was also the King's principal adviser.

Charles then introduced the more advanced French methods of farming, thus bringing a revolutionary factor into the economy and politics of the Czech kingdom. After 600 years the vineyards he founded with vines imported from France are still there, and so are the lakes into which the Lords of the Rose drained their south Bohemian marshland, transforming it into a gigantic fish farm and a district of unique charm. At this time, however, the transition from primitive to more productive methods of field cultivation and animal husbandry resulted in a great upheaval. As long as the man tilling the land could produce a surplus only by the utmost exertion, it was better for the baron to leave him the land and take away the surplus by taxes and dues. But when it became possible to obtain a greater surplus by organizing more intensive and efficient farming, the barons and the Church became eager for direct cultivation of land which so far they had possessed only as superior landlords.

On the newly agglomerated estates fewer people produced more, and soon the dispossessed proletarian farmers started to seek employment in the towns. They often remained unemployed and the products from the improved and enlarged baronial estates remained unsold; so that the boom was followed by a severe economic crisis.

In a truly Keynesian spirit Charles embarked on a grandiose programme of public spending. A period of feverish building activity – the New Town of Prague was developed at this time – gave Matthias of Arras scope which he could never hope for at home in Flanders. But the greatest of Charles's architects was Petr Parléř, the builder of the cathedral on Hradčany (Castle Hill) which forms an essential element of the famous panorama of Prague. The fortification to the south of the Royal Castle on the Petřín hill in Prague is still called the Hungry Wall, as the king's declared purpose in having it built was to provide work for the unemployed. According to tradition, the Charles Bridge spanning the River Vltava, between the Old and the Little Towns of Prague, has for the last 600 years withstood the annual impact of floating ice so well because the king, faced with the problem of agricultural surpluses, had eggs mixed into the mortar.

The building boom gave a great stimulus to arts and crafts. Unfortunately most of the Gothic paintings and sculptures of this period were destroyed by the puritanical zest of the Hussites. But some examples of interiors decorated with semi-precious stones remain, as does the Crown of St Václav which Charles had remade after the model of the Crown of St Louis. The aim of Charles's incessant innovations and activity seems to have been to reshape the whole Czech kingdom on the model of the rich Burgundy and France.

The final effect, however, of the policies followed by this most Catholic ruler, firmly allied to Rome, was the greatest upheaval Rome and the Catholic Church had to face. The agricultural revolution sponsored by Charles was probably the most important factor in the next century's transformation of Bohemia into the cultural, political and military *avant-garde* of Europe. The radical improvement in the efficiency of agricultural production upset the balance of the feudal Czech society and prepared the ground for a political revolution. The progress of the revolt against Rome which ultimately led to the Czech reformation and the Hussite wars reflected the presence of more than two opposing forces.

The growing wealth and power of the Church and of the barons led them into conflicts on the one hand with the central power, the king, and on the other with the lesser nobility and free farmers.

These claimed to be subject only to the king, but the Church and barons wanted to take their land and make them into serfs. They did not dare to take issue with the powerful Charles; they could and did brave his son and successor Václav IV.

Like our own times, this was a period of transition: the search for a new economic and political system took often forms just as bizarre as various contemporary protests against the industrial society. The fourteenth century upheaval was powered by a large variety of sectional interests and forces. No analysis can do full justice to their interplay and combinations but the following description uses three different systems of coordinates: domestic conflict of interests, the clash of national and international priorities, and attitudes to law and freedom.

The domestic power struggle

A visitor to Prague can visualize the pattern of power in the Czech State at the end of the fourteenth century by standing on the Hadčanské Square facing the Royal Castle and the cathedral beyond it. He will see the Archbishop's Palace (now housing the National Gallery) on his left, and on his right, facing the Royal Palace as equals, two palaces of the Schwarzenbergs, heirs of the Rosenbergs who in the fourteenth century owned almost half of Bohemia. They continued to play an important role until recently.

The agricultural revolution precipitated by Charles IV had made the Church and the Rosenbergs, as well as lesser landowners, richer and more powerful. It had increased the antagonism between them and the small gentry and towns, and enabled them to restrict or encroach on the central power of the king. The impoverishment of the peasant farmers who were either dispossessed or could not compete with the more efficient aristocratic estates radicalized the countryside as well as the towns by an influx of unemployed. The barons and the Church were moving towards conflict with the king on the one side and the towns and lower gentry on the other. The new proletariat in the villages and towns was a potential ally of the central power: it feared and hated the landowners and was no less feared by the rich burghers of the towns.

These tensions were kept under control by an alliance between the king, the Church and the barons, but by the time Charles IV was succeeded by his son Václav IV the Church and the barons were so rich and powerful that the king was the weakest member of the alliance. Charles could hold his own because of his international position, personal authority and political skill. Václav possessed none of these, and when he attempted to uphold the central government against the Church and the barons the alliance came to an end: he was taken prisoner by the Rosenbergs. When he regained his freedom he sought the support of the towns and lower nobility. The two main political camps that were to clash during the Hussite wars of reformation, the Church and barons on the one side, and the towns, landed gentry and oppressed and land-hungry peasants on the other, thus began to form long before Jan Huss, the spiritual leader of the Czech reformation, entered public life.

The 'universal' Roman Church becomes too costly

The choice between two different modes of the Christian Church – the one supranational, based on Rome and on Latin as an international language, and the other national in character and language – faced most European countries for the first time in the sixteenth century. The Czechs had long before been confronted with the alternatives: in the ninth century Moravia opted for the Eastern Church, more national in character and using an easily comprehensible Slavonic language; Bohemia had been penetrated from the west by the Roman Church, which claimed the inheritance of the Holy Roman Empire and was always ready to supplement spiritual power with military action. As Great Moravia disintegrated under the Hungarian impact at the beginning of the tenth century, the Czechs became the first Slavs to embrace Roman Christianity. Five hundred years later they were also the first in Europe to revolt against its centralistic, dogmatic and reactionary policies.

The fast growth of the country's economy in the fourteenth century was the decisive force behind the Czech revolt against the Roman Church. But the residual memory of an alternative to the Roman Church must have played its part. Even Charles IV, whose policies were based on alliance with the Roman Church and on peace and cooperation between Czechs and Germans, made an attempt to revive the Slavonic liturgy by building in Prague an abbey, to this day called 'Na Slovanech' (beautifully reconstructed after bombing in 1945), for monks he invited from Croatia. For a Catholic cosmopolitan, educated at the French court and writing his memoirs in Latin, he showed a surprising interest in the promotion of the Czech language. As Emperor he tried by the Golden Bull of 1356 to impose on the Electors – among whom the Czech king was *primus inter pares* – the obligation to have their sons taught Czech (and also Italian). There is a parallel between this and the fact that before attempting to reform the Church Jan Huss reformed the Czech alphabet and spelling by making them phonetical and easy for the child. There has been no need to change it.

Perhaps because Bohemia is a small country wedged into the vast expanse of the German language area, the feeling of national identity emerged early and was already strong when universalism was still supreme in Europe. Although this national awareness clashed with the universalistic concepts of Rome, it was also stimulated by the Roman culture, much more dynamic than the Orthodox Church and freer than the despotic societies of the European east. The Czech state interlocked with the west of Europe as a barrier against Mongol invasions. It formed part of a civilization expanding overseas, first to the Middle East and later to Africa, the Indies and the New World. In the eastern world a dogmatic view of life was retained long after western society had exploded with the rationalism and nationalist thought precipitated by artists, inventors and merchant adventurers.

But more important than historical memory or international influences was probably the new strength and self-confidence of the towns in which the Czech element had been steadily gaining strength. The towns benefited greatly from the order imposed by Charles and the enormous construction programme sponsored by the king and the Church brought them wealth, new skills and with them a feeling of political importance. Charles added to Prague a whole 'New Town' – which still bears this name – laid out according to a plan. Prague became one of the great European cities of the time and as such fulfilled its role as *caput regni*. Moreover the small gentry, always looking to the king for support against the great landed barons and clerics, were becoming a politically conscious class, allied to the towns. Thus political interests, not only the decadence of the Roman Church, called for the development of secular ethics independent of the establishment. The literature of this period includes the first Czech prose work of a philosophical nature. The moral essays of a country squire, Tomáš Štítný ze Štítneho.

In these circumstances the university founded in Prague by Charles in 1348 soon became an intellectual centre of the Czech national opposition to the international Church. The prosperity and experience acquired by the fathers was the basis on which the better educated sons started to search for a revolutionary ideology in preparation for the inevitable conflict.

It is important for an understanding of Czech political ideology throughout the Middle Ages, to note that though the Czechs were defined by their allegiance to the Prague rulers, these rulers were not the state: on the contrary, the state rested on the political nation, the nobility. This constitutional idea which could be called democratic in the Ancient Greek sense which ignored the slaves, survived until the end of the fifteenth century. George of Poděbrad, the Hussite king who spent a lifetime in diplomatic struggle with Rome, could argue in the Czech parliament 'Not the Popes but the barons here assembled are the source of power in this kingdom and elect their kings.'

This fundamentally nationalist concept found a still sharper expression at the beginning of the fourteenth century in *The Chronicle of Dalimil*, where it is already combined with the landed barons' opposition to the growing importance of the towns and the German colonists and settlers invited by the kings. By the end of the fourteenth century the roles were exchanged. The towns, previously linked with the German towns from which the first settlers came, were developing a concept of politics – national in the territorial rather than the ethnic sense. Here, as everywhere in Europe at this time, the towns were becoming alienated from the internationalist and universalist concept of the Roman Church and the elaborate system of feudal ties that stretched across the borders of the emerging national states.

The conflict of economic interests between the Church and the towns became particularly intense when several pretenders struggled for the papal throne and the contending factions were in need of money. The Church used all means to increase its revenue from landed property, dues and inheritances, and from the sale of Church offices and indulgences. A large part of this revenue was remitted abroad. The town craftsmen and merchants would rather have seen the money spent at home. They found the universal Church too much of a burden.

Law and privilege

While the conflict of economic interests was the divisive force between the Czechs and Rome, their widely divergent attitudes towards law, legality, justice and the stability of institutions have been obvious to historians, though most now accept that this clash only mirrored the power struggle between economically opposed sections of society.

Fourteenth-century Czech law, as part of the European medieval system, was far removed from the modern concept of law as a pyramid of norms enforceable and backed by an ethical code. The medieval European legal system was in contradiction to the then professed Christian ethic, based on the Jewish concept of equality before the law, which extends even to the supreme ruler, God, when he enters into contract with man. Instead of one law for everyone, there were different legal systems for different social groups, graded according to the individual's and group's power. Most cases were prejudged, so the task of the court was not to find the truth but provide 'evidence' for a decision already taken. Hence the general use of torture to produce 'confessions' of guilt.

This method of suiting the evidence to the verdict instead of the verdict to the evidence is, of course, not special to the fourteenth century. But the plurality of the medieval legal system is more difficult to grasp. In the Czech kingdom there were four distinct types of courts administering different laws. The ancient common law respected and applied by the rural community was gradually superseded by the feudal lord who, as a judge, would ignore custom to accommodate his own interests.

In towns there were established more elaborate systems of a different type based on codes originating in Meissen, Augsburg and

Nuremberg. Their adoption roughly followed the geographic proximity of the respective Czech town to these three German cities to
the north, west and south-west of Bohemia.

Another set of legal rules was administered by the king, and this
again was not of a uniform nature. As head of the feudal system the
king and his legal officers settled disputes between his vassals. On
royal estates, or on the frontiers, the king's representatives administered justice like any of the barons. The local sheriffs were often
elected but there was the possibility of appeal to the king or his
chamberlain. Finally the king was responsible for upholding law and
order in the kingdom, and in this capacity acted as police or judge in
a wide range of cases from road robberies to disputes between members of different estates, between barons and towns or these two and
the Church.

The Church, in many respects as extraterritorial organization,
administered itself by canon law, regulating not only the appoint-
ments and duties of clerics and the administration of church property and church corporations but also marriage and family, and in
this way had an important say in matters of inheritance. As the
reformist and Protestant movement gained strength, the ecclesiastical courts of the Inquisition trying heresy assumed overriding political power. Excommunication for heresy was followed by death at
the stake administered by the secular power, but there were lesser
punishments like exclusion from the sacraments and interdicts of
religious services imposed on churches or towns. These could turn a
respectable man into an outlaw or force the hand of the government.

Thus in the administration of law, no less than in economy and in
the search for a new political structure, the Church which in earlier
centuries had spearheaded progress was, by the end of the fourteenth
century, obstructing it. The call for its reform became the main
political issue in the Czech kingdom a hundred years earlier than in
Germany because of the faster growth of Church possessions and of
the new bourgeoisie in the booming kingdom.

The revolt against an oppressive institution which had outlived its
usefulness was made easier on the ideological plane by the Church's
loss of moral authority and the corruption of its own standards. It
was authoritarian but was divided within itself: this was the time of
two or three popes. It professed dedication to God and to poverty

but sold its offices as a source of income and political power, while monasteries and nunneries became places of easy and often corrupt living. Finally, it introduced a detested police terror, the Inquisition, to protect a degenerate establishment. In medieval terms it appeared to its opponents as the Church of the Anti-Christ.

3 The first European revolution

Czechs against the Church

The transplantation of what was best in French agriculture, crafts and architecture into a young and fresh society accelerated in the Czech kingdom a movement which elsewhere in Europe came to a head only after another century – against the oppressive concentration of wealth and power in the hands of the Roman Church. Social and economic tensions in fourteenth-century Bohemia were further heightened by an increase in population faster than elsewhere in Europe because of the new prosperity and because the Czech kingdom was spared by the Black Death which decimated the populations of western Europe. Moreover the colonization of the border regions initiated in the previous century was more or less complete, no more forest land was offered to new settlers and, indeed, few would have found such an offer attractive at a time when agricultural products were difficult, even impossible, to sell.

Charles's building programme brought only temporary employment to the surplus agricultural population. What was needed was an expansion of the towns and their manufacturing and trading activities – a structural change rather than emergency measures for the relief of unemployment.

A further increase in wealth in the Czech kingdom was possible only by a redistribution and better use of the existing means of production. Such a redistribution was barred by the Church, which owned between one third and one half of all the land, much property in the towns, and numerous endowments and benefits for churches and monasteries. Economic pressures were further activated by strife within the Roman Church. Since 1378 two popes had been contending for power, and demanding even greater financial contributions from their supporters. An increase in revenue became of paramount importance to bishops keen to recover money they had paid for obtaining office. As a result, the Church was seen by the critical spirits of the time as living in contradiction to the ideals which it professed, and as an obstacle to the further development of the society it had created.

In the later years of his reign Charles IV came to view reform of the Church as unavoidable if the state he had constituted was to function properly. He invited to Prague one of the foremost reforming preachers of the time, Conrad of Waldhauser. Conrad preached at the Týn church, overlooking the Old Town Square, which was to become the focal point of Protestantism. Conrad's successor at this church was Jan Milič z Kroměříže, Vice-Chancellor of the Imperial Court, who founded 'Jerusalem in Prague', a religious community of Czech-speaking priests and laymen – possibly connected with Geert Groote's *devotio moderna*. The reformist and Czech-language-centred school of thought can be followed through Tomáš Štítný ze Štítného, a Czech critical writer, to the Bethlehem Chapel opened in 1391 for exclusive preaching in Czech at a time when the Týn was a German church. Jan Huss was the first priest and preacher at this chapel, which was beautifully renovated in the 1960s.

Even before the Czech intellectual protest gathered force, Petrarch came to Prague from Florence to plead with Charles for the reconstitution of the Roman Empire, an idea rivalling the aspirations of the Church and as symptomatic of the political malaise of Europe as it was unrealistic. Thus the economic, political and ideological roots of the Hussite revolution can be traced back to Charles's reign.

Soon after the sucession of his son Václav IV, in 1378, an important new political issue appeared for the first time in the Czech kingdom: an ethnically based conflict between Czechs and Germans. Many of the towns had been founded by German colonists; more recent Czech settlers outnumbered the Germans and were fighting for better representation. This conflict between the older German and the younger Czech bourgeoisie was particularly evident in Prague, where Germans controlled the administration in the old Town. In many other towns too rich German burghers, though in a minority, still held the town hall.

Curiously familiar as it sounds today, the first revolutionary actions took place among the agitated youth of Prague University.

With more enthusiasm than political wisdom, they coupled protest against the Church with the Czech cause against the Germans. Thus deprived of its originally international character, the Czech reform movement was already doomed. The Czech members of the university were in a minority, for Charles IV had founded it to serve the entire Empire, of which the Czech kingdom was the strongest and richest part but in which the Czech-speaking people were in a minority. Accordingly, it was made up of four national colleges, Czech, Polish, Saxon and Bavarian – the last three for students, mainly but not exclusively German, coming from the north, west and south. Since voting was by college, in a conflict the Germans could overrule the Czechs.

The tension between the richer German and the more numerous Czech townspeople was reflected and magnified by the student community. An ideological spark was the only thing needed for a flare-up. It came from England. The reformist theses of John Wycliffe reached Prague seemingly by accident; they were brought from London by Czech noblemen in the retinue of Princess Anne, daughter of Charles IV who had married King Richard II, and possibly also by Czech students returning from Oxford.

The polemics concerning Wycliffe's philosophical views and criticism of the Church started fairly innocently on an academic plane and at first his views were only adopted by a few Czech masters. But when the German masters denounced a number of their Czech colleagues as heretics and used their statutory majority to condemn forty-five of Wycliffe's theses, the remaining Czech masters and students rallied to the cause of the 'heretics'. The academic dispute quickly became a national issue, and the Czech masters and students demanded an immediate reversal of the voting procedure in their favour. The dean of the philosophy faculty of the university was at that time Jan Huss, who as a reformist priest and spirited preacher at the Bethlehem Chapel had already become a spokesman for the discontented Czech burghers. It was he who presented the demands of the Czech students and masters to the king.

Václav IV found their demands well fitted his immediate political needs. He reversed the German majority in the administration of the Old Town in 1408, and in the following year issued in Kutná Hora a royal patent giving the Czechs a voting majority at the Charles University. Czech historians usually see in this event an important success for the Czech cause and the reform movement. The transformation of an international place of learning into a national one may, under some circumstances, be viewed as a success; but it considerably weakened the reform movement by isolating it within an ethnic framework, thus reducing the chances of the Czech reformation which was already at a disadvantage in being the first in Europe. The Patent of Kutná Hora was followed by the exodus of some 1,200 German students and masters, who established universities in Leipzig and Erfurt, which became centres of a campaign against the Czech heretics.

Statesmanship cannot be expected from students, but the part played by Jan Huss in this affair suggests that his ability to perceive and formulate urgent social needs was not matched by a command of the political strategy required for meeting them at the lowest possible cost in human life and wellbeing.

King Václav IV was even less of a statesman: he was apt to go after a transient advantage and disregard the more serious long-term problems in which this would involve him. In contrast with his much more powerful father, who did not hesitate to withdraw his reforming statute Majestas Carolina, Václav was quick to antagonize the barons without having prepared for himself a position of strength. At one point the barons, led by the Rosenbergs, imprisoned the king and forced him to capitulate. Václav was also in conflict with the Archbishop of Prague and with the Church, richer then than the king and claiming a decisive voice in the affairs of state.

This struggle between the king on the one side and the Church and the barons on the other filled the greater part of Václav's reign. From time to time the political conflict was exacerbated by armed squabbles. Jan Huss and the reformers voicing the needs of towns, lower gentry and common people remained the king's natural allies until 1412, when the king was promised a share in the proceeds from the sale of papal indulgences (the prime target of reformist propaganda) and lost the trust of the reformers without gaining that of Rome.

By punishing the leaders of the demonstrations against indulgences Václav provided the reform movement with its first martyrs and helped to popularize a cause which until then had been more at home in the university than in the streets. The Pope followed with an interdict of all religious services in Prague as long as Jan Huss remained there. Huss moved from Prague to his native southern Bohemia, spreading the reform movement in a country where landless peasants coveted the immense estates of the Church and of the Rosenbergs.

With more time in his rural exile for writing, Jan Huss felt the need to justify his disobedience towards Pope, Archbishop and King. He formulated the thesis to which society reverts whenever its hierarchical organization runs amok and uses subordination as a tool against humanity: 'The ruler who becomes untrue to the law of God', he wrote, 'loses all secular authority.' One should 'punish as a brother' the superior giving evil orders. The theory of the revolution thus formulated, Huss had drafted his death warrant.

He was summoned to the Council of Constance but refused to retract. Declared a heretic, he was delivered for punishment to Václav's brother, the Emperor Sigismund, who had him burned at the stake in Constance on 6 July 1415. In doing so Sigismund brushed aside both a safe conduct which he had issued to Huss and a petition signed by 450 representatives of the Czech nobility. Moreover, in the following year the Council and Sigismund, already seen by the Czechs as perfidious enemies, also executed Jeroným of Prague, a brilliant theologian and Huss's closest friend and associate. Sigismund and the cardinals assembled in Constance must have been singularly uninformed about the explosive nature of the case before them. The explosion came three years later, in 1419.

The Hussite wars

During the four years that elapsed between Jan Huss's execution in 1415 and the first outburst of revolutionary violence in Prague, reformist and chiliastic preachers flocked to deeply stirred Bohemia. One of them was Wycliffe's follower Petr Payne; another, Nicholas of Dresden, attempted to blend the Walden doctrine with the doctrines of Wycliffe and Huss. A new schism appeared, running across accepted social boundaries, dividing the country into Papists and Utraquists. As a result of the work of popular preachers large masses of common people joined the reform movement. One manifestation of the feeling that the existing social order was untenable and had no future was a pseudo-religious expectation that the Last Judgement was near. Much as we now rationalize a similar feeling into pseudo-scientific forecasts of doom from environmental pollution, so in those unsettled times the belief spread that the world would end and the Last Judgement come on 14 February 1420. As government is based on the possibility of manipulating human hopes and fears, such an overriding expectation led to a state of anarchy. No longer faced only with intellectual dissent but with a whole country aflame, Václav fast lost control. When still weak, the Protestant movement was a useful ally for a weak king. Now he shrank before its elemental forces and asked Sigismund to assemble an army against the Czech heretics.

In July 1419 Huss's followers in Prague stormed the New Town Hall and killed their adversaries' leaders by throwing them out of the window. (This established a precedent: defenestration became the preferred method of political coups and was used in Prague again in 1618 and 1948.) This first defenestration of Prague and the subsequent death of Václav IV mark the beginning of the open revolt. The Protestant movement was so strong that once they adopted militant tactics they quickly achieved control, although mopping-up operations and the sacking of the monasteries and other papist strongholds continued for many years. One unfortunate, because irreversible, consequence of the puritan zeal of the Hussites was the destruction of Czech gothic paintings and sculpture, the glory of which can only be guessed at from a few examples that were left untouched.

The spontaneity of the revolt against Rome and the very wide spread of its political base proved its greatest weakness. After Václav's death the country remained without a central government and the unity of the Protestants depended on enemy pressure. When 14 February 1420 passed and the predicted end of the world did not come about, the radical wing of the movement assembled in south Bohemia. These landless peasants, some of them already turned into an urban proletariat, and country squires who could not hold their own against the Rosenbergs and other wealthy barons, felt at a disadvantage to the moderate wing of the movement, who were sheltering in fortified towns. They decided to build a town of their own on the River Lužnice and gave it the biblical name 'Tábor'. It differed very much from the towns which had developed as capitalist alternatives to the feudal way of life. Tábor was the first European commune: those who built it or moved in later were required to surrender all their money and valuables in troughs standing in the main square. The town lived by the rules of a military camp and soon became the focal point of an association of the more radical towns taking part in the revolution.

The Táborites, who proved to be a strong and dynamic revolutionary movement, had a gifted leader in Jan Žižka. A country squire who was dispossessed by the Rosenbergs, he had taken up professional soldiering first in Poland and later in the service of Václav IV. Žižka lost no time in preparing Tábor for a confrontation with the Papists. He ruthlessly suppressed its more radical and anarchic elements, the Adamites, and forced into line the more moderate wing led by Prague. Faced with the threat of seeing their town sacked and burned by Žižka, the Prague burghers promised to give up all thought of a separate peace.

When the armies mustered by the Pope and the Emperor crossed the Czech frontiers they were met by a totally unconventional popular army fighting for its own country and survival. For Sigismund's mercenaries, 'God's Warriors' who went into battle singing hymns proved a terrifying experience. This psychological weapon alone was often enough to turn a heavily armed Catholic formation to flight. The Táborite forces moved into battle under the cover of walls formed by heavy peasant wagons for protection against the invaders' armoured heavy horses – the same wagons that transported the families of the fighting men, and supplies and arms. As a mobile fortification, linked end to end, they effectively enclosed the Hussite camp. This original military tactic was dictated by the impossibility of leaving families behind, exposed to the enemy. It enabled women to take part in the action, thus doubling the fighting strength of the Táborites. The weapons their army used were unconventional too, mostly farm tools adjusted for the purpose such as flails studded with nails, scythes and forks.

The terror which the Táborites spread through Central Europe was due not only to their novel form of warfare but also to their egalitarian and communist concept of society. The rich burghers of Prague, who shared the Táborites' hostility towards the Church, were not convinced that Tábor's radicalism and hostility to wealth were not the greater danger. They attempted to come to terms with the Emperor Sigismund and only when their mission was un-successful did they accept Tábor's protection. It did not take many years for them to find it very oppressive.

The third – and most conservative – faction of the Hussite move-ment was formed by the Protestant nobility who acquired much of the land taken from the Church and feared that the Táborites might turn it over to peasant communes.

The different war aims of the three factions were the main weak-ness of the Hussite movement. The Protestant barons just wanted to hold what they had; Tábor's radicals headed for a sort of 'cultural revolution'; Prague wanted to have the best of both worlds with moderation. After much controversy Tábor accepted the so-called Four Articles of Prague as a minimum programme, tabling at the same time twelve more radical articles of their own.

The Four Articles of Prague show beyond any doubt that what-ever other tensions contributed to the development of the revolution-ary situation, the revolution itself was directed against Rome, which in modern terminology could be described as a multinational com-pany exploiting the local population. Its aim was a reformed church that would no longer stifle progress and whose members would enjoy equality before God. The Czech Protestants wanted to do away with priestly privilege, economic, legal and spiritual.

By demanding that the Gospels should be freely preached, the first article aimed at freedom of opinion, of speech and of the press. This aim was never attained, neither in sectarian Tábor from which Žižka chased the anarchic extremists, who then founded a smaller Tábor of their own, nor in Prague where the radical preacher Jan Želivsky met with a violent death. Far from being tolerant, this revolution, as any other, was destroying its own followers.

The second article aimed against the privileged position of the clergy, demanding that not only priest but all church members should partake of both bread and wine at the mass. 'Not cross but chalice' was the emblem of the Hussites, still to be seen on the churches of the Czech Protestants. This purely symbolic demand was only mildly controversial and was ultimately conceded by Rome.

The crux lay in the third article which demanded that the Church should have no worldly dominion; that is, that it should give up the estates amassed in the course of the past hundred years. This part of the programme – the most generally acclaimed by the Hussite movement – was carried into effect during the wars. The sequestration of church estates was not reversed by the subsequent *modus vivendi* agreed with Rome.

The fourth article aimed against inquisition and indulgences was accepted by the Tábor radicals only under protest. It demanded that mortal sins should be publicly punished 'by properly instituted authority'. The anarcho-communists of Tábor did not like the limitation contained in the last words.

It would be wrong, however, to attribute such revolutionary zest to the whole Hussite movement, and even more incorrect to assume that the movement upset the established structure of society. While a small army of peasants under Žižka was constantly on the move, the majority of the rural population worked and paid dues and taxes to the barons. Even the revolutionary parliament of 1421, which deposed Sigismund and instituted a provisional government eliminating the Church from a position of political influence, assumed the continuation of monarchy. Žižka favoured as candidate a relative of the Polish king. He did not succeed and his idea of joining Poland and the Czech kingdom was accomplished only after another fifty years.

In spite of this political ferment the Catholic 'iron knights' were repeatedly defeated by the popular army, led first by Žižka and after his death by a soldier-priest, Prokop Holý. Under his leadership the Hussites even invaded enemy territory – one expedition reached the Baltic Sea. Subversion reached even farther afield: Hussite manifestoes, sent where expeditions could not go, gained the Czech Protestants many sympathizers and kept the Inquisition busy all over Europe.

Though the Protestant barons and well-to-do burghers saw their possessions threatened by the radical doctrines of Tábor, they feared still more a victory by the Catholic armies, for this would cost them their lives. Unity in the Hussite camp was therefore maintained as long as Rome and Sigismund insisted on a military solution. The situation changed after a crushing defeat of the Catholic armies near Domažlice, on the Bavarian frontier, in 1431. Rome then recognized the need to seek a political solution, and by this decision immediately turned the balance in its favour. The reluctant allies, whose unity was enforced by military confrontation, were soon driven apart by Rome's diplomatic offensive. In the end the Protestant barons joined with the Catholic barons and defeated the Táborites at Lipany in 1436, thus paving the way for a negotiated settlement with the Church, the Kompaktáta. This ended the war, restored Sigismund to the throne, and represented partial recognition by Rome of a Czech reformed church. Although Rome was able to delay the ratification of the Kompaktáta and the two sides interpreted them differently, Rome's universalism suffered here its first serious blow: it was obliged to negotiate and to accept a *modus vivendi* with the Czech heretics.

Modern Czech history and politics cannot easily be understood without some knowledge of the effect of the Hussite wars on the Czechs. Three images, all interrelated, are lodged in their collective memory. First, they remember Jan Huss, and in a country where generation after generation has been obliged to compromise and conceal its true views to survive, the contrasting image of a man, who was ready to die at the stake rather than give up his vision of truth, has a redeeming magic. Huss's slogan 'Truth prevails' was chosen for the Czechoslovak presidential standard. Interpreting these images for their own time, the Czechs of the nineteenth century – seeing themselves as patriots of a small ethnic island in a sea of Germans – drew comfort from the thought that though small in numbers the Hussites were able to withstand the onslaught of the German Catholic armies. The historiographer František Palacký formulated the philosophy of his period: 'Whenever we won, it was rather by spiritual strength than by physical force.'

In 1930, on the eve of the Nazi rise in Germany, Masaryk, the first President of the Czechoslovak republic, proclaimed 'Tábor is our programme,' and in 1945 the Communists were quick to make the same claim for different reasons. In 1968 many people looked back to discover a strange parallel between many aspects of the Christian revolt against Rome and the corrupt Church and the Communist revolt against Moscow and the corrupt Party. Although there was only non-violent resistance in 1968, as in the Hussite wars the presence of a foreign army produced a unity which could be eroded only by political means. Lipany, where the fratricidal battle took place in 1436, no less than Tábor, is still very much an important point of reference in Czechoslovakia today.

Back to international cooperation

The kingdom which Sigismund regained was tired, embittered by
long wars and divided within itself. Whoever ruled the country between 1437 and 1618 had to strike a careful balance between the
interests of the Protestants and the Catholics, who in fact formed two
nations within one country. Soon, however, new forces began to
overshadow the conflict between the Czechs and Rome.

The Turks were advancing into Central Europe and the pattern of
international trade changed, inland trading routes conceding much
of their importance to overseas trade. The Turkish expansion could
be halted only by the establishment of a Central European power
joining the Czech kingdom with Poland, Hungary and Austria.

While Central Europe was preoccupied with defence against the
Turks, the maritime nations of Western Europe were experiencing
great commercial expansion overseas. The influx of cheap silver
from the Americas was a blow to Czech silver mining, and it was
made harder by a general fall in the prices of the products normally
exported from Bohemia and Moravia. The pattern of trade was also
changing and the expansion of overseas trade by-passed landlocked
Bohemia.

While the towns were hit by depression the landed aristocracy
prospered through improved techniques of agriculture and gross exploitation of their subjects. From this period date the first processing
industries on aristocratic estates, not only mills and breweries but
glassworks and foundries. Freed from the supremacy of the Church,
the nobility competed successfully with the towns. The rise of the
barons to political and economic power was enhanced by the importance they had as the military caste in face of the persistent Turkish
danger at a time when the royal treasury was hit by the fall in silver
prices.

This was an unhappy time for the peasant population. They had
no protection from the weakened central power and no refuge in
towns suffering an economic crisis. A series of peasant uprisings
indicates that the barons' oppression of the rural population was very
intense.

Changes in the fundamental economic and political structures
were reflected by great intellectual activity. The aristocratic culture

was inspired by Italian humanism and Renaissance art. But also in the peasant masses a new quietist stream mixed with the aggressive mood of the Italian *Quattrocento*. The doctrine of non-violence and non-resistance to evil, formulated after the Hussite wars by Petr Chelčický, a peasant preacher in South Bohemia, can be viewed as the Czech resonance to Buddhist attitudes which had reached Europe earlier – for example in the form of the cult of St Francis of Assisi. Here and now it was a reaction to the cruelties and devastation of the long wars. The writings of Chelčický formed the beginning of the sect called the Czech Brethren, better known in the west as the Moravian Brethren. By their spiritual and cultural energy the Czech Brethren created that unique breed of stubborn, high-principled, bible-reading peasants and small-holders which functioned as a storage battery of ethnic identity after the Czechs lost their independence. A group of Brethren working in Králíky translated and printed the Bible and thereby brought the Czech literary language to a new peak of development. The Kralická Bible, a work of love, uses the living, colloquial language of the time and achieves great beauty and impact through its simplicity, earthiness and emotional restraint. In Slovakia the Czech of this Bible became the literary language and only in the nineteenth century was it replaced by the Slovak vernacular.

Sigismund hardly had time to clear up pockets of ardent Táborite resistance before he died in 1437. In accordance with the mutual succession treaty between Charles IV and the Habsburgs, Sigismund was succeeded on the Czech throne and in Hungary by Albrecht, Duke of Austria. He died after two years, leaving a posthumous son, Ladislaus, who lived and died at the Imperial Court in Germany. The task of pacifying the country and picking up the threads of international cooperation, so necessary in view of the mounting danger from the Turks, fell to George of Podiebrad (Jiří Poděbradský), the Hussite king.

George of Podiebrad was a Czech Protestant baron, far from the richest, but a man who combined a zest for power with considerable political skill. A widely reproduced nineteenth-century painting (by Brožík), of the 'unanimous' election of George of Podiebrad to the throne after Ladislaus Habsburg had died in 1457, is completely misleading. By that time the Czech Estates – barons, lower nobility and towns – had hardly any choice but to vote for George, who was already the undisputed master of the country. As the Captain of the Boleslav region and later of the federation of east Bohemian regions he broke by force of arms the military resistance of one county after another. When he finally gained control of Prague, he established himself as regent for the absent Ladislaus. Notwithstanding the doubtful legality of his advancement, George of Podiebrad was successful as regent and later as king he restored peace and order and secured the economic recovery of the war-ravaged country though not forgetting to increase his family possessions at the same time.

At home, he relied on the support of Protestant towns and lower nobility and a carefully maintained balance between the opposed groups of Protestant and Catholic barons. In contrast to the rigidity of his domestic policy, George's foreign policy was extremely flexible and dynamic. But in all his changing of alliances, broken promises, friendships and betrayals alike, George was guided by two overriding aims: to secure international recognition of the Utraquists, the Czech Protestant Church, and the ratification by Rome of the Kompaktáta of 1437 in the spirit they were interpreted in Prague; and to achieve a Central European and possibly wider defence agreement against the Turks. These two aims were, of course, complementary: joint defence against the Turks precluded the possibility of a new religious war against the heretic Czechs.

The style of his diplomatic offensive suggests that he was a far-sighted statesman. The first project concerned a radical reform of the Holy Roman Empire which would secure the Imperial throne to the Czech kings. The second was conceived after Rome withdrew from the Kompakatáta: George proposed to all the European courts a sort of United Christian Nations Organization for joint defence against the Turks. The first paragraph of the provisional charter, drafted by the King's diplomatic adviser, Antonio Marini of Grenoble, provided for the renunciation of the use of force in the settlement of disputes between members.

Neither the reform of the Holy Roman Empire nor the federation of christian princes against the Turks was practical politics. As so often before, the only realistic scheme was to attempt a personal, monarchical union of Poland, the Czech kingdom and Hungary. For this reason George recommended that the Czech Estates should elect as his successor not one of his two sons but the Polish Prince Wladislaw of the Jagellon dynasty.

Not even this project, however, was fulfilled in the way envisaged by George. Between 1471 and 1490 Wladislaw reigned only in Bohemia, while Moravia, Silesia and Lusitania were taken by the Hungarian King Matthias Corvinus, a personality like George in stature and origins. After a short war Wladislaw concluded peace with Matthias after whose death he was elected also to the Hungarian throne. He could not effectively control his large realm and its mighty barons, and the peasants were exploited and virtually enslaved. Wladislaw's rule and that of his son Louis (Ludvik) are marked by peasant revolts in both the Czech kingdom and Hungary. The lawlessness of the period prompted the first compilation of the Czech law completed by Victorin Kornel ze Všehrd, a Czech lawyer educated at the University of Bologna.

The Jagellon period saw the brief revival of Czech silver mining and of gold, tin and copper mining in Slovakia. In 1516 new silver mines were opened in Joachimsthal, and the Joachimsthaler silver coin – '*thaler*' for short in German, and '*tolar*' in Czech – established the name now employed for the American currency.

The peasants were not the only section of society to suffer from the arrogance of the barons. The barons encroached on the manufacturing privileges of the towns, opening breweries, distilleries, mills, timber yards, foundries and glassworks. Thus the Jagellon period gave rise to a clash of economic interests and a lasting antagonism between towns and landed nobility. In another hundred years this proved fatal for the kingdom, which, divided within, lost its independence and parliament for which the splendid Wladislaw Hall was built on the Prague Castle. Its austere grandeur now provides the stage for the prearranged election of Presidents.

The economic conflicts between towns and barons often reached the intensity of a civil war. The nobles claimed the return of land acquired by towns during the Hussite wars. Merchants were molested and robbed on the roads. In retaliation the towns organized punitive expeditions capturing and beheading robber knights. The two antagonistic factions of the establishment were, however, pushed together by common danger: at home they were threatened by the discontented peasant masses and abroad by the advance of the Turks into Central Europe. In 1470, to prevent a popular uprising the towns and the nobles concluded a civil peace treaty, for which the towns had to pay dearly by economic concessions.

Unable to assert their authority at home, the Jagellon rulers of Poland, of the Czech kingdom and of Hungary were in no position to muster an army that could withstand the Turkish onslaught. In 1526 King Louis was defeated by the Turks at Mohac in Hungary and died in the Danube marshes. For 150 years after this defeat most of Hungary remained occupied by the Turks.

The Jagellons were weak rulers and could not keep in check the barons who obtained from them the legalization of serfdom and constantly encroached on the privileges of towns. This made the towns join together and raise an army of their own so that in addition to frequent peasant risings the country was on the brink of civil war. Only in 1517 was an agreement reached, on St Wenceslas's day, confirming that burghers could be tried only by town courts and that the jurisdiction of the regional courts extended solely over nobles.

Although unsettled politically, the period of the Jagellon attempts to rule was also a time of cultural growth stimulated by the humanistic influences reaching the country from Italy. The first printing press was opened in Plzeň in 1468 and was another stimulus to literary output in Latin and in Czech. Architecture flourished in a splendid late Gothic, sometimes – as in the Wladislaw Hall of Prague Castle – already touched by Renaissance elements. All pointed to a great change, which came with the Habsburgs in 1526.

4 The Prague Habsburgs

Halfhearted adversaries

The Czech throne was claimed by the Austrian Duke Ferdinand of Habsburg on the basis of the succession treaty between the Habsburgs and the Jagellons. George of Podiebrad had not been the only ruler striving for a large Central European dominion in the face of the Turkish advance. Maximilian, Duke of Austria and Burgundy, the Emperor who, backed by England and Savoy, laid the foundation to the Habsburg encirclement of France, concluded in 1491 an alliance with the Great Prince of Moscow whose aim was to make the Polish Jagellons give up Hungary. But by 1515 the Turkish threat was so great that he felt obliged to negotiate with Wladislaw Jagellon a mutual succession treaty. Wladislaw's son Louis was betrothed to Maximilian's granddaughter Maria. This treaty led ultimately to the marriage of Maximilian's grandson Ferdinand to Wladislaw's daughter, Anna of Hungary (in 1521). When Louis Jagellon died in 1526, Ferdinand claimed the Czech throne.

The Czech Estates denied the validity of this agreement, claiming that Czech kings could be appointed only by Parliament. After some hard bargaining, Ferdinand of Habsburg finally obtained the support of the Czech nobility and towns, promising to respect the religious *status quo*. Presumably the steady advance of the Turks, who in another three years were to reach the gates of Vienna, increased the interest of both parties in reaching an agreement. Although the Turkish threat should have worked for the Habsburgs even better in Hungary Ferdinand's claim to the Hungarian succession was rejected.

The Habsburgs were by this time the most powerful ruling family in Europe – too powerful for the liking of the Czech barons, who over-confident after fifty years of weak Jagellon rule, believed that the Czech kingdom would benefit externally while limiting the Habsburg power at home by Parliament. However Ferdinand soon moved some offices of government to Vienna and introduced an improved system of tax collection which enabled him not only to finance wars with the Turks but also to further his dynastic aspirations. As soon as he was established on the Czech throne he lost no time in laying the foundations of an empire in which national parliaments had a diminishing importance. These centralizing measures, and his later harsh treatment of Czech Protestant towns, overshadow the positive aspects of Ferdinand's rule. He was an educated man, a student of the writings of Erasmus, and sought allies among the more liberal Utraquists against their puritanical faction.

After the long wars, with Sigismund's armies, with the Hungarians and with the Turks, Bohemia was thankful to move from the centre to the fringe of European affairs. A certain relaxed feeling can be detected in the art as well as the politics of this period. Although Renaissance architecture had already entered Prague during Wladislaw's reign, the first purely Renaissance building in a light and cheerful style was the Belvedere which Ferdinand built, employing Italian architects, for his wife Anna.

The first revolt against centralization and the dictatorial rule of a foreign dynasty came in 1546-7 when Ferdinand was preparing an expedition against Protestants in Germany. The Czech towns and nobility not only refused to provide him with an army but mustered one of their own to help the Germans. However, in the 110 years that had passed since the end of the Hussite wars, antagonistic forces in the various sections of Czech Protestantism had come into play and its revolutionary spirit had petered out. The Czech Protestants were halfhearted in their intention of helping their German co-religionists, and their army waited near the frontier to see who would get the upper hand. When Ferdinand scored a limited victory the nobility was quick to recant, leaving the blame on the towns which suffered severe retribution, approved by the 'Bloody Parliament' of 1547. There were executions, and for the first time in Czech history the king established police officers in towns, which also were subjected to confiscations and a special tax.

The abortive revolt also provided an opportunity for persecution of Moravian Brethren – many had to emigrate. With the help of the Jesuits, Ferdinand started a counter-reformation policy but had to move carefully to try to avoid a confrontation with the Ultraquist Church, whose freedom was guaranteed by law.

The Bloody Parliament of 1547 proved only a small foretaste of the final defeat of the Czech Protestants in 1620 in the same way that the conflict between Catholics and Protestants in Germany, ended by the Peace of Augsburg in 1548, was only a foretaste of the Thirty Years War. On the other hand, the Peace of Augsburg established in the German lands of the Empire the principle *cuius regio eius religio* (who rules also determines religion). This was never accepted in the Czech kingdom and was explicitly rejected by the Majestas Rudolphina in 1609, which confirmed religious freedom for Catholics and Ultraquists alike, irrespective of the religion professed by the lord on whose possessions they lived.

The Augsburg treaty, which became an essential part of the imperial constitution, was concluded as the Turks moved into Central Europe – a danger which obliged both sides to show a certain moderation. Rome viewed it as a compromise, and with a divided mind: it seemed to tolerate it in 1555 but later Paul IV is believed to have contemplated in 1558 accusing Ferdinand of condoning heresy. Ferdinand was certainly no hardliner, either in Catholic or in specific Habsburg terms.

Ferdinand had been well exposed to liberal influences in his youth, but his reasons for pursuing a moderate policy were, of course, political: the strength of the Lutherans in the German lands, the possibility that the Czechs would rise to support them – as they almost did in 1547 – the Turkish advance and the unlikelihood of getting much support from the Spanish Habsburgs in the case of trouble – all this left him with hardly any options. A realistic assessment of his situation led Ferdinand to take a reformist stand and to ask the Council of Trent in 1561 to approve communion in both kinds for the laity (as practised by the Utraquists) and to allow priests to marry, in the hope that this would open to married Lutheran pastors the possibility of returning to a reformed Catholic Church.

This leaning towards Protestantism became still more pronounced in Ferdinand's son and successor Maximilian II, who declared himself privately as 'neither Catholic nor Protestant, but Christian', had a married confessor, and, like the Utraquists, practised communion in both kinds. Moreover, his personal inclinations and beliefs reflected the political antagonism between the Europe-oriented Prague Habsburgs and the Spanish Habsburgs, whose political interests spanned the world.

Threatened by the Turks in the east, the Prague Habsburgs wanted peace in the west. Maximilian was therefore greatly worried about the possible consequences of the massacre of the Huguenots in France on St Bartholomew's Eve. Using the services of Wratislaw Pernštýn, a Czech nobleman, he tried to mediate between Philip II of Spain and the Protestant Netherlands.

In his efforts to preserve peace in Europe Maximilian aimed for an alliance with the Poles and even detained in Prague the envoy whom Philip of Spain sent to the Russian Tsar, Ivan the Terrible. Ivan was negotiating an agreement with the Turks, and was therefore an enemy of any occupant of the Czech throne – the fact that he was also a Habsburg made little difference.

Maximilian's successors in Prague, Rudolf II and Matthias, were not only completely anti-Spanish but also dominated by a growing feeling of impotence and resignation: they could appease but not reconcile the Protestants, who were deeply suspicious after the experiences of their co-religionists in France and the Netherlands. They could not prevent Madrid and Rome trying a hard line where their own soft line failed.

The political aspirations of the two Habsburg branches merged only when Spain finally recognized that her world ambitions could not be pursued in the face of English seapower without complete domination of Europe. The energies of both dynasties turned to European affairs: the mounting anti-Habsburg opposition in Europe was no longer to be appeased but crushed. War became inevitable and was to last for thirty years.

Centre of research and arts

As if sensing the end of an era Prague was seething with new ideas. The Prague court was the backwater of European politics presided over by a frightened but intellectually curious, art-loving Emperor. Rudolf II appears to have been a man sensing the approach of a scientific revolution. Though still thinking in terms of the outgoing era, his alchemists and astrologers were preparing for a breakthrough in science and astronomy. The imperial court – like some university foundations of our day – provided a living and easy mutual contact for outstanding and active minds.

In an observatory built for him at Nové Benátky, forty miles north of the capital, Rudolf's court astronomer Tycho de Brahe assembled over a long period accurate observations of the planets and their satellites. Brahe's thinking was still shackled by the Ptolemaic geocentric theory and he took enormous pains in fruitless attempts to explain his data by assuming always more complicated rotation of spheres round the earth. His successor, Johannes Keppler, applied the new heliocentric concept of Copernicus to Brahe's data and evolved the three theorems expressing the relationships between the mass, speed and orbits of planets and their satellites. Similarly, though in a less spectacular way, the alchemists whom Rudolf paid to discover how base metals could be transformed into gold (they lived in the tiny houses of Golden Street – still a highlight for sightseers in Prague) assembled data useful for the development of chemistry.

Astronomy and, in particular, mathematics, connected the walled Jewish quarter with the Royal ghetto, for this cosmopolitan society of scientists was perhaps even more separated from contemporary Czech society than were the Jews themselves. The Jews in fact provided the Charles University with its first professor of mathematics, Master Kaménck. This was also the time of the Cabbalist Rabbi Loev whose grave is now a place of Jewish pilgrimage. He is best known in legend as the creator of Golem, the robot made of earth and given life by '*shemah*', the Jewish profession of belief in one God.

Rudolf II amassed in the castle a great collection of paintings and other art treasures. Even what remained of this collection after looting during the Thirty Years War, removals to Vienna and sales ordered by the utilitarian Joseph II in the eighteenth century, still fills an impressive gallery at the Prague Castle. Many were discovered only in 1966 in stacks of unclassified paintings in the lofts and storerooms of the castle, bringing to light unknown masterpieces of Renaissance art.

The doomed revolt

Textbooks, literature and political oratory have firmly established in
Czech minds the oversimplified ideas that the independence of the
Czech kingdom was lost in the battle of the White Mountain in
1620; that as the first victim in the common struggle the Czechs
were betrayed by their Protestant allies who concluded in 1648 the
Peace of Westphalia without them and to their cost. This historical
image lets a self-pitying reaction be substituted for hard political
analysis whenever the country joins the right cause but is abandoned
by its allies or sympathizers, as happened at the time of Munich, of
Yalta and in the spring of 1968. Virtue betrayed four times over
suggests some fundamental fault in political thinking and a greater
awareness of this might prevent a fifth repeat of the historical pattern. A country rarely loses its independence in a single battle, and
the Czech kingdom certainly did not lose it in the two-hour skirmish
outside Prague in 1620. This defeat only revealed the internal weakness of the country and the naive view which its leaders took of the
European politics of the day.

Far from being the result of a political misadventure in 1618-20,
the end of Czech independence was coming throughout the second
half of the sixteenth century. The peasant masses, oppressed and on
the brink of revolt, were moving back to the radicalism of the Hussite wars but lacked the leadership which would channel their radical
mood into action. They no longer had a common cause with the
Protestant nobles who had become their oppressors. The Czech
towns, which in the Hussite wars had formed an uneasy alliance with
both Táborites and the Protestant barons, now feared their own poor
no less than the barons feared their serfs. The burghers also distrusted the nobility which had betrayed them in 1547. Ferdinand I's
punishments broke the economic power of the towns and this had a
disastrous effect on the social development of the kingdom. Already
overshadowed by the flourishing overseas trade of western Europe,
the towns had to struggle against domestic difficulties. The whole of
Czech society became introverted, immersed in internal strife between Protestants and Catholics, between nobles and towns, between
barons and the common people.

Even the struggle of the Protestant nobility against the Habsburgs for the maintenance of their privileges and freedoms was heavily marked by this provincialism of Czech politics. They seemed to underestimate the effort required to prevail against the Habsburgs whose dominions stretched from south-eastern Europe to America. The Habsburgs, on the other hand, could view the Czech revolts as a mere nuisance so long as their position in Europe was secure.

The self-confidence of the Protestant barons was further strengthened during the reign of the two Habsburgs who appeared exceptionally uninterested in politics, Rudolph II and Matthias I. During their rule the barons scored two easy victories. In 1609 they succeeded in obtaining the Majestas Rudolphina, a decree establishing complete religious tolerance in the Czech kingdom. It enabled Protestants to build their churches on Catholic domains and gave similar freedom for Catholics on the estates of Protestant barons. Under Matthias the nobles went even further and forced him to sign an unprecedented document guaranteeing that their property would not be confiscated for political offences.

The euphoria generated by the relative ease with which the Czech Protestants advanced their constitutional position under Rudolph and Matthias survived when the imperial succession passed to Ferdinand II. It was as if the Czech political leaders failed to notice that Ferdinand's accession meant a change in regime. The new emperor was a man of action, a statesman holding his court in Vienna where he was safe from the threats of force which the Czech Protestant barons could employ against his two predecessors who lived in Prague.

The Czech Protestants were also encouraged by the opposition to the Habsburgs, rising all over Europe, not realizing that the threat presented by this opposition would oblige the imperial regime to consolidate its power in Bohemia and Moravia, its most important base after Spain. As long as their domination of Europe was unchallenged, the Habsburgs could afford to be tolerant towards the Czech Protestants and to treat their political games as a mere nuisance. Ferdinand, however, faced a changing, explosive situation in Europe in which the growing militancy of the Czech Protestants must have appeared as a serious risk.

Another Czech miscalculation concerned the strength of the Protestant camp in Europe. The Czech Protestants appear to have been tragically out of touch: their information was out of date. There was only one well-informed Czech Protestant magnate and he took a sceptical view of the situation. In considering potential allies in 1615, three years before the revolt took place, Karel Starší ze Žerotína (Charles of Žerotín the Elder) wrote that a Protestant union was unlikely to come about in Germany, that Gabor Bethlen, the ruler of Transylvania, was unreliable and that the Elector of Saxony could not be trusted. He realized that after the death of Henry IV of France Europe was different and that the England of James I would no longer be able to give the Protestant movement on the Continent the support it had received from Elizabeth I.

If lack of information led to a strategic error in timing, an almost incredible political clumsiness deprived the Czech Protestants of the last chances they had.

The revolt against the Habsburgs was very much in the air ever since Ferdinand had started to encroach on Protestant liberties, and the Catholic Church, taking its cue from him, started to be tough with Protestants on its estates. The situation became explosive when almost simultaneously two Catholic lords, a bishop and an abbot, ordered two Protestant churches built on their land to be pulled down, thus openly disregarding Majestas Rudolphina.

However, the Protestant nobility, and still less the towns, were by no means ready to strike. Leading members of the radical wing of the Protestant movement were so uncertain of support that they tried to force the issue: they took a large group of unsuspecting Protestant leaders to the castle under a false pretence of demonstration and protest, while the intention was to assassinate Ferdinand's men. However, even the radicals must have been halfhearted about the intended murder: two of Ferdinand's governors and their clerk, when thrown out of the window of their office at the castle, fell softly on a heap of rubbish and went to Vienna to report. This second defenestration of Prague sent to Ferdinand advisers well informed about Czech weaknesses.

After the Protestant leaders had been personally involved in a treasonable act, it was easier for the radicals to convince the Estates that Ferdinand should be deposed. More tactical mistakes followed. The Protestant confederation adopted a constitution which completely eliminated any central power and would have led to the same state of aristocratic anarchy that became the fatal weakness of Poland, where any lord could veto a decision. This in itself was enough to put off potential supporters and to make the vacant Czech throne a less desirable prize.

The Czech Protestant nobles took an even more disastrous step by proceeding immediately with the election of a king, instead of letting the several candidates compete for the throne by providing help against the Habsburgs and establishing a military presence in Bohemia. They settled on their western neighbour, the Count Palatine, Frederick, arguing that a personal union between the Palatinate and the Czech kingdom would create in the heart of the Empire a bloc linked with England, since Frederick was married to Elizabeth, daughter of James I. Unfortunately the Palatine treasury was empty and the Czech nobles proved incapable of mobilizing their own resources. England was too far away, and the question of help for the Czech Protestants became an issue of English internal politics. No real aid was forthcoming from this quarter.

Another potential ally, the Elector of Saxony, lost interest when the throne was offered to Frederick, while the Habsburgs promised him Lusatia for help or neutrality. Gabor Bethlen, the Protestant ruler of Transylvania, was interested in the Czech revolt only if he could make money out of it and this did not seem likely. The little principalities of Germany organized in the Protestant Union were on the Czech side but not of much assistance at this stage. Only the Netherlands sent help but that came too late because of internal political strife between the anti-Spanish radicals and the party of the commercial faction. Sweden, which under Gustavus Adolphus was to play a decisive part in the Thirty Years War, was too far away to intervene at short notice.

The Vienna Habsburgs were reluctant to engage in the war advocated by Spain and therefore took two years to prepare their diplomatical and military intervention – giving Frederick time for more political blunders in Prague. The choice of the Count Palatine not only failed to secure outside help but also failed to unify the anti-Habsburg forces at home – on the contrary Frederick managed to become yet another faction, disliked by both Utraquists and Lutherans. When the imperial army finally moved it made fast, practically unopposed, progress to Prague, where the Czech Protestant army was assembled on the White Mountain. They attacked the Habsburg army as it approached on the road from Plzeň but were defeated in a battle that was over in about two hours. Frederick, 'the Winter King', and his English wife fled from Prague without any attempt at resistance.

The retribution that followed the White Mountain left the country stunned for centuries. While the Czech barons, confident that by the guarantee obtained from Matthias their property would not be confiscated, viewed the whole affair as a political game, the Habsburgs and the Catholic Church determined to eradicate Czech Protestantism and independence once and for all. Twenty-six Protestant leaders and one Catholic who joined them were condemned for high treason and mutilated and beheaded in front of the Old Town Hall. It can be assumed that a larger number of less prominent people lost their lives at the same time. The property of Protestant nobles and sympathizing Catholics was confiscated. Peasants tied to the land were forcibly converted to Catholicism and free Protestants, nobility and burghers, were given the choice of conversion or emigration. It is estimated that 300,000 emigrated, including almost the entire educated stratum and many peasants who fled although they were required to stay. Some, like John Amos Commenius, Bishop of the Moravian Brethren, and Hollar, the engraver, ultimately found their way to England. Many more writers, painters, clergymen, craftsmen and traders who did not want to give up their faith or to live under fear and oppression, left in the hope of returning in better times, and never came back.

Writing in 1968, a Czech historian, Miroslav Hroch, came to a conclusion that brings to mind the events of his own time:

The Czech uprising in the years 1618–20 can hardly be cleared of the charge of a certain amateurism. The drama enacted in those unhappy years was written carelessly and the players were not very good. The fact that many of them had in their hearts the self-sacrificing enthusiasm of amateur actors makes it all the sadder. It was an uprising born of rashness, of insufficient political erudition, of the radicalism of a small group of enthusiasts whose honourable intentions could not be questioned. This uprising decided for centuries not only the fate of the ruling class but the fate of the entire nation. Here in this tragedy without glory lies the essential tragedy of the defeat on the White Mountain.

PART II

1620–1914

5 The Catholic transformation

The European Citadel

The Protestant revolt of 1618 was not well prepared, nor did it enjoy popular support. A large section of the political nation, including the towns, remained neutral. The Protestant aristocracy saw it purely in a local context, as just another political move this time taken a step further against the absentee ruler. The Habsburgs, however, saw the Prague events in a wider framework. Aware of the mobilization of anti-Habsburg forces in Europe and threatened by a major conflagration, they hit back hard. Yet things were allowed to drift too far and their brief and effective expedition of 1620 did not go down in history as a successful pre-emptive strike but as the first in a series of wars that scourged Europe for fully thirty years.

The crushing of the revolt was fateful not only for the Czechs. The end of an independent Czech kingdom was also to be a turning-point in the history of Europe. In that tense situation, when hawkish parties were getting the upper hand in both the Protestant and Catholic camps of Europe, the news that the Habsburg governors had been chased from Prague must have had the same electrifying effect as, 350 years later, did the news that the Czechs were trying to free themselves from Soviet domination.

It is painfully obvious that the actors in the drama did not have a full grasp of the wider scene. Frederick, the Count Palatine, elected King by the poorly informed Czech nobility, on the eve of the storm had nothing better to do than to antagonize not only the Catholic minority but also the Czech Utraquists and the German Lutherans by cleansing with Calvinistic vigour Prague churches of altars, paintings and statues. The crucifix on the Charles bridge offended his English wife by its nudity and she had it thrown into the river. Her father, James I, was not in such a radical mood. He moved only when the Spanish threatened the Palatinate and even then only to try to appease the Habsburgs as mediator.

The same reluctance to engage in a major war existed also on the side of the Vienna Habsburgs but they were steadily pushed towards it by the Spanish branch. Both armies fighting the fatal battle of the White Mountain were made up mostly of mercenaries, the Protestants being commanded by Thurn and two other Germans and the Habsburg army by Johann Tserclaes de Tilly, a Dutchman. Yet, almost symbolically, the soldiery from Italy, Burgundy and the Netherlands included in its ranks a future warlord, Wallenstein, and a future philosopher, René Descartes, who between them did more to change the political and spiritual scene of Europe than all the princes who paid them for risking their skin on the outskirts of Prague on 7 November 1620.

Though the Spanish were not much in evidence, the Czechs realized that they were the real enemies, pressing for a European showdown between the Catholics and the Protestants. Protestant propaganda warned that the Habsburgs had sold the Czech kingdom to Spain and the Czech pamphlets and cartoons distributed at that time in Europe had a strong anti-Spanish edge.

The Prague defenestration was taken by the Catholic party as the final provocation. In much the same way the German Protestants were set on the warpath by the publication of Ferdinand's Edict of Restitution, the product of pressure from Spain and Rome, which demanded the restoration of church lands appropriated by Protestant princes since 1552 (the Treaty of Passau). Even those princes who had so far been neutral or allied to the Catholics now rose against the Emperor who threatened their possessions. The Protestant reaction to the Edict of Restitution – speeded up the disintegration of the Holy Roman Empire. The reaction to it obliged the Emperor to become an independent military power: in the past he had had to rely on armies provided by the Princes of the Empire. And by a supreme irony of history it was the son of a Czech Protestant family, Albrecht z Valdštejna, known as Wallenstein, who created for Ferdinand a self-supporting army and a war economy ensuring supplies of equipment and armaments, and thus became the first modern European warlord.

Wallenstein's success against the North German Protestants led by the Danish King Christian IV was demonstrated by the emergence, for the first time in history, of an Imperial Navy in the Baltic. It became evident that in an expanded world every isolated European conflict becomes universal. Gustavus Adolphus of Sweden, who entered the conflict at this stage as leader of the Protestants, said that 'things had come to such a pass that all wars being waged in Europe were mixed up together and became one war'. And it was about this time that Bohemia came to be seen as the citadel of Europe.

In the first ten years of the mounting storm, from the defeat of the Czech revolt in 1620 to the entry of the Swedes into the conflict in 1630, this citadel of Europe was transformed into a Habsburg province – and at the same time, by a dialectic evolution, emerged as the power bloc generating not only the military strength of the Habsburgs but also their new, distinctly Central European, as opposed to German, imperial policies. Those who lived through the transformation of the independent kingdom into the Habsburg citadel had a hard time. A new constitution imposed by the Habsburgs in 1627 established them as a hereditary dynasty, no longer dependent on election in the Czech Parliament, whose powers they severely curtailed. The new constitution, called the Renewed Establishment, recognized only the Roman Catholic religion and gave its clergy an important place in the Parliament and in the Administration.

Not relying on constitutional changes, the Catholic party, led by foreigners, made sure by execution and expulsion of Protestants and by confiscation of their estates that there would be none left to attempt a come-back. Land held by Protestants and the goods of Catholics accused of participation in the revolt were given to officers of the imperial army of occupation. Nobles and burghers were allowed to emigrate, but peasants were not and had to accept conversion. Their exploitation by forced labour on the estates of the new foreign barons was stepped up and their movements, personal freedom and consumption were restricted by new regulations.

These political changes profoundly altered the economic structure of the Czech countryside. After confiscation small estates were integrated into large units and could now be administered bureaucratically. The last traces of paternalistic relations between the lord and his peasants disappeared. The possibility of unrestricted exploitation of serfs removed the need for technological progress in agriculture. The economy of the Czech towns suffered in more than one way. The market surplus of the small, private plots of land was extremely small and peasants were allowed to buy food and drink only from the enterprises of their lords. Cut off from European trade and surrounded by a depopulated countryside stripped of purchasing power, the towns had no chance to recover.

Wars ravaged the Czech lands several times and reduced the population through starvation and pestilence. When finally in 1648 peace was concluded in Westphalia between Catholics and Protestants, the Czechs ceased to exist as a political nation and their lands were left under foreign occupation.

Commenius and Wallenstein

While the Czech kingdom was rapidly sinking after 1620, the fight for the preservation of the national political and cultural heritage continued on two fronts. Abroad, exiles vainly tried to convince Protestant powers that the restoration of Protestantism in an independent Czech kingdom should be made part of any peace settlement, though they succeeded, in disseminating some of the literary and artistic achievements of their country. The other front was at home, where a few collaborators and the silent majority each in their own way tried to salvage as much as possible, by putting a new coat on the old body politic. One man did more than anybody to uphold the Czech cultural heritage, and he could do so only in exile in Poland, Sweden, England and Holland. Jan Ámos Komenský (Commenius) was the last bishop of the Czech (Moravian) Brethren. He left the country in 1627 and spent the rest of his life in Poland and in the Protestant countries of Europe, writing textbooks, satirical pamphlets and philosophical works and taking an active part in educational activities and the organization of schools. His textbooks and educational works were based on the then novel concept that people learn only if their interest is aroused and that the teacher must appeal not only to the ear but also to the eye. *Orbis Pictus*, an illustrated language textbook, is probably the first audio-visual textbook.

In a bitter satire entitled *The Labyrinth of the World and the Peace of the Heart*, Commenius lifted the veil of pious pretence to reveal the senseless cruelty of the world much the same as Cervantes did before him and Voltaire after him. Only six years spent as a political prisoner enabled me to understand why Commenius gave up all hope of reforming adults and turned his energies to improving the world by better education of children.

It is characteristic of the meek view the Czechs take of their national destiny that they look to the exiled Commenius, to the wandering 'Teacher of Nations', as one of the great men, perhaps the greatest man the country has produced, while they see only a hostile alien in the other son of the country who was raised high by the waves closing over the sinking kingdom. They accept as their own the humble teacher but not the great statesman and soldier – Albrecht of Wallenstein, Duke of Friedland, Generalissimo of the Imperial Army. Outwardly the two have nothing in common – the educationalist and bishop of a quietist sect, an exile dependent on friends and his writing, and the warlord who built himself palaces of outstanding splendour from the business of death and cruelty. But the lives and work of the two had a common feature. In their mutually opposed callings, each on his own side of the political barrier dividing Europe, they attempted to expand and transform the essentially Czech experience – one that of learning and happiness, the other that of power and politics – into a wider European context. With absurdly disparate weapons they opposed each other on the political scene of the war-torn Continent. Yet there is a great affinity in their achievements: they both salvaged the heritage of the sinking kingdom by transporting it into the newly-emerging, modern world.

In contrast to Commenius, Wallenstein's actions were certainly not prompted by patriotism. But in pursuing his considerable greed for possessions and power, he analysed correctly the political forces of his time and almost succeeded in restoring the independence of the Czech kingdom. Born in 1583 in Heřmanice in Bohemia, Albrecht Václav z Valdštejna received the education appropriate to a boy from a Czech Protestant family of no great means. He also travelled in Germany, France and Italy and realizing the political blindness and provincialism of the Czech Protestant nobility, lost no time in changing camps. After having joined the Habsburg military service as a member of the Czech contingent against the Hungarians in 1604, he was converted to Catholicism in 1606 and made his first fortune by marrying Lukrecia Nešková, an elderly widow with large estates in Moravia.

During the 1618-20 revolt his estates were confiscated by the Czech Protestants but Wallenstein, as he now called himself, did better than redeeming them. The regiment which Wallenstein brought to Ferdinand contributed much to the Habsburg victory and he was appointed Governor of Bohemia and made partner in a coin-minting monopoly. With debased currency he bought up nearly sixty estates belonging to executed or banished Protestants. His second wife, whom he married in 1623, was suited to a man who owned all north-east Bohemia and sought greater political influence: Isabela Kateřina, daughter of Karel Harrach, a Czech Catholic baron and chief adviser to Ferdinand.

Wallenstein's progress is marked first by the organization of an army for Ferdinand; then by the consolidation of an economic base of his own in the Duchy of Friedland, a self-enclosed region in the north of Bohemia; finally by his great attempt to join the Adriatic to the Baltic seas by a chain of countries welded into a political unity centred on Prague. This political concept, pursued by all great Czech rulers – Přemysl Otakar II in the thirteenth century, Charles IV, George of Podiebrad – stemmed from the economic need of a landlocked country to secure trade by making links with distant sea-ports, combined with the political need to seek allies north and south against enemies in the east and west.

Wallenstein's north–south project was in harmony with Spanish interests: it could help to eliminate the competition of the Nether-lands. Wallenstein occupied Jutland and was subsequently appointed general of the Baltic and the North Sea. His plan was to join the two seas by a canal so that his imperial navy could link up with the Spanish fleet in the North Sea. The plan was wrecked by the opposition of the Hanseatic towns. Lubeck, Hamburg, Rostock, Luneburg and Stralsund refused to provide ships for the Emperor, fearing the Spanish as friends no less than the German Protestants as enemies. On 6 July 1630 the Swedes landed a small army in Pomerania and later that month Wallenstein was dismissed at the insistence of the Catholic princes.

Wallenstein remained out of office until 1631 when he was re-called to save the situation after Gustavus Adolphus defeated imperial forces at Breitenfeld, near Leipzig. When Gustavus Adolphus was killed in battle the following year, Wallenstein remained the only great man on the Central European scene, combining the qualities of an administrator, general, politician and statesman.

After being recalled to power, Wallenstein's first step was to regain control of Bohemia, then occupied by the Elector of Saxony. The temptation to resurrect the Czech kingdom and to make himself its king as the first step to becoming emperor was so obvious that the Viennese court could not believe that Wallenstein would not ultimately act upon it. The Catholic princes whose lands Wallenstein allowed to be devastated by the Swedes fanned this suspicion, and Father Joseph, Richelieu's adviser on foreign affairs, let it be known that in 1619 – before the battle of the White Mountain – Wallenstein had confided to him the ambition to found his own kingdom in Germany and recapture Constantinople from the Turks. Whether true or not, this gossip must have appeared to Father Joseph both plausible and likely to weaken the Habsburg camp.

In a style not novel in power politics – and most recently used by Stalin in his pre-emptive strike against potential Titoists in the satellite countries – a secret tribunal in Vienna decided that Wallenstein must die before he betrayed the Emperor. Unlike Stalin, the Emperor was not in a strong enough position to use the paraphernalia of justice: Wallenstein was not executed but assassinated on 26 February 1634 at Cheb (Eger) in the western tip of Bohemia.

Wallenstein's death frustrated the independent power complex based on Bohemia and the Habsburgs could now finally take possession of their Czech heritage. From that time until 1918, Bohemia and Moravia were the mainstay of the Viennese Habsburgs' power which, severed from Spain, remained in latent or live conflict with the German states until the fatal alliance which led to the First World War. Like all rulers of Bohemia before them, they were bound to expand their possessions and influence south and north.

In the following year the Treaty of Prague, concluded between the Emperor and John George of Saxony, marked the beginning of the end of the long wars but the war-weary Swedes received a new impetus from France. Cardinal Richelieu declared war on Spain and for thirteen more years Bohemia suffered at the hands of the French and the Swedes. The Swedes sacked Wallenstein's palace in Prague and took its art treasures, together with those they found in the royal castle and elsewhere, to Stockholm. The university was defended by its students on the Charles Bridge. The statue of a student musketeer which can be seen in Klementinum, the old Jesuit university, commemorates this event.

The devastation of war and disease in Central Europe lasted thirty years and population reduced to as little as forty per cent of its former number – even governments saw in the end that no one could win. The warlords were losing interest as there was little left for their armies to pilfer and live on. A feeling was abroad that it was now necessary to find a way to co-exist.

The Peace of Westphalia was concluded by the first all-European peace conference. It was held in Münster and Osnabrück in 1648 and gave expression to the need for the coexistence then called 'toleration' of different sovereignties and creeds. Neither the territorial acquisitions of Sweden and France nor the settling of accounts and possessions between the Catholic and Protestant princes of Germany matched the importance of the fundamental restructuring of European society east of the Rhine to which the Peace of Westphalia bears witness. In 1648 the pretence of the continued existence of a pyramidal feudal society of princes and barons, headed by the Pope and the Emperor, was finally abandoned.

The Czech kingdom was not represented at the peace conference: – the Protestants who had revolted in 1618, as well as the Catholic warlord Wallenstein, who could be seen as heir to the political power complex of the Czech state, were dead. The Viennese Habsburgs, defeated in their ambition to impose Catholic imperial rule on Germany, were confirmed as the hereditary rulers of the Czech crown lands. The Golden Bull of Charles IV, the constitutional document which had confirmed the leading position of the Czech kingdom in the Holy Roman Empire became obsolete. It was replaced by the Peace of Westphalia as the new constitution of a disintegrating Empire of which the Czech kingdom was to form part only in political theory. When after another 200 years the imperial tradition was invoked in the efforts leading to the unification of Germany and the Czechs were invited to send a delegation to an Imperial Diet in Frankfurt, František Palacký, historiographer of the Czech Kingdom and 'Father of the Nation', refused. In agreement with most of his contemporaries, he thought the place of Czechs was in the new society of nations, mostly Slav, ruled by the Habsburgs.

Baroque in the Czech lands

The peace of Westphalia did not bring universal peace to Europe. France and Spain remained at war, but east of the Rhine, in Central Europe, there was to be a long period of peace from 1648 until the wars fought by Maria Theresa to defend her succession to the Habsburg throne in 1740. Internal peace was necessary to Central Europe if it was to hold its own in the struggle against the Turks in the east and against France in the west. The external dangers in their turn contributed to the coherence of the empire of the Austrian Habsburgs. In this period Spain rapidly declined from a world power to the prize for which other countries went to war; the Scandinavian countries slackened, the military power of the Swedes was broken by Peter the Great, who centralized Russian government in the hands of the tsars and initiated the westernization of Russia.

As the pressures from Sweden and Spain diminished, and while Russia had not yet grown strong, the offensive power of the Turks was broken. Austria, England and France emerged as the supreme powers, producing three outstanding statesmen and generals: Prince Eugene of Savoy, Marlborough, and Louis XIV.

The feeling of achievement, the fortunes made while wars were fought abroad, all are reflected in the baroque style, the relaxed architecture of open palaces and country houses built where self-enclosed fortressess had stood before. The style speaks from a position of strength, attained through a sequence of protracted and degrading wars. This explains its search for the soul and preoccupation with death.

In the European context, baroque is the style of the centralized state. In Bohemia and Moravia its ideology formed part of an ideological warfare against the Protestants. The new rulers and the victorious Catholic Church filled the war-ravaged country with churches and palaces that made it into another Italy north of the Alps. While these beautiful monuments still strike the eye, the psychological effects of this ideological campaign are now less immediately obvious. Nevertheless, the 150 years of baroque and counter reformation effected a brutal turn in Czech history and, for some time, succeeded in suppressing the people's consciousness of its past.

For this reason Czech historians often speak about the 'lost centuries'. But there is no such thing as lost time; every impact sends waves of events in space and into the future. When the Czech kingdom came to an end, there began a new Czech nation, stripped of its traditional political classes but for that reason also less inhibited and more egalitarian: a sort of young America in the heart of an old continent, even if the country emerged in a state of amnesia.

Another label used to identify this period is 'the age of darkness'. Like all labels, it is an oversimplification, but there is some truth in it. It was not only the darkness of persecution and oppression but also the darkness in which water gathers underground before it emerges as a stream. Many streams in the national character of the Czechs can be traced back to the formative influences of the baroque period.

The Prague executions in 1621, which were staged with all the paraphernalia of a theatrical performance mark the beginning of European baroque. In Central Europe, at least, such a psychologically-aimed display of cruelty was something novel. It became typical in the period of the Counter Reformation, when it was used to present heretics with an earthly and easily understood image of hell and damnation. It obviously provided both an outlet and a stimulus for sadistic and masochistic tendencies, but on a national scale Catholicism did not achieve such an acceptance of cruelty as despotic governments did with the Protestant Prussians and the Orthodox Russians.

There were also some positive effects. Preoccupation with death and suffering in hell was a means to an end. The character, feelings, behaviour and impressionability of the people to be terrorized into conformity and obedience had to be studied. Baroque statues, nowhere better seen than in the avenues of Virtues and Vices on the terraces of the castle-like home built by Count Špork for war veterans in Kuks, in north-eastern Bohemia, remain as evidence of the deep psychological interests of the time. This was manifested also in the Jesuits' psychoanalytical approach to confession: Sigmund Freud, born in Moravia, and the Viennese psychological school have roots deeper than nineteenth-century Vienna. Life and death, morality and nature, buildings and countryside – these were the polarities producing the tension or passion which the baroque was striving to overcome in the quest for harmony; the imprint of this quest can be best seen in the Czech countryside.

In Hejnice, a small village on the Wallenstein estate in north Bohemia, there was a handsome Gothic church with the conventional east–west orientation of the nave cutting across the splendid panorama of mountains rising from the plain to the north. With a superb disregard for convention Fischer von Erlach, one of the great baroque architects, built a new nave facing north instead of east, reducing the original main nave to a transcept: the two spires of the rebuilt church now appear to be flanking symmetrically a distant mountain peak, giving a unique sense of harmony to the approach through a long avenue of lime trees.

The conditioning of the mind by the harmony of landscape with man-imposed statues and buildings against the contrasting experience of war destruction, as well as the image of death either approached through martyrdom or leading to eternal suffering, had a profound influence on the Czech character: there is a certain reluctance to fight, an outward submission to foreign domination made bearable by an unyielding mental reservation. These attitudes can be termed cowardice and hypocrisy; the Czechs transformed them into an ironic art of survival.

Moving from the general to the more specific features of the Czech character rooted in this period, we come to the hatred of censorship, seen as an instrument of foreign oppression and feared as a threat to national existence. Koniáš, the name of the Jesuit who organized the collection and burning of heretical books (including the Czech translation of the Bible) is still after 300 years the byword for the hated figure of censor. The real Antonín Koniáš was so efficient, and his definition of heresy so all-embracing, that for almost 200 years Czech ceased to be a literary language in the Czech lands. It only survived as such in Slovakia, where the Kralická Bible continued to be read by Protestants sheltering on the estates of Calvinist barons.

The language-fixation of the nationalism of the nineteenth century, which so affected relations between Czechs and Germans, not only in the Habsburg monarchy but even in the 1918-39 republic, can be traced back to this period of the Counter-Reformation and late Germanization programme of Maria Theresa and Joseph II.

Also the questionable notion that the political, cultural and artistic life of an occupied country can be continued abroad is given substance by the example of the seventeenth-century exiles. Apart from Commenius a large number of politicians, writers and artists were active abroad. The two historians of this period, Pavel Stránský and Pavel Skála ze Zhoře, worked in exile, as did an outstanding portrait painter, Jan Kupecký, and Václav Hollar, the engraver, who settled in London.

The fact that Czech baroque artists worked abroad and were at home replaced by Italian and German architects and sculptors in the service of the new foreign aristocracy is often used as an argument for the view of the baroque in Czech lands as alien style. True, it was imported by foreign occupants but it was nevertheless assimilated. The injection of foreign, mostly southern talent greatly enriched the local style of building and of living, and the new lightness, elegance and sparkle did not remain restricted to aristocratic society. The art and music of Catholic churches, and the Italian and Spanish fashions of the aristocracy had a lasting influence on the music, folklore and costumes of the peasants. Czech folklore is a marriage of baroque and Slav forms and colours, of baroque drama and peasant values, of baroque rhythm and local melody. For better or for worse modern Czech art and drama, literature and music still draw heavily on the underground sources originating in the baroque period and continue to strive to express local reality through the formal means of European art.

Traditionalists and Rebels Attempt a Revival

After 1620, the political and cultural traditions of the country were transposed into modern terms by two men, Commenius and Wallenstein; then the baroque styles imposed on the country from outside were assimilated by the people. Looking closer at the process by which this was achieved over some 150 years, we can distinguish its contradictions, made up of various forms of submission or acceptance on the one hand and of rejection and rebellion on the other. Though both reactions were present in some degree all the time, it was only natural that the initial terror of war and anxiety of occupation gradually wore off and that the invasion of foreign ideology, administrators and artists was followed by the rising tide of a national revival.

The Arts

The influx of foreign rule, thought and art, repulsive as it must have appeared to those who watched it in submission, produced monuments of great beauty and grace: churches and palaces built by Kilian Dienzenhofer, Fischer von Erlach, Georg Hermann and numerous Italian architects; statues by Brokof, Mathias Braun and Georg Raphael Donner.

Music, the least political of the arts, provided the first signs of revival, and local talent, stimulated by the instrumental music introduced by the Catholic Church, produced many baroque composers for the Church and for the aristocratic courts at home and abroad. The works of František Mícha, Bohuslav Černohorský, Jan Stamic, Jiří Benda and Josef Mysliveček, all belonging to this period, continue to be performed and loved in Prague.

Czech painters, absorbed and modified the baroque style. Václav Vavřinec Reiner has the sharp, dramatic quality of the Italian and Spanish paintings of the period; but portraits by Petr Brandl and Karel Škréta are in mellower style, looking for drama in the soul rather than in the actions of their subjects.

Science

In 1621 Jan Jesenský, an eminent Slovak surgeon and Rector of the Charles University, was beheaded and the university taken over by the Catholics. Protestant students and teachers dispersed all over Europe, and what remained was in 1656 integrated with the Jesuit university established by Ferdinand II in Klementinum. Hence for some centuries, it was called the Charles-Ferdinand University.

A hundred years after the Jesuit takeover it reverted to its tradition of critical thought: Jan Marcus Marci, a physician and physicist of this period, has only recently been rediscovered as an original and penetrating mind of the Newtonian brand, though not of Newton's calibre. The practical orientation of this new generation of scientists and intellectuals – often parish priests or members of monastic orders – is best represented by Prokop Diviš who invented the lightning conductor in 1754.

While in the Czech lands one can speak of a resuscitation of the national traditions within a foreign-imposed framework, in Slovakia the Counter-Reformation stimulated the first activity on a higher educational plane. The Jesuit university established in Trnava in 1635 educated the first generation of Slovak medical men and lawyers. Not until 1667 did the Protestants, mainly Calvinists open a school of advanced learning, the Collegium in Prešov. Isaack Caban, a Slovak philosopher of atomistic orientation, was a product of this period.

Czech Society

In the hundred years from 1650 to 1750 the Catholic Church retreated to the defensive, fearing for its new wealth in face of the centralized administration of the monarchy. At the same time it underwent an inner transformation. It started by replacing the cult of the reformer Jan Huss with that of his contemporary, Jan of Nepomuk (secretary to the Archbishop of Prague and very much the man of the Catholic establishment). By the end of this period Jan Huss was virtually forgotten and Jan of Nepomuk became the patron saint, and recipient of the prayers of the poor, his statues came to adorn bridges, crossroads and village greens.

For the second time the *Ecclesia Victoriosa*, the Victorious Church, became very rich in Czech lands, and perhaps a little too powerful for the liking of the Court. The Church's leaders sensed this danger, which ultimately materialized as wholesale sequestrations of church property by Joseph II.

A hundred years is three generations, and before this time had elapsed even the ranks of the Jesuit order, that spearhead of the Counter-Reformation, included the sons of the Czech aristocracy and of the burghers, born in the country and connected with its people through numerous links.

In the first period of persecution Koniáš, the Jesuit censor, had burned Czech books; in 1672 another Jesuit, Bohuslav Balbín, wrote in Latin a *Defence of the Czech Nation* and did much to revive interest in its history.

While the intellectual revival profited from the cosmopolitan orientation of the Church and the Jesuit Order, the political reaction of the aristocracy to foreign rule was conspicuous in its provincialism and historicizing traditionalism. When speaking of the aristocracy of

Bohemia and Moravia one has to keep in mind that in the seventeenth and eighteenth centuries the ethnic and the geographic concepts competed. Even Germans living in Bohemia and Moravia would be accepted as and would feel themselves to be in the geographical sense, 'Bohemians', the same as the Czechs. As one of their leaders said: '*Ich bin weder ein Tscheche noch ein Deutsche, ich bin ein Böhme*' ('I am neither a Czech nor a German, I am a Bohemian').* The aristocracy of the Czech crown lands was ethnically more German than Czech and included a good measure of foreign blood which arrived in the country with the Habsburgs after 1620. But by the end of the seventeenth century it had merged its interests with those of the local families and had found the provincial parliaments useful for trying to get taxes reduced and for pressing claims to government posts. The new constitution imposed in 1627 stripped the Czech kingdom of all independence and power but allowed it to exist in name.

Under the 1627 constitution the country was governed from the Court Office, Vienna, and the principal officers of the Czech crown could become politically influential only when taking the Habsburg side. Thus Balbín's *Defence of the Czech Nation* can be seen as voicing the bitterness of the aristocracy against the Chamberlain of the Czech kingdom, Ignatius Bořita z Martinic, who was accused of having sold out the economic and social interests of the aristocracy to the Court. The Czech aristocracy was careful to preserve the vestige of statehood, in their claim that the Habsburg rulers must after succession be crowned as Czech kings, thus establishing constitutional claims which were instrumental in transmitting the idea of a Czech state to the bourgeois politicians of the nineteenth century.

On the whole, however, they were a 'loyal opposition' kept out of office and out of touch with real politics. This alienation was a manifestation of the trend visible in France, for example, in the reduction of feudal lords to the status of courtiers by Louis XIV. But there was no Versailles to substitute court intrigue for real activity in Bohemia and Moravia. The apolitical aristocracy turned its energy elsewhere. Some brought farming and forestry on their estates to a

---

* It is almost impossible to say this in the Czech language in which 'Bohemia' is 'Czech land' and there is no one word which embraces both Czechs and Germans living in Bohemia.

high degree of perfection. For example, the Schwarzenbergs, heirs to the Rosenbergs in southern Bohemia, who later expanded their farming interest to Latin America and Africa.

Most of the aristocracy, however, turned their interest from politics to art and literature – some of their paintings and books are preserved to this day, others were dispersed or even destroyed after 1945. They give us the picture of a landed gentry familiar with contemporary thought and which had a refined taste for gardens, sculptures, paintings, libraries and private theatres. The contrast between them and the contemporary, politically active landed gentry of England could not be greater.

The absence of political life in seventeenth and eighteenth century Bohemia and Moravia had another cause. In western Europe, with the advance of capitalist economies, the political role of the aristocracy was passing to the bourgeoisie. It was this bourgeoisie which finally broke the back of despotic monarchies, and spearheaded the arrival of centralized state administration in Europe. In contrast, the economic strength and political spirit of the Czech towns was weakened in the sixteenth century and finally destroyed by the consequences of the Thirty Years War. The resulting political vacuum explains not only the unhindered progress of Viennese centralism but even the lack of political realism in more recent Czech history.

The only element of Czech society which retained full vitality in this period was the peasantry. The peasants could not escape from their situation, and historical traditionalism, so dear to the owners of the estates to which they were attached as serfs, offered them no comfort. There were peasant revolts during the second half of the seventeenth and throughout the eighteenth century both in the Czech lands and in Slovakia. Some of these revolts were only local in character, for example, the 1631-2 uprising of the Slovak and Hungarian serfs in eastern Slovakia, suppressed by mercenary armies, and the 1672 uprising in the poor, mountainous Orava in north-west Slovakia – Kašpar Pika, a local landowner, and twenty-five village sheriffs who led the uprising were executed after cruel torture. Some uprisings reached national dimensions, as when a few years after the Slovak rebellions Czech and German serfs rose against their landlords in western and northern Bohemia and the movement spread rapidly into the Moravian frontier districts.

It was suppressed with great cruelty; and an Imperial Patent issued to regulate the services of the serfs made their position even worse.

One peasant uprising, though only of local importance, more than any other seized popular imagination and became very much a part of Czech national consciousness. This was the 'rebellion' of the eleven villages of the Chods,* the free peasants settled by the Czech kings near the border town of Domažlice to guard the frontier with Bavaria. After the defeat of the Czech Protestants in 1620 these militarily organized and autonomous villages were 'given' to an imperial officer, Laminger; for a further seventy years the Chods continued to believe in the sanctity of their 'royal privileges' until these were confiscated by the Czech Court Office in Vienna, and their leader, Jan Kozina, hanged in Plzeň in 1695.

It is of considerable importance for the understanding of the politically more vigorous present mentality of the Slovaks to realize the difference which separated the seventeenth-century uprisings in Slovakia from those in the Czech crown lands. The rebellion of the Chods, for example, was backward-looking, historicizing in its ideology, isolated from other political forces of its time. The Slovak uprisings were led by the local aristocracy and the towns, they often enlisted Turkish support, and always banked on the external threat which this presented to the Habsburgs. At the beginning of the eighteenth century, the Transylvanian prince Francis Rakoczi II placed himself at the head of a large peasant uprising in north-east Slovakia and for many years controlled the whole of Slovakia. While the Chods had been told, after their revolt was broken, to keep *perpetuum silentium*, the defeat of Rakoczi's army was followed by a peace treaty between the Habsburg government and the aristocratic leaders of the rebels.

The contrast is even more striking between the Czech hero Kozina and the contemporary Slovak hero, Jánošík. Both were hanged, one for trying to argue the case of his people with the lawyers of the Court Office in Vienna, the other for taking justice into his own hands and for many years carrying on partisan warfare from the mountains against the lords of the valleys.

The transformed nation emerging from the 'lost centuries' consisted of an oppressed peasantry without leadership, a weak and

---

* A *chod*, (in modern Czech *chodec*) is a walker. The Chods were supposed to 'walk' along the frontier on guard duty.

diffident bourgeoisie and an aristocracy partly foreign and mostly apolitical. The country could easily be governed from distant Vienna.

6 The Habsburgs' new role in Europe

The freedom of the Habsburg Empire

In 1683 the Grand Vizier's army ravaged Lower Austria. The Turks besieged Vienna and controlled approximately that part of the country which after 1945 was the Soviet zone of occupation. The Ottoman Empire's westward pressure had steadily been gaining force since 1526 when Ludvik Jagellon died while trying to stem the Turkish advance in Hungary, and Ferdinand of Habsburg was elected to the Czech throne.

After 1526 the organization of common defence against the Turks was the main *raison d'être* of the Habsburg rule in Central Europe. In 1683 it faced the ultimate test. For two months the Turks besieged Vienna. The capital was rescued by the combined action of the Polish king, Jan Sobieski, and the Duke of Lorraine, and two years later the last Turkish units were cleared out of southern Slovakia. In 1717 Eugene of Savoy took Belgrade, and the Turks, though still entrenched in the Balkans, ceased to be a danger to Central Europe.

While the Turkish danger subsided, in the West France still loomed large as the Habsburgs' hereditary enemy. After the 'iron ring' of Habsburg possessions encircling France was broken in the Wars of the Spanish succession, France gradually applied a similar policy of encirclement to the Austrian Habsburgs. Bavaria was the traditional rival for Austria's leading role in Central Europe but a new rival and a more formidable one was emerging in the north of Germany: Prussia was being organized by the Hohenzollerns as a totalitarian militaristic state and was clearly set on an expansionist course. This new configuration of the political map of Europe enhanced the strategic importance of Bohemia. Throughout the eighteenth and the better part of the nineteenth century the Habsburgs never lost sight of the crucial importance of Bohemia as the corner-stone of the Danubian realm.

The coronation of Charles VI as Czech king in Prague in 1722 was performed with great pomp to demonstrate Habsburg dominion in the Czech crown lands, Bohemia, Moravia, Silesia, and Lusatia.

Charles had reason to fear for *these* Habsburg possessions. A family treaty, the Pragmatic Sanction, regulating Habsburg succession had been concluded in 1713, to forestall all claims that could be raised or supported by France and Prussia. Charles spent the best part of his rule (1711–40) in intense diplomatic activity trying to get the Pragmatic Sanction accepted as constitutional law by the estates in his countries and as international law by other European powers. Treaties and promises, however, could not make up for real strength.

When Charles died and was succeeded by his daughter Maria Theresa in 1740 the storm broke loose. The Duchy of Silesia, and Lusatia – the two smallest of the four Czech crown lands – became the immediate bone of contention between Maria Theresa and Frederick II of Prussia. Silesia was at that time the most developed economically of the Czech crown lands and the significance of its cession to Prussia lay not so much in the loss suffered by the Habsburgs as in the gain made by the Hohenzollerns. The conquest of Silesia gave Prussia the economic power for a major role in European politics. It also placed Prussia in a convenient position to invade the remaining two Czech crown lands, Bohemia and Moravia, and thus strike at the heart of any Danubian power.

As Maria Theresa recorded in one of her numerous letters, it was always her foremost objective to defend her good Czechs against the wicked Prussians. Harrach, Kinský, and later Kaunitz, all members of the Czech nobility with vested interests in Bohemia and Moravia, were her principal ministers. She was a great, simple woman, uneducated but with an instinctive grasp of the essential rules of successful power politics: resist while the defensive position is still good and not after it has been lost; keep trust of supporters and allies, yielding to blackmail only increases the blackmailer's demands. She distrusted the unprincipled cleverness of her advisers, who were concerned only with the intricacies and short-term aspects of the diplomatic game which started in 1740 and was to keep European chancelleries busy for the next fifteen years.

The first move in this game – which ultimately established Prussia as a European power and thus planted the seeds of two world wars – was made by Britain. With a strange disregard of the long-term consequences such a policy was to have on the European balance of power, Britain, while still an ally of Maria Theresa, pursued towards Prussia a policy of appeasement (which in 1755 evolved into an alliance). When, in 1741, France and Prussia concluded an alliance against Austria, the British Ambassador insisted that Maria Theresa should surrender Silesia to Frederick while she still had a chance to buy peace in this way. Maria Theresa did not, and fought three Silesian wars to regain that duchy and to hold Bohemia and Moravia.

In 1742 Bavarian and French troops occupied Prague and for a short time controlled Bohemia before the Austrians chased them out. In the following year Maria Theresa was crowned Czech queen during the short peace she bought from Frederick by the treaty of Breslau, allowing him to keep Silesia.

In 1742 Britain entered the war on Austria's side against France and Spain, and while Austrian troops were in Alsace (on the way to recover Lorraine from France), the Prussians invaded Bohemia and held Prague for ten weeks before they were expelled by a joint action of the Prague population and Austrian troops. For the second time Maria Theresa regained Prague but was obliged to renounce Silesia, this time by the treaty of Dresden concluded with Frederick in 1745. In return Prussia recognized the election of her husband, Francis of Lorraine, to the no longer real dignity of the Holy Roman Emperor.

The Seven Years War, fought between Britain and France for overseas possessions, was seen from Prague and Vienna as the third Silesian war. The precedence of immediate overseas interests over long-term issues of European policy can perhaps explain why Britain had already in 1741 pressed Maria Theresa towards appeasement of Prussia. In 1755 this, and the concern for Hanover, led Britain to conclude an alliance with Prussia, thus bringing about the great reversal of the European alliances.

In 1756 Prince Kaunitz, a brilliant career diplomat from an aristocratic Moravian family and Maria Theresa's Foreign Minister, signed in Versailles treaties establishing for the first time an Austro–French alliance. Later this alliance was to become a recurring element of European politics, until Prussia grew strong enough to put a stop to it.

The reversal of alliances – Kaunitz's answer to the British appeasement of Prussia – was the first attempt at the great continental
system. France, Austria, Russia and Sweden were united against
Britain and her new ally. In another fifty years Napoleon, after
defeating the Austrians and Russians at Slavkov (Austerlitz)
in Moravia, almost succeeded in uniting, by force, the whole
of the continent against Britain. Later still, Hitler too started
his conquest of the continent by the occupation of Austria and
Czechoslovakia.

In 1757 Frederick tried again to pull the Bohemian lynchpin out
of this continental system but suffered a serious defeat at Kolín,
about sixty miles north-east of Prague. Two years later he was defeated at Kunnersdorf but, to his great surprise, the Russian generals
failed to exploit their victory, demanding that Austria should open a
'second front'.

In the meantime France, defeated by Britain on the seas, pulled
out of the war and so did Sweden. The next year a great *volte-face*
took place in Russia. The new tsar, Peter III, concluded a separate
peace and alliance with Prussia. Suddenly outflanked, Maria Theresa
was obliged to sign away Silesia for the third and last time at the
Peace of Hubertusberg in 1763.

Peter III was soon deposed by his wife Catherine the Great who
repudiated the alliance with Prussia. But Prussia was already established and in another nine years was so strong that Frederick could
engineer the division of Poland, in which Maria Theresa participated with a divided mind. She could not oppose both Prussia and
Russia single-handed. To abstain would only leave a greater share of
Poland to Prussia. Prince Kaunitz, and Joseph, the heir-apparent,
were quite eager to acquire a part of Poland, but the empress was
reluctant to see a small country violated by great powers. She felt it
would pay better to uphold moral principles in this case, when to
desert them would strengthen Prussia still further, open to the Russians the gate to Central Europe and severely jeopardize relations
between the Habsburgs and the small Slav nations which formed the
greater part of the Danubian Empire. The tears Maria Theresa shed
on this occasion were better justified than she could know: the dismemberment of Poland further weakened the political stability of
Europe and created a dangerous precedent. There were to be three
more divisions of that unhappy country, the last between Hitler and

Stalin in 1940, and in 1945 it was simply pushed westwards on the map of Europe.

The fate of Poland has always had a direct bearing on the situation of the Czechs. The partitioning of a potential ally sealed the dependence of the Czechs on Vienna and at the same time stirred up feelings against the Habsburgs. Although the Austrian part of Poland advanced economically and culturally faster than the rest, the Polish exiles contributed much to the view of the Habsburg Empire as a 'prison of nations' and prepared Western, particularly French, opinion for its liquidation in 1918.

After long wars Maria Theresa ruled another fifteen years in peace. She is better remembered by the Czechs than any other Habsburg ruler; no stately home is complete without her portrait. But none of the castles can claim a more intimate connection with the great mother-empress than a humble inn in Bubeneč village, now a suburb of Prague. The inn is called Na Slamníku ('On the Strawsack') because it was here that Maria Theresa was delivered of one of her eighteen children after beginning labour while hunting nearby. The anniversary of this event used to be celebrated each year by a local fête attended by a female member of the Habsburg family. It was amusing to see that Alice, daughter of President Masaryk, kept up this Habsburg tradition after 1918. In 1947 Mrs Beneš, the wife of the last freely elected President, took part in the most recent public celebration in memory of Maria Theresa, Czech queen and defender of the kingdom against the Prussians.

Maria Theresa and Joseph II – reforming and revolutionary monarchs

The loss to Prussia of Silesia and Lusatia, and of Kladsko, a province of Bohemia, was not due to any lack of determination. Maria Theresa fought her three Silesian wars with a remarkable singleness of purpose. Her inability to preserve more than the naked core of the Czech crown lands, Bohemia and Moravia, and the resulting deterioration of the strategic position of the Danubian empire, was primarily due to the economic weakness, loose administration and educational backwardness of the Habsburg realm. In the last analysis, it was the enforced re-Catholicization of Bohemia and Moravia in the previous century, accompanied by the imposition of a regressive neo-feudalism, which obliged the Habsburgs to concede to Prussia a position in Central Europe from which a direct way led to the formation of the German Empire by Bismark in 1871.

The confrontation between the well-trained Prussian army, backed by a ruthlessly efficient, authoritarian regime, and the bizarre assembly of regiments provided for Maria Theresa by noblemen who paid no taxes and ruled their estates like so many little kings, made the need for change more than evident. Vienna had still to catch up with the mercantilists, and what Maria Theresa attempted with her reforms did not go much beyond what Colbert had done for Louis XIV before she was born. But once the ice was broken the stream gathered force and the measures taken by her son, Joseph II, outstripped by far the mercantilism of western Europe, covering the ground of the French Revolution before it took place. By 1790 this polite, peaceful 'revolution' brought Bohemia, Moravia and Austria to the stage at which France settled after the restoration of the Bourbons in 1815.

The enlightened despots of Vienna gave the Czech nation a new lease of life. This was certainly unintentional, but actions have a life of their own, quite independent of the intentions prompting them. Maria Theresa and Joseph envisaged a centrally governed and uniformly German-speaking state, but by freeing the peasant serfs – the only section of the population still speaking Czech – and by giving them human rights and the possibility of economic improvement and education, they provided the means to a national revival. In another two generations a Czech-speaking and politically conscious nation had rediscovered its role and was claiming a greater share in decisions concerning its future.

In broad outline these are the causes of the reforms and their unexpected effect on the Czechs. More must be said, however, to explain why the Czech nation re-emerged with such a uniquely egalitarian character and how its respect for legality, its bureaucratic leanings and its acceptance of a beneficent father-figure can be traced back to this, its second childhood.

To gain a better understanding of this crucial period in modern Czech history, it may be useful to contrast the situation in Bohemia and Moravia with that in the lost Lusatia and Silesia. Their development began after 1620 when the Elector of Saxony succeeded in protecting the Protestants there from the fate of their co-religionists in Bohemia and Moravia. As a result, they retained their ties with the progressive Protestant world of Western Europe, gradually moving into the capitalist era. In Bohemia and Moravia, meanwhile, the Catholic Church and the neo-feudal Catholic aristocracy tried to protect an outdated political and economic system and its ideology against the penetration of progressive ideas from Germany, the Netherlands and Britain, by keeping frontiers closed to cultural and commercial exchanges. Czech towns were sealed off from ideological contamination, and also deprived of all stimuli which could lead to a new development of their productive forces. Their decline was thus perpetuated. Unbelievable lack of foresight and stubborn conservatism cost the Habsburgs their former position as the ruling house of Europe, and now, their first and only female ruler had to draw up the balance and count the losses.

General de Gaulle once said that no regime is capable of reform from within. This has not been so clearly evident in Central Europe as it has been in France, but with a certain licence one can view Joseph II as an ideological and political outsider, hated by the establishment over which he presided. He foresaw the revolution in France, and vainly tried to warn his sister Marie Antoinette. At home he took resolute action to pre-empt the outburst in his realm, battling against the establishment with all the exaggeration of a revolutionary.

Not so his mother. Maria Theresa believed and behaved as a Catholic monarch and the head of an aristocratic, neo-feudal establishment. She employed its members, appealed to their sentiment and loyalty, appeased them by gifts and favours. Her objective was to preserve as much as possible and to reform as much as necessary. However, even to carry out the limited changes to which she was driven by dire need, she had to call in many outsiders. Wilhelm, Count Haugwitz, whom she employed to centralize administration and the collection of taxes, was a Silesian civil servant from a Protestant family. His father was a general in the service of the King of Saxony. Gerhard van Swieten, a Dutch physician, was appointed Chief Censor to liberalize the censorship which so far had been completely in the hands of the Jesuits. He not only reformed the university but also laid the foundations for the future greatness of the Viennese medical school. Marshal Daun, who started the reform of the army, was from a noble Austrian family; but Lacy, an Irishman, was chosen as his successor.

This choice of foreign advisers, mostly with a Protestant background, was on a lower level paralleled by invitations extended to foreign traders and entrepreneurs. The reason for this not only lay in the general backwardness of the domestic scene, still largely overshadowed by the educational monopoly of the Catholic Church. Maria Theresa also needed intellectual help from outside against the nobility, which opposed reforms likely to jeopardize its political and economic interests.

Czech nationalistic interpretation of this period has often been at pains to sort out the 'good' reforms from the 'bad', – 'good' or 'progressive' being those which freed the serfs, improved their education and legal status and reduced the power of the Catholic Church. The 'bad' reforms were the attempt to make German the universal language in the realm and the disbanding in 1749 of the Czech Court Office, the last vestige of the unity and separate entity of the Czech crown. These distinctions, of course, make as little sense as giving a surgeon a bad mark for the cut and praising him only for the stitch.

To be able to reform at all, Maria Theresa had to create central government departments independent of the traditional administration of the lands and counties then completely in the hands of the reactionary nobility. She replaced the Czech Court Office by two central government departments, one for administration and finance and the other for the administration of justice, with jurisdiction over both the Czech and Austrian Habsburg lands – but not the Hungarian crown lands where the nobles were always ready to revolt.

These new departments started to reorganize regional administration, infiltrating the Land Offices with imperial civil servants and diluting as much as possible their autonomous and aristocratic character. The dissatisfaction of the aristocracy had to be appeased in 1762 by changing the name of the central government office from 'Directorium in Publicis et Cameralibus' to 'Czech and Austrian Court Office', but it remained a central office serving the sovereign and branching out not territorially but according to departments of government. Local noblemen continued to preside over the Bohemian and the Moravian Land Offices but they were appointed by Vienna and had very little real power. In the same way the administration of counties passed under the control of the central government in Vienna.

Those who made up the newly created civil service were selected for ability, and the use of academic titles, still widespread in Central Europe, was originally introduced as a counterweight to aristocratic titles. Gradually a doctorate in law became the condition of appointment to the service. Reading the reports and recommendations presented by civil servants of the period, one cannot fail to be impressed by their broad vision and the lucidity with which it was expressed. To resist aristocratic pressure and corruption by the newly emerging entrepreneurs, the Viennese court had to imbue its civil service with a strong *esprit de corps* and pay its members relatively well.

To a nation that was only coming to life again in its dispossessed classes, without an aristocracy or bourgeoisie of its own, the civil service represented one of the very few channels of advancement and security. The Austrian civil service therefore came to be staffed to a large extent by Czechs or at least men of Czech origin, and to be employed by the state became the general ideal of security for most young men and their parents. In the long run this led to prestigious official positions in government service for a few; for far too many it meant humble clerical jobs, employment by the post office or, later, the state railways, so that the enterprising spirit of the nation suffered and acceptance of a bureaucratic order became deeply ingrained.

The reform of the administration was primarily aimed at breaking the local nobility's resistance to innovation, but it also loosened the ties which held the lands of the Czech crown together. Direct links, by-passing Prague, were established between the Viennese central government and Moravia and the two remaining Silesian provinces, Opava and Těšín. Gradually the Habsburg rulers ceased to be spoken of as Czech kings, though they retained this title in a string of others, and came to be called Emperors – Holy Roman Emperors first and after 1804 Austrian Emperors. They remained kings of Hungary: hence the double-barrelled description of all organs of the Austro–Hungarian state: 'imperial and royal'.

This partial dissolving of the Czech kingdom into the Habsburg empire also had its positive aspects. The removal of customs tariffs between the Czech crown lands and Austria increased the market for Czech textiles and glass. There was a revival of mining, and trade and industry were encouraged by the construction of imperial highways and by the opening of rivers to navigation. The privileges of guilds of craftsmen were gradually reduced in favour of a new type of entrepreneur heralding the belated arrival of the capitalist era in Bohemia and Moravia.

The textile industry employing cottage workers in the mountainous regions of north-east Bohemia expanded but there was no labour for factories. The serfdom preventing the agricultural surplus population from seeking employment in industry continued throughout the reign of Maria Theresa. It was only abolished by Joseph II in 1781 in the Czech crown lands and in Austria, and four years later in Hungary, though there it took much longer before the measure became fully effective. *Robota*, the obligation to provide service and to work without pay on the local lord's estates, was discontinued by Joseph II on crown estates only, but it became gradually less and less oppressive until it was abolished altogether in 1848.

Not all the aristocracy of Bohemia and Moravia were blind to the opportunities existing in new forms of economy and many tried to introduce them on their estates, particularly in mountainous regions where field crops did not pay. This led to an expansion of the textile industry – mainly cottage industry – especially in the weaving of linen, as well as some development of ore mining and the traditional glass industry. The first industrial exhibition to be held in Prague was organized in 1791 by such noblemen with mercantile interests. However, all this activity was not only belated in the European context, but also much too small.

The new ideas of the Age of Reason were only trickling in through aristocratic channels. How secretive and exclusive these channels were is indicated by the important role of masonic lodges, the first of which opened in Bohemia in the early years of Maria Theresa's reign.

The revolutionary impact of the Toleration Patent issued by Joseph II in 1781 can be understood only in reference to this background. The granting of religious freedom was not in itself of staggering importance. The number of secret Protestants was by this time too small to be of political significance and the Catholic Church could well afford – and after the disbandment of the Jesuit order did have – a much more liberal approach to ideological matters. The revolutionary impact of the Toleration Patent consisted in the opening of frontiers to the Protestant world, in which feudal orders were already receding before the advancing capitalist forms of production.

The ideological barrier separating the Czechs from the Protestant world was not the only one pulled down by the revolutionary Emperor. By freeing the Jews, until then confined to ghettos, Joseph II also pulled down the internal barriers – visible ones at which guards were mounted – which obliged the Jews to live as a separate nation-within-a-nation. Jews have lived in Bohemia and Moravia since the twelfth century at least, and they started to settle in Prague earlier. They belonged to the Crown, which ran a protection racket extorting special taxes from them, but was unable to make them really safe against periodic pogroms. During the thirteenth-century expansion of the Czech state the Jews were given by Přemysl Otakar II equality before the law, but this liberal attitude lasted only as long as Prague rulers retained their ambitions in European trade. Sometimes, as in the unsettled times before the Hussite Wars, the ransacking of the Jewish quarter was probably viewed by the Crown as an expedient diversion for the discontented population. At other times the Jewish town enjoyed a slummy and overcrowded prosperity. The spiritual expansion under Rudolph II about 1600 can be explained by the intensive interest of the court in the sciences. Also the Prague Habsburgs of the time, more progressive and liberal than the Spanish, hoped for a peaceful coexistence with the Protestant world with which the Prague Jews kept in touch through Jewish communities in the West. Much the same pattern of governmental interest, but under a more favourable political constellation, induced Joseph II to allow the Jews to settle outside the ghettos as traders and craftsmen. Some of them later became farmers, but many more, landless as they were, eagerly seized the new opportunities offered by the development of industry.

The culture of the Jewish ghettos was bilingual, Hebrew and Czech, but the freeing from the ghettos was accompanied by the obligatory replacement of patronymics by family names, and these had to be German. This produced the puzzling phenomenon of the Czech and Moravian small towns, where Jewish families lived integrated with the non-Jewish Czech population, assimilated to a degree rarely reached since Arab rule in North Africa and Spain but distinguished by German names. In Slovakia the liberal attitude of the government led to a great influx of Jews from Galicia (joined to the Habsburg realm after the division of Poland in 1772), but their integration never reached the same degree.

The interaction between the Czechs and the Jews, whom centuries of confinement and persecution had made more enterprising and inventive, was an important factor of change. But the main generator of change was provided by far-reaching educational reforms. The only proper schools existing before the eighteenth-century reforms were the Latin schools or gymnasia, which until 1773 remained under Jesuit control as did the Prague University. The reforms begun under Maria Theresa provided for a uniform system of education for all children. This new system formed a pyramid based on 'trivial' schools established in every parish to teach the three Rs. 'Main' schools were opened in provincial towns and in the capital towns of each land there were 'normal' schools with departments for the training of teachers.

Joseph II provided this secular educational system with a firm financial basis, by creating a school fund out of the confiscated property of closed monasteries. The rest of some 60 million gulden worth of property taken from the Church was converted into a religious fund for the provision of parish priests. In this way both schools and parish priests became at least partly dependent financially on the government departments administering the two funds (later merged with the treasury). In addition to reducing drastically the number of monks – from 60,000 – and nuns, and leaving undisturbed only the teaching or nursing orders, Joseph II also secularized, in a manner of speaking, the parish priest, opening this office to poor candidates from Czech peasant families.

The Czech-speaking parish priest, the village school in which children were taught to read and write their native language, the new freedom to move and seek employment in the towns, the emergence from seclusion of the few Protestants who had secretly preserved a few Czech books and continued to read the Czech bible – all this was of much greater consequence than the fact that in the high schools teaching was in German only. The Czech village boys who made their way up through the German schools did not forget. In 1791, a year after Joseph II died, a chair of Czech language and literature was established at the Prague Charles–Ferdinand University and it was recalled that Jan Huss was a reformer not only of religion but also of Czech orthography, which he had made simple, phonetic and economical.

Thus Joseph II was the Germanizer who opened the floodgate of Czech national revival; the despot who in fighting the nobility laid the foundation of an essentially democratic society; the revolutionary who by leaving in the subconscious memory of the Czechs an imprint of a beneficent father-figure condemned them to be the least revolutionary people of Europe.

The making of a nation

At Joseph II's death in 1790, the inhabitants of the Czech crown lands formed two nations. One, Czech-speaking, consisted of the peasants and the population of small towns, also mostly engaged in agriculture. The other, including the more affluent burghers and the nobility, spoke German. Only the second counted as the political nation, which was still geographically conceived. At this time the barriers of class and wealth were still stronger than those of language. But new forces were already at work, released by the emancipation of the peasants and by the educational and legal reforms. The iron curtain which since 1620 had separated the Czech kingdom from the Protestant capitalist world had been lifted. A new political nation was in the making and its strongest driving force was the Czech-speaking peasant. This explains why even after a process of occupational differentiation and uneven accummulation of wealth lasting 150 years, the Czechs remained essentially a single-class nation.

The Napoleonic wars speeded up the development initiated by the reforms, not only by spreading the ideology of national liberation as by causing a shortage of food and British industrial products. War-generated inflation made it easier for the peasants to pay taxes – which were fixed in absolute money terms – while prices of agricultural produce rose. The standard of living of the peasant population rose in proportion to the fertility of the land; more quickly in the plains irrigated by the rivers Elbe and Morava than in the hilly regions on the borders. The more prosperous peasants created a market for industrially produced implements and consumer goods, so that the less prosperous population in the hills could find employment in industry. In Slovakia, which is almost entirely covered by mountains and was deprived of the benefits of the reforms by the resistence of its Hungarian lords, things were very different. The plight of the Slovak population was so bad that large-scale emigration appeared to leaders of public opinion as the only solution. Indeed, until 1914, and on a diminishing scale between the wars, Slovaks used to seek employment, and many stayed for good, in the more fertile regions of the Balkans and in the United States.

Napoleon's continental blockade provided a great incentive for the Czech textile industry, the skills for which had already been developed by cottagers. By 1810 the number of persons employed in the manufacture of linen alone numbered 600,000 – a threefold increase since 1780. The sugar industry, based on beet grown in the lowlands, expanded to meet the demand in a market to which cane sugar could no longer be imported. A new iron and steel industry based on local coal and ore deposits developed to provide material for the manufacture of armaments needed by the suddenly increased armies and long wars.

This period of rapid industrialization had started with the first industrial exhibition – still under aristocratic patronage – held in Prague in 1791. In 1784 the Prague Private Learned Society was transformed into the Czech Society for Sciences, the nucleus of the present Czechoslovak Academy of Sciences. The Polytechnic, opened in Prague a little later, evolved into the present Technical University.

The relative prosperity of agriculture and the development of industry led to a substantial increase in population. Between 1781 and 1846 the population of Bohemia, Moravia and the remaining parts of Silesia increased from 4.5 to 6.5 million. The increase occurred mainly in the villages; towns remained small – indeed most Czech provincial towns started to expand only shortly before 1939 and some have preserved their medieval or baroque core to this day.

The expanded population had reason to feel much more secure, for the commission of lawyers appointed by Maria Theresa completed its work in the first decade of the new century and the civil code which it produced came into force in 1811. Together with the penal code drafted during Joseph's reign it still represents the basic body of family, property and contract law in modern Czechoslovakia. The lucidity of these statutes has not yet been surpassed. Many of the recent attempts to revise the penal code and the law of family and property from a so-called Marxist position fell short of this standard and had to be withdrawn after a few years.

A clearly defined, coherent system of norms, codified in precise, plain language, free from any legal jargon, is one of the essential conditions of real equality before the law. Non-codified common law and case law lead to a monopoly of knowledge by skilled professionals whose services are costly. By making rights and duties generally known, the new civil and penal codes helped to improve the relative position of the poorer, Czech-speaking population.

Rationalist and romantic nationalists

At the beginning of the nineteenth century there were two streams of thought which were both remarkably tolerant when compared with manifestations of nationalism towards the end of the century. The first was represented by the older generation of intellectuals, their thinking rooted in the Age of Reason. Its leading personality was the Catholic philosopher Bernard Bolzano (1781–1848), whose writings, though in German, deeply influenced Czech thinkers. (Even Josef Dobrovský (1753–1829), often called the 'father of the Czech national revival', wrote the first Czech grammar in German.)

The 'Blue abbé', as Dobrovský was also called because of his preference for the blue of the masonic lodge to which he belonged, was very typical of the way talented boys from the Czech villages made their way up, first supported through grammar school by the Catholic Church or local nobles, later attracting attention in the seminary and ending as house chaplain and tutor in an aristocratic family. This sort of life provided the contacts, leisure and material security required for the pursuit of the arts and sciences.

The second group of thinkers was inspired by the equally tolerant, romantic nationalism mostly associated with the movement started in Germany by J. G. Herder. They were the first generation of German writers who were Czech patriots: J. G. Meinert, who paid an enthusiastic tribute to the Hussite movement in his *Ode on Bohemia*; Alfred Meissner and Moritz Hartmann, whose German poems glorified the Czech Protestant warrior Jan Žižka.

Parallel with these German writers and inspired by the same ideals, a new generation of Czech intellectuals was being drawn from the untapped reservoir of talent in the villages. The publisher of the first Czech-language newspaper, *Česká Expedice*, and also head of an itinerant theatrical troupe performing to Czech audiences in the provinces, Václav M. Kramerius is a legendary figure of the period. František Martin Pelcl was first professor of Czech language at the University of Prague. As a pioneering Czech linguist he was followed by Dobrovský, whose work was developed by the author of the first Czech-language dictionary, the grammarian and translator Josef Jungmann (1773–1847).

The rationalist Czech revival also produced a number of highly creative scientists and medical men, such as J. S. Presl and Jan Ev. Purkyně, whose contributions laid the foundations of Czech medical research, particularly in the field of physiology, and whose study of human sight brought him very close to the invention of cinematography. The Purkyně Society still survives in Prague as a voluntary association which promotes medical research and the dissemination of its results.

Soon, the romantic German writers, enthusiastic for the Czech past, were joined by a Czech romantic movement which from then on kept reappearing in essentially rationalist Czech politics, literature and art, not always to the greatest benefit of the country. This romantic approach was launched by two Slovaks of Protestant background, Jan Kollár (1793–1852) and Pavel Josef Šafařík (1795–1861). Both were influenced by the contemporary German obsession which tempered glorified national history and folklore by a tolerant humanism as expressed in the writings of Herder. Both are significant for the new consciousness of the wider community of Slav nations which later developed into the pan-Slav political movement promoted and exploited by Russia.

The uncertain first stages of modern Czech as a literary language can be seen in Kollár's unlucky attempt to follow Russian in using a quantitative metre in Czech. This produces a ridiculous effect – as generations of Czech students asked to memorize the opening verses of Kollár's *Slavia's Daughter* (1824) discover with some hilarity.

Twelve years later Karel Hynek Mácha published *Máj* (May), a Byronic poem, which firmly established the Czech language as a poetic medium of outstanding richness. Pavel Josef Šafařík, the other outstanding Slovak author of the romantic period, followed the same pan-Slav ideas as Kollár, but in prose. In 1836 he published an essay on the interrelation of the Slav literatures and in the following year a book on the pre-history of the Slav nations.

The great Czech historian and conservative political leader František Palacký also belongs to the generation born in the last decade of the eighteenth century. Unlike Kollár and Šafařík, who were Slovaks, Palacký was a Czech from Moravia, though he studied in Bratislava and only settled in Prague in 1823. His interest in history appears to have been inspired by romanticism and a desire to enhance the political consciousness of the Czechs though his method was scholarly. He found support from patriotic nobles who created for him the office of historiographer of the Czech kingdom. His monumental work, *The History of the Czech Nation in Bohemia and Moravia*, proved to be the final act in the process by which the Czechs rediscovered their national identity. Paradoxically, but characteristically, the first volume of Palacký's history, which appeared in 1836, was published in German. The first volume of the Czech version, mainly written in Rome and Nice, appeared in March 1848. Palacký was the first of the modern Czechs to look westwards, over Germany, from which his precursors and most of his contemporaries derived their notion of the wider world. His method was influenced by English historians.

As later, in Masaryk, the founder and first president of the Czechoslovak republic, in Palacký the influence of German romanticism was blended with Anglo–Saxon pragmatism and realism. Palacký oscillated between the two manners of thought. His history of the Czech nation, carried up to 1526, glorifies Přemysl Otakar II, who ruled in the period of the great Czech expansion in the thirteenth century, and it probably exaggerates the importance of the Hussite wars for Europe. But though his tenet is that whenever the Czechs won, this was always by strength of spirit rather than by force of arms, he assembled in his great work all the facts necessary for a more materialistic interpretation of history. His pragmatic and realistic features are expressed in his Austro–Slavism, which aimed at the transformation of the Habsburg empire into a federal state, in which the Slav majority would have a dominating position within a democratic framework. In this he was supported by Karel Havlíček Borovský, an important journalist and political publicist, whose distrust of a Russian-led pan-Slavism was based on personal experience of the backward Tsarist regime. Ladislav Rieger, Palacký's son-in-law, and František Brauner were the main political figures of this conservative stream.

The more radical wing of Czech politics which emerged in 1848, found its spokesmen in the younger generation, including Josef Václav Frič and Václav Sabina. The former was an inspiring hero-figure of romantic leanings, the latter more of a politician appreciating the support which the radical cause could get in the emerging class of industrial workers. It is believed that Sabina ended as a police confidant.

Prague and the revolutions of 1848

The Paris revolution of February 1848 set things on the move in Prague as it did in other European capitals. For some time the new nationalist and socialist movements had been prevented from appearing on the political scene in Prague by the harsh regime maintained by Prince Metternich and his police minister Sedlnicky. However, a relaxation towards the end of the first half of the century allowed these groups to come into the open.

The Emperor gave in to the general reluctance to tolerate the Metternich regime any longer, and appointed new government, promised constitutional rule and to the Czechs a separate Constitutional Assembly, a widening of the electorate, the reconstitution of the supreme offices of the Czech kingdom in Prague, and the recognition of Czech as another official language of equal status with German. However, the subsequent appointment of Prince Windischgraetz as commander of the Prague garrison was interpreted as a threat to the revolutionary movement. There were incidents between the reinforced garrison and students and workers, and in May 1848, one month after the announcement of constitutional changes, Windischgraetz put his troops into the factories on the outskirts of Prague.

The tension generated by these events affected the course of the Slav Congress which opened in Prague on June 2. The conservative wing of the nationalist movement, led by Palacký, hoped to obtain an endorsement of the Austro–Slav programme and an expression of loyalty to Habsburg rule. The conservatives failed to achieve this. In the excitement generated by the military suppression of demonstrations the radical wing prevailed and the congress adopted a Manifesto to All European Nations, protesting against the oppression of

Slav nations and demanding freedom for all nations of the world. The congress was interrupted by bloodshed. A demonstration of students and factory workers converging on the present Wenceslas Square – the traditional place of political demonstrations in Prague – was attacked by the army. The radicals, including also the revolutionary section of the German population, took to the barricades. Windischgraetz (whose wife was killed by a stray bullet in their home in the centre of the city) withdrew his troops from Prague and by artillery bombardment broke the rising in six days; assisted, no doubt, by the reluctance of the pro-Austrian conservatives to take part in a revolution against Vienna.

The suppression of the revolutionary movement in Prague as well as the support which could be expected from the conservative, pro-Austrian, Czech politicians enabled Vienna to deal more effectively with its other problems. In addition to those posed by the democratic revolutionary movement sweeping Europe and by its socialist undertones, the Habsburgs also had to face the Pan-Germanic movement which promoted the idea of a great German empire including Austria with its German as well as Slav population. The Pan-Slav movement must have appeared even more serious at a time when the unification of Germany was only a dream, but when Russia already was a great power which had made the decisive contribution to Napoleon's defeat. The third danger to the Viennese regime was the Hungarian aspiration to re-establish the crown of St Stephen as an independent dominion over all the Slav nations in the Balkans. Windischgraetz therefore moved from Prague to Vienna and broke the revolt there. By the middle of the following year the Hungarian revolution, led by Lajos Kossuth, was brought under control with Russian help. In March 1849 it was becoming clear that the Hungarian revolt was doomed. The Viennese government dissolved the Constitutional Assembly that had been sitting in Kroměříž (in Moravia) since the preceding November. Even in the short period of its existence it had revealed what was to be the main issue between Prague and Vienna for the rest of the century. The Czech delegation proposed the monarchy be federalized. Vienna insisted on a centralized rule for the non-Hungarian part of the empire. It only reached out to a federal solution in 1917, on the verge of a great military defeat, when it was too late.

Constitutionalists claim autonomy for the Czech Kingdom

The Metternich regime did not distinguish between German, Czech or Hungarian nationalisms. The revolutions of 1848 were crushed with equal harshness and determination whether in Prague, Vienna or Budapest. But the one in Prague was easiest to defeat because the greater part of the newly emerging Czech bourgeoisie was not really revolutionary. They had been drawn into the tumultuous events of May and June 1848 reluctantly. Closely allied to the patriotic nobility of Bohemia and Moravia, they looked backwards, to the resurrection of the aristocratic constitution of the Czech kingdom within the Habsburg realm, rather than forwards to the abolition of the surviving neo-feudal orders, which was the aim of the young radicals and students. The new class of industrial workers was still too small, weak, and lacking in political leadership to lend any reality to the enthusiasm of the romantic intellectuals.

However, the process of change initiated by the reformers Maria Theresa and Joseph II, and halted by Metternich, was stimulated by the events of 1848. The emancipation of the peasants was completed and true industrialization of Bohemia and Moravia began. Agricultural methods were improved rapidly and the food industry expanded fast. Mining for non-ferrous metals, which with all its vicissitudes had had a prominent place in the Czech economy since the twelfth century, was now overshadowed by mining for iron ore and coking coal. Bituminous coal from the already established mining regions of Kladno near Prague and Ostrava in Silesia, as well as from mines opened in north-western Bohemia, was needed for the new blast-furnaces and railways. In 1859 the privileges of the guilds were terminated by the Trade Act, which established freedom of enterprise. Finally, the tariffs between the Hungarian and Austro–Czech parts of the Empire were abolished; this was of as much significance to Czech industry as the Repeal of the Corn Laws in 1846 was to British industry.

Imports of cheap grain from the Hungarian plains led to further redundancies in Czech agriculture, thus in one stroke providing developing industry with workers and cheap food for them. More labour was made available by the modernization of the textile industry introducing steam-engine-powered machinery. However, there was very little Czech capital to make use of the available human and natural resources; the development of coal mining and of the iron and steel industry and engineering relied mainly on investment from Vienna and France.

Many of the great Czech industrial corporations were founded in this period. The engineering works opened in Plzeň by Count Wallenstein passed in the 1860s into the hands of Emil Škoda, and in the course of time became the principal armament and heavy engineering supplier of the Habsburg monarchy. The Ringhoffer and Daňek works, which form the core of the present C.K.D. electrical engineering group, were also established in the 1850s and 1860s.

While promoting change in the economy the Viennese court did its best to prevent its spreading into the political and ideological sphere. In 1851 the Emperor Franz Joseph I (1848–1916) revoked the constitution of March 1849 and reverted to absolute government. Alexander Bach, a prime minister whose name became synonymous with censorship and police rule, concluded with the Pope a concordat, which returned to the Catholic Church many of the privileges it had lost under Joseph II, including the control of lower education.

The Bach administration aimed to create a new Austrian patriotism which would counteract the centrifugal forces of both traditionalist, geographical patriotism (for example, of the Czech and German nobility in Bohemia and Moravia) and the new, ethnic nationalism. It revived the old idea that the unity of the realm could be enhanced if all subjects spoke one language, namely German. This language policy, which was harmless in the time of Joseph II when it was counter-balanced by the economic upgrading of the Czech-speaking population, now proved politically disastrous for the Habsburgs. It linked the Vienna regime with the richer German- and Vienna-financed capitalists, who were seen by the young Czech bourgeoisie and intelligentsia as foreign competitors and exploiters. Consequently an important part of Czech political opinion ceased to see the Germans in Bohemia and Moravia as potential allies against Vienna. Although the Czech population was stabilized at 65 per cent in 1857–90, the idea of settling differences with the Germans not at home but in Vienna gradually gained ground.

The identification of the Habsburg regime with the German competitor at home was further enhanced by the appeasement policy which Vienna adopted towards its German population in order to counteract the pan-Germanic propaganda emanating from Prussia. For the Czechs, the temptation to join a Hohenzollern Reich simply did not exist. When, on the other hand, in spring 1848, the Prussians extended to the Czechs, as members of the defunct Holy Roman Empire, an invitation to send representatives to an Imperial Diet in Frankfurt, Palacký, the 'Father of the Nation', rejected it out of hand. Nor did the temptation from the east, the pan-Slav programme and hopes of regaining independence under the protection of the tsars, take root in practical Czech politics. When the Russian army had helped Vienna to crush the Hungarian revolt in 1849, it had become evident that independence gained with Russian help would be a step backwards in terms of social and economic development.

The realization that without the Habsburg Empire, the Czechs would fall under either German or Russian domination was striking a chord of historical experience. Since the eleventh century all Czech rulers powerful enough to pursue their own policies had endeavoured to establish or fortify a Central European empire. In the early 1860s Palacký's famous dictum 'If there were no Austrian Empire we would have to create one' appeared to be expressing the general consensus of Czech public opinion.

The process of differentiation between the richer bourgeoisie allied to the nobility, and the small shopkeepers and entrepreneurs with more radical political views, which had begun around 1848, later led to the formation of two political parties, one conservative and the other liberal. Both political streams were agreed in seeking a satisfaction of their national aspirations within the Habsburg Empire. Gradually, as the anti-German element of these aspirations gained the upper hand over the traditional concept of an autonomous Czech kingdom of 'Bohemians' who spoke either Czech or German, the local aristocracy became more and more detached from Czech politics. This separation weakened the Czech cause in Vienna at a time when the Hungarian nobility, always in the forefront of national resistance against the Habsburgs, scored important successes, ultimately leading to the dualist organization of the Austro–Hungarian Empire. While reducing the weight of Czech demands in the eyes of Vienna, this separation of the aristocracy from the mainstream of Czech politics also freed Czech society from a retarding influence and enabled it to begin to formulate a liberal and democratic national programme. It ensured that the political and economic demands of the working class were more readily accepted later on and explains why in Prague there was never the armed conflict between bourgeoisie and workers that took place both in Budapest and Vienna during 1918-38.

In the early 1860s, however, the immediate weakening of the Czech position was of greater consequence than the long-term benefits accruing from the loss of aristocratic support.

As long as the police regime of Alexander Bach lasted, the Czech political programme was not much more than an intellectual exercise. It was put to a practical test only when the government was brought to a sudden end in 1859 by the depletion of state finances during the Crimean War, followed by defeat in northern Italy. In October 1859 Emperor Franz Joseph renounced absolute rule 'for all time' and promised to restore the constitutions of the countries forming the Habsburg realm. But the constitution decreed in the following February placed the Czechs at a great disadvantage: it gave voting rights only to taxpayers above a certain income limit and this ensured a dominant position not only for the ultra-conservatives but also for the Germans, who had a majority in the higher income groups. The Czech deputies, representing 65 per cent of the population, found themselves outvoted by German deputies, even in the regional parliaments of Bohemia and Moravia. Similarly the deputies representing the Slav majority of the Empire were in the minority in the Viennese parliament, the Imperial Council.

Frustrated by their inability to achieve anything by parliamentary methods and by the Government's reluctance to compromise, the Czech deputies, like the Hungarian deputies before them, ceased to attend the sessions of the Imperial Council and adopted a policy of passive resistance. It was during this period that the differences within the Czech camp led to the constitution of two parties, the conservative 'Old Czechs' and the liberal 'Young Czechs'.

Disillusion with the February constitution also led to doubts as to whether it would be at all possible to achieve national aspirations within the Habsburg Empire. Even Palacký, who for the greater part of his life had been a protagonist of Austro–Slavism and believed that the Empire was indispensable to Czech national security, now had second thoughts. His *Idea of the Austrian State* published in

1865 closes with the adamant statement 'We existed before Austria and will survive her'.

Such negative attitudes towards Vienna were further strengthened in the course of the following decade. In 1866 Prussia defeated Austria at Hradec Kralové, in northern Bohemia, and confirmed her supremacy in Germany. The potential control of Bohemia opened to Prussia the road to victory over France at Sedan and to the establishment of the German Reich in 1871. This was the practical meaning of Bismarck's theory that whoever controls Bohemia is the overlord of Europe.

Hard pressed in the west, Vienna tried to win the support of Hungarians in the east by granting them far-reaching concessions. The settlement of 1867 divided the Habsburg Empire into two autonomous parts, Austria and Hungary, united in the person of the monarch and in common armed forces and foreign affairs. Contributions to the common budget were subject to annual negotiations between the two countries.

The promulgation in December 1867 of a new constitution embodying this settlement led to a wave of protest in Moravia and Bohemia. Czech deputies stopped attending the regional parliaments, Czech political leaders paid a demonstrative visit to Russia and popular demonstrations were organized at historically significant places and in connection with the return of the crown of St Wenceslas and other Czech royal insignia from Vienna to Prague.

Aware of the new importance of Bohemia as a bulwark against the Hohenzollern Empire, Vienna was ready to make concessions. The Czechs did not demand the same degree of independence as that achieved by the Hungarians but asked only that the Czech regional parliaments and civil servants should be given greater scope. They also wanted to revive the office of a Czech court chancellor who would represent Bohemia and Moravia in the Vienna government.

Eighteen 'fundamental articles' were agreed between Hohenwart's government and the Czech representatives and approved by the regional parliaments in Bohemia and Moravia. They provided for a regional government in Prague, responsible to a regional parliament. In addition to defence and foreign affairs, finance, trade and transport were to be administered directly from Vienna. Bohemia and Moravia were to be divided into Czech and German districts and the German minority in the regional parliament was to be given the right to veto certain measures affecting their ethnic interests. On 12 September 1871, Franz Joseph signed an Imperial Rescript acceding to the Czech demand that he be crowned as Czech king to symbolize the special position of the Czech crown lands within the Austrian part of his realm.

This compromise, if it had been realized, was likely not only to reconcile the Czechs with the Habsburgs but also enhance the position of other Slav peoples in Austria–Hungary. Such a development would have given a different turn to the foreign policy of the Austro–Hungarian Empire and precluded its plunging into a world war at Germany's side in 1914. In 1871, however, the fear of such an ascent of the Slav element within the Empire led the Hungarian government to join the Austrian Germans in their opposition to the deal. When finally Bismark assured Vienna that the new German Reich would take no hostile action against Austria–Hungary, the Government withdrew from talks with the Czechs in October 1871, defaulting on the agreement which the Czechs believed confirmed by the Imperial Rescript issued a month earlier.

Vienna's default caused a deep trauma in Czech politics, disturbing the basic assumption that an agreement with Vienna could and should be reached. The disappointment led to a new period of passive resistance and of abstention from all legislative bodies. The nation's mood was one of national defiance, most forcibly expressed by Prince Karel Schwarzenberg, by far the greatest landowner in Bohemia. It is understandable that the aristocratic and conservative faction of Czech society was most upset by the 1871 defeat. They stood to gain most from a historical revival of an autonomous Czech kingdom. They were also least impressed by the liberalization which found its expression in the December constitution of 1867. But the Czech liberals did not see things quite so blackly.

8 Search for national aims

New politics

The constitution of 1867 had signalled that the Habsburgs were finally withdrawing support from the feudal order and were going to link their fortunes with the rising class of capitalist entrepreneurs. This explains their reneging in 1871 on the promise to revive an autonomous Czech kingdom: the young German-speaking Austrian bourgeoisie was much more nationalistically minded than the German-speaking aristocracy, which still cultivated the cosmopolitan spirit of the feudal era. Hence the paradox of Czech politics in the second half of the nineteenth century: by strengthening the Czech nationalists this Habsburg liberalization turned its political representatives into reliable allies of the more conservative – which in that time also meant less chauvinistic – upper classes of the German-speaking population.

The Czech politicians' boycotting of the legislative assemblies proved to be of little effect as Vienna had no reason to fear that they would evoke a revolutionary spirit in Bohemia and Moravia. The people had a peaceful temperament and an ingrained belief that governments will ultimately carry out the reforms and changes necessary for their preservation. The Czech bourgeoisie had also been doing very well both economically and culturally, profiting from its first real industrial boom in the capitalist era and the new civil freedoms. Soon they realized that though non-cooperation might be an effective weapon for a big landowner like Prince Schwarzenberg, whose privileges were being gradually eroded by government, it was not advantageous for a class expecting from that government new concessions, facilities and contracts. The Czech entrepreneurs, now backed by a big bank of their own, the Živnostenská Banka opened in Prague in 1868, feared that the policy of abstention from parliament and office would only benefit their German competitors.

In 1878, Czech deputies returned to the regional parliament and in the next year to the Imperial Council in Vienna. From then on the Czech delegations pursued an 'active' policy, trying to obtain whatever concessions and advantages they could and often accepting seats in the Government and other offices. The radical factions, clinging to the 'constitutional programme', sneered at this as a 'policy of breadcrumbs'. However, in a period of an economic and cultural boom, the Czech political leaders could well afford to ignore their criticism.

They even had some success in the difficult area of language politics with which both Czechs and Germans of the time seemed to be obsessed. In 1882 Czech was given equal status with German in contacts between government offices and the citizens in Bohemia and Moravia; German continued to be the only official language for the internal use of government departments; it lost this privileged position only temporarily, in 1897, when the government of Kazimir Badeny, a Polish count, gave the Czech language full equality for the short time he remained in office. A period of violent friction between Czechs and Germans, mainly focused on language problems, was ended in Moravia in 1905 by a pact conceding to the Czech majority of the electorate also majority representation in the regional parliament and the regional executive committee. In Bohemia, however, the strife between Czechs and Germans continued unabated. There the Germans formed only thirty per cent of the electorate and had a minority representation in the regional parliament, while they were part of the German majority in the Imperial Council in Vienna. By obstructive tactics this German minority finally succeeded in paralysing the regional parliament of Bohemia in 1908 and its executive committee in 1913. The Vienna government then appointed an administrative commission which remained in charge of the regional offices in Bohemia until the monarchy disintegrated in 1918.

Looking back, one realizes how the language problem and other similar issues were used by both sides to divert attention from the mounting social problems. By 1900 over half of the population of Bohemia was employed in industry, transport and trade, and only about a third remained in agriculture and forestry. Bohemia and Moravia were experiencing their early capitalist period with all the social degradation that goes into the formation of an industrial labour force. Accumulation of capital for further investment depended on hard toil and low consumption. Moreover there were two periods of unemployment, during the economic crisis which led to state bankruptcy in 1873 and in the recession of 1900–1903. In addition to the clash of interests between employers and employees in industry and agriculture, the interests of small and large entrepreneurs were diverging. Many small or weak enterprises could not weather the economic crisis of the 1870s and had to close down or be taken over by stronger competitors and banks. The electorate's more radical mood found expression in a more fervent nationalism.

Conservatives

The Old Czechs, the conservative party allied to the aristocracy, never really recovered from the débâcle of 1871 when its programme of constitutional revival was betrayed by Vienna. In the years that followed, while still the leading Czech party, the Old Czechs lost much of their public image by agreeing in principle to a division of the country, as far as language was concerned, into Czech and German districts. The impossibility of presenting as a practical goal, the 'historical' programme on which the Old Czech party was founded, its association with the richer capitalist and aristocratic stratum and the consequent lack of national radicalism, led to the decisive victory of the liberal party, the Young Czechs, in the elections of 1891.

Liberals

The 1890s saw the emergence of all the political factions that were to play an active role in the next thirty years. The Young Czechs could not uphold for very long the radical nationalist programme on which they were elected. A revival of economic activity following the 1900–1903 depression as well as the shortlived language concessions made by the Badeny Government in 1897 facilitated a return to a gradual policy aimed at securing economic advantages for the Czech bourgeoisie.

The more radical faction, composed mainly of students and politicians aiming at working-class support, became more active soon after the elections of 1891. In 1893 the Vienna government provided them with publicity and a halo of martyrdom by holding a political trial of their leaders. Among those sentenced for high treason was Alois Rašín, who later became the first Minister of Finance of the Republic.

This radical–nationalistic faction with socialist overtones remained within the party of the Young Czechs until 1897 when it seceded as the Radical Progressive Party. Two years later another splinter group formed the Radical Constitutional Party, returning with a new vigour to the revivalist programme on which the Old Czechs failed.

Other small parties started to draw away the support on which the Young Czech Party was based. One of them was the Czech Popular Party (better known as the 'Realistic Party'), founded by a group of intellectuals around Thomas G. Masaryk.

Finally the Popular Progressive Party under the leadership of Adolf Stránsky split from the Young Czechs. Reorganized in 1906 by Karel Kramář, the Young Czechs continued after 1918 as the National Democratic Party. Kramář, who entered politics as a textile manufacturer, was a very efficient political leader of the bourgeoisie in its patient and successful struggle for economic and cultural equality in the Empire. Political issues and the pan-Slav programme were used by him mainly as rhetorical devices, to glamorize his day-to-day politics, which were – in essence – that Czechs should pay fewer taxes and get greater allocations in the budget. Kramář retained great personal influence on Czech politics even in the first years after liberation in 1918, though his party continued to decline.

Agrarians

One of the fundamental reasons for the decline of the Young Czechs was the loss of a following among the agrarian population. The Czech farmers, that is those who were qualified by sufficient taxable income to vote, had decided the election victory of the Young Czechs in 1891. The formation of farmers' associations had been begun by Alfons Štastný in the 1880s but during the 1891 election they were still affiliated to the Young Czechs. A separate Agrarian Party was formed in Bohemia in 1899 and in Moravia in 1904. In contrast with the political atomization of the urban population, most of the farmers supported the Agrarian Party and this was to become the leading party of the coalition governments which ruled the Republic until its end in 1939.

Catholics

One other group was seriously competing for the agrarian electorate, the Catholics. The Catholic National Party was originally established by Mořic Hruban as in 1896 in Moravia and three years later in Bohemia. Jan Šrámek, a Catholic priest turned professional politician organized the Christian Socialist Party, another Catholic party aiming also at working-class support, and united the two in 1899. This united Catholic party was known in the 1917–48 period as the Czech Popular Party.

Sokol

By the end of the century the gymnastic movement Sokol (Falcon), founded in 1862 with the support of the Young Czechs by M. Tyrš and J. Fuegner, had become a political force of considerable importance. Local units established throughout the country met regularly for gymnastic training and social activities. Gymnastic festivals were held each year in provincial towns and on a national scale in Prague once in four years.

The cultivation of a patriotic spirit bordering on chauvinism was as much part of the movement as physical culture and with the uniforms, marches and high degree of discipline the movement represented a paramilitary organization of the Czech bourgeoisie. It was to play its part in the independence movement during the First World War and in establishing the authority of the new republic.

Labour

The origin of the Czech labour movement can be traced back to workers' clubs and brotherhoods for the mutual support of members, of much the same type as existed earlier in Western Europe. It was consolidated into the Social Democratic Party in 1878 and participated in elections for the first time in 1891 when it obtained 2.8 per cent of all votes cast in Bohemia. In the intensely nationalistic atmosphere of that time, the internationalist Social Democrats had to overcome a very great psychological barrier as the first and only party professing allegiance neither to the 'constitutional' nor to the 'linguistic' aspects of the national programme. But it had the support of the emerging trade union movement and soon placed itself in the forefront of the struggle for a general and equal right to vote, independent of income. As soon as the income test of voters was somewhat lowered in 1896, the Social Democrats won in Bohemia and Moravia eleven seats in the Imperial Council, of which five were taken by Czech and six by German deputies. Soon afterwards the Social Democratic Party split according to nationality. In the election of 1907, the first in which voting was general and equal, the number of Czech Social Democratic deputies elected to Vienna rose to twenty-five.

Catholic attempts to gain labour votes had diminishing success. Prior to the splitting-off of the Communists in 1921, the only Czech party seriously competing with the Social Democrats for workers' votes was the National Socialists established under the leadership of V. J. Klofáč in 1897. The ranks of this party included industrial and farm workers as well as shopkeepers and small entrepreneurs and a very large proportion of railway workers and state employees in the clerical grade. It also had a good following among teachers and the intelligentsia. With its wide spread of membership the National Socialist Party was a product of the unique classlessness of Czech society. Its political programme was inevitably vague and though it tended to promote the interests of the lower-income groups it was not socialist. After 1918 the National Socialist Party became the main supporter of Edward Beneš, first as Foreign Minister and later when he became President.

The deputies of all these parties made up the Czech delegation to the Imperial Council until its final adjournment in 1914. The Czech delegation was deeply divided in its attitude to the Vienna government, not so much because of the differences between the parties composing it as because of the lack of a unifying aim. By the beginning of the First World War the Czechs had succeeded in organizing themselves as a political force but remained rather uncertain about the objective for which this could be used.

Sentiment above reason

This absence of a positive unifying national or social aim is reflected in the work of Czech writers, artists and musicians active from 1850 to 1914. Their intellectual activities appealed mainly to emotions and to sentiment. Music, painting, sculpture and poetry flourished. Humour and satire, the negative ways of dealing with the problems of life, were brought to a high degree of perfection. The search for national aims and for a political programme produced some outstanding polemicists and publicists. There were some good short-story writers, chroniclers of country life. But only one novel of the period – written at the very beginning – has that claim to greatness which springs from a singleness of mind uniting the writer with his readers.

The Grandmother, by Božena Němcová – 'Our Lady Božena Němcová' is what a modern Czech poet calls her to express the esteem in which she is still held by the Czechs – is about the life of a village in the pre-natal period of modern Czech society. The story of a grandmother, whose aims in life and moral values are so well defined and accepted by the village society, has been maturing for thirty years and is told by her granddaughter as if in a single breath. Though the time and place are narrowly circumscribed, the novel with its tale of war and love, the curse of insanity and the blessings radiated by a courageous soul is universal. The apotheosis of the grandmother-figure, standing for established conventions, shows how much the author, who lived at times in the utmost poverty, missed them in a young bourgeois society with too much greed and too few graces.

In the years following 1848 Božena Němcová was one of the few writers who satisfied the true spiritual needs of the nation. Most turned their attention to the need for reassurance and flattery felt by a small nation reappearing on the political scene, whose urban society was competing with a German bourgeoisie backed by the formidable establishment of the Habsburg Empire.

The romantic tendencies which were an emotional counterpoint to the mainly rational roots of the national revival degenerated towards the end of the century into rampant, historicizing patriotism. In this climate it required a heroic nature to deal critically with the country's history or society.

In contrast to writers, Czech musicians and artists had the advantage of an uninterrupted tradition because language was no barrier to them. The Catholic Church, whose insistence on Latin and denial of the Bible to the laity had an anti-literary and alienating effect on the common people, nevertheless provided music every Sunday. In addition to its ecclesiastical traditions Czech music also had a living source in the folksong of the people. Unlike the aristocratic audiences of the pre-Mozart period, the young Czech bourgeoisie was still very close to its village origins and fond of its melodies.

The two great composers of this period, Bedřich Smetana and Antonín Dvořák, drew freely on folksong and their music sounds homely and natural to the Czech ear, though Smetana's operatic work was influenced by Richard Wagner. Ironically, *Libuše*, an opera about the mythical Czech priestess-queen, which suffers most from Wagnerian romanticism and noisiness, is still the standard piece given on state occasions in the Prague National Theatre. But while *Libuše* is accepted as a part of national pageantry, the opera most cherished by the Czechs is *The Bartered Bride*. Characteristically, this is a comic opera based on a story taken from contemporary village life. It treats with warm-hearted humour love's victory over peasant greed for land and money.

Smetana died in 1884, a year after the opening of the National Theatre which marked a turning-point in the cultural life of Prague. The theatre, bigger and more ostentatious than the aristocratic 'Theatre of the Estates', in which Mozart's *Don Giovanni* was performed for the first time a century before, served as a status symbol for the bourgeoisie, who provided for its construction by voluntary contributions.

Dvořák (1841–1904) was more relaxed in many ways: he used folk melodies, generally Czech and Slav, as themes of his music but the stories on which his operas are based have a more general, human interest. He spent many years abroad, particularly in the United States, freely absorbing Red Indian melodies into his music.

Smetana found a lesser heir in Fibich, while Janáček (1854–1928) continued Dvořák's relaxed exploitation of folk melodies, mainly Moravian and Silesian in origin. But his musical language is very different from Dvořák's and belongs clearly to the dissonant trends of the first decades of the twentieth century.

The specifically Czech themes treated musically by Smetana appear also in the works of Josef Mánes (1820–71), the great figure in Czech modern painting. The work of Josef Navrátil, the fine romantic landscape painter of the preceding period, was continued by Adolf Kosárek, and the tradition of baroque portrait painting was revived, in a realistic and forceful style, by Karel Purkyně. The succession went to the draughtsmen, Mikoláš Aleš 1852–1913), who still chose mainly historical or folk subjects, and then Max Švabinský, the portrayer of flowers, butterflies and statesmen, who lived long enough to record truthfully, though always very politely, the prominent personalities of three different regimes. Julius Mařák and Antonín Chittusi who used a realistic style for essentially romantic landscapes had a whole band of followers leaning towards Impressionism, which was brought to its highest point by Antonín Slavíček. Art Nouveau had its protagonists in Josef Hinais, Jan Preisler and Alphonse Mucha. Švabinský, strongly marked by this style in his youth completely outlived its mannerism.

The master of Czech sculpture, Josef Václav Myslbek (1848–1922), differed from contemporary painters by his restraint, confronting the dramatic baroque statues which surrounded him with his neo-classical heroes, saints and allegories. These are often noble and elegant but always cool and static. Jan Štursa (1880–1925), his gifted discipline, readmitted movement and drama to Czech sculpture, preparing the way for Otto Guttfreund, who later used a very modern language to return to the soul-searching quest of baroque sculpture.

Folksongs, fairy tales and stories told on long winter evenings on the farms provided a whole generation of poets with imagery and a musical language offering a rich diversity of sounds. But to the Czech patriots the gift of this rich, flexible and poetic language was not enough. At a time when the Germans were making so much of the *Ring der Niebelungen,* the lack of a national saga gnawed at the Czechs' patriotic pride. When Václav Hanka announced that he had found two eleventh-century manuscripts containing an epic saga of the early Premyslids, including that of Libuše, the matriarch-priestess who married the first Přemysl, the Czech bourgeoisie was overjoyed: although they were still not equal to the Germans in the unromantic field of trade and industry, at least in the field of poetry they could match the Niebelungen with a saga almost a thousand years old. It was later proved – though there are some who do not accept this – that Hanka in fact wrote the manuscripts himself in a reconstructed ancient Czech. The 'Fight for the Manuscripts', or rather Masaryk's public campaign against the uncritical and romantic patriotism with which they were associated, has an important place in Czech cultural history. All the same, Hanka, if indeed he was a misguided patriotic falsifier, must be acknowledged as one of the country's great poets.

Together with Karel Hynek Mácha and Ladislav Čelakovsky, whose poems echo Czech and Russian popular epic songs, Hanka is a member of the first generation after Jan Kollár. The next generation of poets, emerging after 1850 around the literary magazine called *Máj*, after Mácha's principal poem, included Karel Jaromír Erben, who delighted in tense and often morbid epic poems told with a natural flow of language, Vítězslav Hálek who spoiled his talent by writing sugary love-songs, and Jan Neruda whose bitter-sweet sonnets always ring true. Neruda, who through journalism became a master of the *feuilleton* and the short story, started the Czech tradition of humour, using it for social criticism as Maupassant used his tragic stories. Another journalist, probably the greatest the country has had, Karel Havlíček Borovský, is not normally classed as a poet, but he produced two satirical poems, one aimed at Russian and the other at Austrian despotism, which have a lasting place in Czech literature.

At first sight it seems strange that Božena Němcová belonged to the same generation as these social critics. She does not appear to be concerned with the hypocrisy and self-importance of the townsfolk which occupied the humourist and the satirist. Her novels are about village folk and enlightened aristocrats; her fairy tales are records of ancient country tales. Nevertheless, she was writing for the same young urban society in search of new values. These are your origins, she seems to say, the values to which you must be true to be happy.

The generation of the 1870s centred on *Ruch*, another literary magazine, lacked the intensity of Neruda and Němcová but probed the field farther. Josef Sládek, an indifferent poet in his own right, contributed greatly to Czech literature and theatre by his trans-lations from German and English and in particular by making Shakespeare's plays available to the National Theatre. Svatopluk Čech was the first poet who added to patriotism a strong plea for social justice. This was at the time when the Social Democratic Party rose to political importance in Austria and sensitive writers realized that conflicts between classes of the same ethnic group might soon overshadow the old frictions between Czechs and Ger-mans. Jakub Arbes, author of stories somewhat reminiscent of Edgar Allan Poe, was also a writer conscious of social problems. This is even more true of Karel Sabina, a tragic figure – a gifted left-wing, almost revolutionary essayist, turned police informer. The in-famy would have cost him his place in the textbooks of Czech litera-ture but for the fact that he also happened to be Smetana's librettist and has a share in the national opera *The Bartered Bride*.

Alois Jirásek, who also entered the literary scene through the magazine *Ruch*, was different from the rest of his generation. His historical novels like those of Walter Scott, reliably patriotic and with a good measure of adventure, kept appearing in a steady flow for almost half a century. In his best works he succeeded in making his heroes human and in endowing his heroines with charm, but he was best of all when portraying the young, whom he learned to know well as a grammar school teacher.

After *Máj* and *Ruch, Lumír*, named after one of the heroes of Hanka's contested 'manuscripts', was the next literary magazine to herald yet another generation of poets and writers. Its circle was conspicuous by undiluted neo-romanticism. In Julius Zayer it at-tained a religiously mystical quality, while Jaroslav Vrchlický kept closer to the everyday level of human existence.

The extraordinary facility with which Vrchlický poured out per-fect verse and his lifelong devotion to literary work soon won this half-Jew the position of the Czech national bard. His poetic works hold their own, alongside his truly gigantic effort to transpose into Czech all that was best in western literature. Translations of Shake-speare's plays are as good a signpost of succeeding waves of literary fashion as of changing modes of life and attitudes in Czech society. That Vrchlický felt the need to produce a new Czech Shakespeare so soon after the appearance of Sládek's translation shows how fast the

literary language was developing and how acutely felt was the need
to add a greater sophistication to the translation, without departing
from the basically romantic, heroic interpretation of the plays. In
spite of all his merits, in language and in opening the country's
windows to the wider world, Vrchlický was a tame spirit and did
not touch the issues of the day – nor its vices, passions and heroic
aspirations.

It was left to men of lesser talent to speak out for the nonconform-
ists against the establishment. One of them was Petr Bezruč, whose
real identity remained undisclosed for a long time and is still sometimes questioned. His *Silesian Songs* are a passionate outcry against
the exploitation of the coalminers in Silesia by the Germanizing aristocratic mineowners and their sycophants. These harsh yet melodious
poems advanced Czech patriotism from petty competition between
shopkeepers to the struggle of a social group for survival.

Josef Svatopluk Machar, the second poet and writer who attacked
the establishment of the pre-1914 period, did so on a much wider
front. Though his more prolific writings were of a less revolutionary
character, he shocked Czech society by making a prostitute the
heroine of one of his novels. He attained a real grasp of the
human condition in his less controversial writings, for example in a
diary he kept while in hospital. He was essentially a humanist in the
Czech meaning of the word, which signifies a belief that the interests
of human beings and of humanity should be placed above those of
profit or party, of Church or Government. His ideology was greatly
confused and could easily open him to suspicion of Nietzschean leanings, though he remained an honest rebel to the end of his days. A
bank clerk before 1914, he spent part of the war in Austrian prisons,
accused of treason. After 1918 he was made Inspector General of the
Czechoslovak Army but soon resigned this post to return to his role
of intellectual opponent of the establishment – this time represented
by his lifelong friend Masaryk.

Of the writers of this period one should also mention Václav Klic-
pera, whose comedies of manners written more than 150 years ago
still fill the theatres, and Josef Kajetán Tyl, whose sombre and
patriotic historical tragedies are now rarely performed but whose
name was given to Prague's oldest theatre, the Tylovo, formerly the
Theatre of the Estates. A whole succession of accomplished writers
recorded the life of the Czech peasantry, among them the brothers

Alois and Josef Mrštík, and the prolific chronicler of south Bohemian village life, Josef Holeček.

An attempt to do justice to all the writers and artists would probably obscure the direction taken by the mainstream of Czech thought and make it still more difficult to understand why the subsequent history of Europe has been at frequent intervals punctuated by events either initiated by the Czechs or tolerated by them, as in 1918, 1938, 1948 and 1968.

Long after the Czechs had matured in art and science, in letters and industry, they still lacked practical experience of international politics. Actually aware of this shortcoming, they looked back to their history for direction.

The search for a political programme and an attitude to life that would be both practical and satisfying usually took the form of endless discussions about the Czechs' historical mission. In the early days attention was focused on Přemysl Otakar II, the thirteenth-century king who created a Central European empire. Palacký oscillated between the knowledge that such an empire – be it under Habsburg or other rule – was essential for the security of the country and the hope that the Czechs would survive its disintegration if it could not satisfy their national aspirations. This wavering drove him towards non-militancy in spite of his admiration for the Hussites and their revolt against Rome. His dictum, 'Whenever we won, it was rather by spiritual weapons than by force of arms', was adopted by the Czechs more sincerely than was good for their future. His non-militancy was drawn from the collective memory of the beneficent rulers who fought the reactionary classes and made it unnecessary for the people to revolt.

When the Habsburg regime joined the European reaction after Napoleon's defeat, and again after the revolutions of 1848, the Czechs made up for political weakness by glorification of the past, by pinning their hopes on the tsars and – though this never applied to the best men of the country – by substituting the Jews for the stronger real adversary.

Those who had the courage to fight, like Karel Havlíček Borovský, the brilliant journalist who opposed the police regime after 1848, were also able to see that the tsarist regime was not better but worse. Later generations have ignored the main tenet of Havlíček, that the Czech romantics in their pan-slavism and historicism were dangerously avoiding the real issues, and only remember him for his few years of comfortable exile in an Austrian village.

In 1882 the Charles-Ferdinand University in Prague was split into two, one Czech (the modern Charles University) and the other German, and Tomáš G. Masaryk, a lecturer at the University of Vienna, was called to the chair of philosophy at the Czech university. He quickly took up Havlíček's role as the nation's conscience. But there is no doubt that the Czech politicians of the period viewed the future founder of the Republic as an impertinent outsider. He made two sorties into public life which left an imprint on the country. One concerned Hanka's manuscripts – he asked patriots to admit that they were not genuine and instead of basing national pride on a fake to turn their mind to the everyday 'small jobs' for a better future. The second campaign which brought him no fewer enemies, was the Czech parallel to the Dreyfus affair, with Masaryk playing the role of Zola. The Czech 'Dreyfus', appropriately, was a poor country Jew tried and sentenced for the 'ritual murder' of a Gentile girl. Many years later the brother of the girl confessed on his deathbed to murdering her.

These two public campaigns were astutely aimed. Glorification of the past and anti-semitism were the two most important props in the covering up of the inadequacy of Czech nationalist political parties. The third was pan-slavism, the pinning of national hopes on Russia. Masaryk turned his attention to this problem and placed it into a wider context in his book *Russia and Europe*. Like Havlíček, Masaryk found the tsarist regime obscurantist and backward. But he no more liked the extreme quietist, Christian opposition to it expressed in Tolstoy's philosophy of non-resistance to evil. Masaryk – and this is probably the secret of his popularity with the Czechs – was a thoroughly practical philosopher, and he rejected Tolstoy's doctrine as impractical.

The programme he offered the country as an alternative to anti-semitism and pan-slavism was remarkably tame: for a small nation, sustained activity on everyday problems ('small jobs' rather than great deeds) was the best way to success. This is another expression of the same obstinate non-militancy which in Palacký took the form of extolling spiritual strength over armed combat. In Masaryk's reading, Czech history represented a constant striving for a more truthful, tolerant, non-denominationally Christian, socially just, rational, democratic society – an open-ended system with a human face. Having unmasked German romanticism and Russian pan-slavism, Masaryk turned to the young United States for a basically Protestant and manifestly democratic ideology. Unfortunately the question of how Czechs could live according to such humanitarian ideals, wedged as they were between the two totalitarian powers of Russia and Germany, still remained to be answered.

PART III

1914–1971

Introduction

Measured by time alone, the fifty years filled by the history of the Czechoslovak republic before its occupation by the Soviet Army in 1968 appears disproportionately brief compared with the thousand years of the Czech kingdom. However, the pace of history quickens as our sights shift from distant times, about which we know little, to our lifetime crowded with events of which many are not easy to forget.

After a lapse of three hundred years Prague was again a focal point of European history. The effects of decisions taken in London, Paris and Berlin, in Washington and Moscow, were often recognized by those who were taking them only after years had passed. In Prague they were felt almost immediately, and rarely as a blessing. Indeed, the whole history of Czechoslovakia is about the efforts of a small country, more egalitarian than Sweden, more democratic than Britain, and more concerned about the everyday comforts of human existence than France, to weather the storms of European conflicts. It is also about survival under the two totalitarian powers to which it was sold in quick succession, first at Munich and then at Yalta. These efforts rarely reached the level of heroism and were often bogged down by narrowmindedness and cowardice to the point of betrayal of the values that were to be saved. But like the Jews, the Czechs have developed humour and irony to a fine art of survival: to see the ridiculous aspects of power saves one from despair; to laugh at oneself while wriggling under the oppressor's boot preserves the soul.

The tensions and conflicts of the outside world were reflected inside the new state established by the union of Bohemia, Moravia and part of Silesia – the 'historical lands' of the former Czech kingdom – with Slovakia, which since the tenth century had been part of

Hungary. One third of the population of Bohemia and Moravia was German and while ethnic division and sentiment greatly strained the historic links between the Czechs and Germans, the great historical division has often proved to be stronger that the close ethnic affinity of the Czechs and Slovaks. In the course of these fifty years the gap between the economic levels of the two parts of the country was reduced by the industrial development of Slovakia and many new links were forged between the Czechs and Slovaks while almost the entire German population was expelled and settled in West Germany in accordance with the Potsdam Agreement reached between the Four Powers in 1945.

In 1918, however, the divisive forces were more in evidence than anything else, except perhaps a feeling of surprise shared equally by Czechs, Slovaks and Germans when the new state was proclaimed on 28 October 1918.

9 Czechoslovak Independence Movement 1914–1918

A dream at dawn

A whole generation of Czech politicians maturing in the years before 1914 saw the Habsburg empire as the only bulwark capable of stemming the flood of pan-Germanism. Their main fear was of the ascent of Hohenzollern Germany, with its imperialist designs, its mounting influence on the German-speaking population of Austria. The Habsburgs, for their part, feared the Hohenzollerns no less than the Czechs did, and they were supported against the alliance of the Ruhr industry and Prussian militarism by the Catholic Church, the aristocracy, and by Czechs of almost all political shades.

As the great European conflagration of 1914 approached, the traditionalist party, the Old Czechs, who were joined with the nobility and the richer stratum of the bourgeoisie in aspiring to a revival of the defunct institutions of the Czech kingdom, were of steadily diminishing importance.

One of the more important streams of Czech politics was represented by Dr Karel Kramář, the leader of the Young Czechs, and was based on a neo-Slav programme. The second Slav Congress held in Prague in 1908 (the first sparked off the revolt of 1848) was a demonstration against pan-Germanism. Kramář saw the Russian support for the smaller Slav nations as part of an alliance between the tsar and the Habsburgs. He organized the Slav Congress with the approval of Vienna, which at that time was engaged in direct talks with the Russians.

The Czech Social Democrats, which since 1899 formed a united front with the Austrian Social Democratic Party, also aimed at the reform and not the destruction of Austria–Hungary. Their programme called for the transformation of Austria into a 'democratic,

federal state'; thus their aims were opposed to the 'historical' programme of Czech independence seen as a continuation of the Czech
kingdom under the Habsburgs. The Social Democrats proposed the
formation of new territorial units respecting ethnic boundaries – and
the joining of the dispersed ethnic enclaves into 'associations', one
for each nationality, with autonomy in ethnic matters.

Finally there was the small Realistic Party led by Masaryk. To
him the German despotism appeared more dangerous than the Russian because it used not only brute force but also intelligence and
expertise; but both to him were equally detestable. He viewed
Kramář's hopes for Russian support of the Slav peoples of the Austrian empire as wishful thinking. He admitted the possibility of Russia in the future, becoming a power counterbalancing the influence of
Germany, but thought that the Japanese victory of 1905, revealed a
weakness in the Russian empire which the 1905 revolution did not
cure. Masaryk did not believe that the fall of the despotic regime in
that year brought about a sufficiently radical change. Moreover he
doubted the sincerity of Russia's intentions: he feared that the
tsarist government saw the small Slav nations of Central and Eastern Europe only as pawns in the Russian power game.

Before 1914 Masaryk's political programme envisaged gradual reform achieved by steady, patient work towards the improvement of
Austrian institutions. His long-term emphasis was on democratic
rule and social justice, on respect for the life and dignity of each
human being, rather than on national independence. In this period
he spoke only vaguely of the need for the small nations of Central
Europe to join forces in defence against German despotism, and only
in 1908 did he admit that it might be necessary to use force and
revolutionary means in the pursuit of reform, though the idea clearly
appeared to him as distant and unreal. If Masaryk's pre-war political programme was so vague this was due to the absence of any real
prospect that the western democracies, to which Mararyk was linked
by marriage and ideology, could provide a counterbalancing force
against both Germany and Russia.

By going to war on the side of Germany in 1914 the Habsburg
Empire at one stroke changed both the domestic and the international assumptions on which pre-1914 Czech politics were based.
For the first time since 1620 there was a chance of linking the fate of
the Czechs with that of the Western world. Few Czech politicians

had been aware of such a possibility and still fewer would have been ready to risk the future of the country in such a chimeric venture. Masaryk was one of the handful who soon went into voluntary exile, to formulate a programme of national independence based on the assumption of an Allied victory.

After the rise of Prussia in the eighteenth century the enmity between Habsburg and Hohenzollern had been the crucial element of the balance of power in Central Europe: if one of the two was allied to Britain, the other compacted with France. To the east, the rivalry between Russia and Turkey (until 1914 with a foothold in the Balkan peninsula and in control of the Middle East) completed the European security system.

At the beginning of the twentieth century the expansive drive of Germany, powered by a belated, exceedingly fast and self-intoxicating industrial growth, was turned to the Balkans and the Middle East, while a rapid build-up of naval strength lent force to German claims in Africa. The Habsburg Empire, straddling the German road to the Balkans and the Middle East, could not remain neutral. It had only two options: to try to stop Germany or to become its partner and share in the spoils which, if left to Germany alone, would make it the master of Europe. The first option would have led to a reassuring alliance with Russia, which Austria–Hungary bordered in the east along a long frontier running south from the Baltic deep into the Balkan peninsula.

Seen from Vienna, the choice between the two options appeared closely linked with the internal power struggle which had dominated the political life of Austria–Hungary for well over fifty years: would the Germans and Hungarians retain their politically decisive position or would they concede a full share of power to the Slavonic majority. The pan-Germanic movement and the attractive image of industrial prosperity in the German Reich predetermined the issue. To preserve and strengthen the position of Germans and Hungarians, Vienna linked its fate to Berlin.

By taking this step the Habsburg Empire lost the main reason for its existence which from the European point of view was the containment of Germany and from the Czech point of view protection against the Prussians. Russia joined France and Britain in a Grand

Alliance encircling the central powers of Germany and Austria, temporarily supported by Italy.

All Czech political parties had based their programmes on the existence, improvement and strengthening of the Danubian Empire, and the unexpected turn of events left them utterly perplexed. A war on the side of Germany could not be a Czech war, still less one started by the occupation of Serbia and fought against idolized Russia. So much was clear to all, but there was no other line of positive action open. The Czech population adopted a negative, evasive attitude, exploiting all that was absurd in the expectation that individuals could be made into heroes against their own interests. It was at this time that 'the Good Soldier Švejk' was born, the nihilistic, foul-mouthed, full-blooded anti-hero with tongue in cheek who always says 'Yes Sir' but never obeys. Unfortunately that is also his limit. He can paralyse armies but remains incapable of organizing a football team.

The confusion of the Czech political leaders was possibly even greater than the frustration of the Czech private soldier. The Catholic party's obsession with the Most Catholic dynasty could not be dispelled quickly. The Czech Social Democrats, closely associated with the Austrian Social Democrats, lived in the belief that workers everywhere would rise and stop another war. Instead they saw themselves voting with the Austrian Social Democrats for the war, as social democratic deputies in 1914 did in all the parliaments on both sides of the front dividing Europe. The pan-slav programme of the Young Czechs was based on the assumption of an entente between Petrograd and Vienna and the outbreak of war deprived it of the last semblance of reality.

The Russian military successes during the first year of the war gave the pan-Slav leanings of the Czechs a more radical turn. Although expansion in the Balkans and the occupation of Constantinople were the main Russian war aims, the tsarist government was also anxious to annexe East European territories populated by Ukrainians and Poles. A proclamation issued by the Grand Duke Nikolay Nikolayevich, the Russian supreme commander, promised the Slav peoples of Austria–Hungary 'restitution of their rights' and protection of their language and religion. Though it was mainly aimed at the Orthodox population in the Balkan peninsula, the Czechs soon gave it a much wider interpretation: Czech soldiers from the units on the eastern front gave themselves up in thousands rather than fight a German war against their Russian brothers.

Vienna tried to repress the spread of this feeling by arrests and executions. In 1915 Karel Kramář, the leader of the Czech pan-Slav movement, was sentenced to death and put behind bars. This proved a most unpolitical move. Kramář, a rich textile manufacturer from north Bohemia, was a most unlikely revolutionary leader in any case, but whatever danger he represented to Vienna disappeared in May 1915 when the Russian front was broken and pushed away from the Moravian border. On the other hand, the removal of Kramář from the Czech political scene relieved Masaryk, who had been active in France and Britain since the end of 1914, of the fear that a public proclamation of his western-oriented independence programme would be disclaimed at home by pan-Slav Czech politicians.

In September 1915 Masaryk was joined in Paris by Eduard Beneš, a secondary-school teacher who established communication with the Czech underground political network formed after the outbreak of the war. Later there came Josef Durich, an Agrarian deputy representing the Russian-oriented section of the Czech independence movement. On 14 November 1915, the Czech Committee Abroad, which had been formed under Masaryk's leadership in June to represent all Czech communities in France, Britain, Russia and the United States, issued a proclamation calling for an independent Czechoslovak state. This proclamation, published with the approval of the underground network at home, marks the beginning of Masaryk's political action abroad and the first public move towards the establishment of an independent state uniting Czechs and Slovaks.

So far Masaryk's contacts in the West had been mainly with academics and journalists. In France it was Ernest Denis, the author of *The End of Czech Independence*, a multi-volume history of the Czech Kingdom until 1620. (His statue in Prague surprises French tourists who have never heard the name.) In Britain it was R. W. Seton-Watson, editor of *The Times*, who invited Masaryk to explain the Czech position in the newspaper and later made him accept a chair of Slavonic Studies at London University.

Masaryk's first memorandum, submitted to the British Government in May 1915, argued the need for an independent Bohemia which – together with a proposed Yugoslavia – would form a barrier against the German *Drang nach Osten*. It also introduced the theme of the 'reborn Europe'.

In 1914 the Allies had none of the ideological armaments which later became the stock-in-trade of any government preparing for war. The Germans were seen as just another expansionist power, trying to take a piece of our cake. Masaryk's memorandum brought in the element of moral indignation; he saw the Germans as having moved towards totalitarianism ever since Nietszche published *Also Sprach Zarathustra*, an ode on the superman, and contrasted this with the Anglo-Saxon model of democracy which was his ideal for 'reborn Europe'. This programme, propounded with zest in *The New Europe* (which he founded with W. Steed in October 1916), had a similar function in the 1914–18 war to that which the Atlantic Charter formulated by Churchill and Roosevelt had in the political warfare of 1939–45. This explains why Masaryk left a deeper mark on British public opinion than could be expected from a lesser political figure of a small and little known nation.

Masaryk's academic and ideological approach, his attempt to influence the Allied governments through public opinion, was supplemented by a more direct approach to political circles in France when Masaryk and Beneš were joined by Milan Rostislav Štefánik, a young Slovak astronomer who worked at the Mont Blanc observatory and had wide social and political contacts. He arranged Masaryk's first meeting with the French Premier, Aristide Briand, which led to official French support for the Czech independence movement.

From the British and French points of view, Masaryk's independence programme, while useful as a weapon of political warfare, was of doubtful value in its proposal to stem the German advance towards the Middle East by a disintegration of the Austro–Hungarian Empire. In 1916 there were huge losses of men at Verdun and on the Somme. The Central Powers, having rolled back the Russian front in 1915 then broke the new Russian offensive when it reached the Carpathian Mountains in 1916. They controlled Serbia and towards the end of 1916 occupied Romania. At the turn of 1916–17 the President of the United States, Woodrow Wilson, accepted Vienna's initiative and started secret talks for a 'peace without a victory'.

The French government was interested in the Czech independence movement mainly because the Czech and Slovak P.O.W.s who had surrendered to the Allies because they did not want to fight them, might be included in the Foreign Legion. The first Czech units were formed in France in 1916 and in December of that year the French government signed an agreement with Masaryk's Czechoslovak National Council (Conseil National des Pays Tchèques) into which the Czech Committee Abroad had been transformed in February 1916 for the formation of a Czechoslovak army fighting on the Allied side. The bulk of this army was to be brought from Russia, where Czechs and Slovaks had surrendered in great numbers.

While Allied doubts about Masaryk's independence programme were intensified by hopes of concluding a separate peace with the Habsburgs, the position of the Czechoslovak National Council based in France was greatly weakened by the formation of a rival National Council in Russia. Durich, who in 1915 had cooperated with Masaryk and Beneš in France, moved to Russia in the following year. The tsarist government, which was bearing the brunt of the fighting with Austria–Hungary, claimed a decisive say in any future settlement of the Empire. It was in the Russian interest to control any Czech independence movement. Durich therefore received encouragement and financial support in the formation of a second council, which deprived Masaryk's movement of the support of the numerous and relatively prosperous Czech and Slovak settlers living in Russia and of the possibility of bringing the prisoners of war to France. Moreover the splits between the independence movement in France and Britain on the one hand and Russia on the other led to conflicts among the Czech and Slovak communities in the United States.

The Czech independence movement, split into Western and Russian factions, was almost extinguished by new efforts of Austria–Hungary to make a separate peace. Charles, who had succeeded Franz Joseph in 1916, tried to gain support for his peace efforts by a new policy designed to free the Habsburg regime of its dependence on the German and Hungarian minority. In a government newly formed in Vienna the offices of Premier and Foreign Minister were given to two members of the Czech nobility, Clam-Martinic and Czernin, and much was made of the somewhat exaggerated suggestion that by this the Czechs had become the leading element in the monarchy. The Czech politicians Kramář, Rašin, Klofáč and others sentenced to death for pro-Russian activity received an amnesty, with the result that the pro-Austrian faction in Czech politics was resuscitated. When the Allies included in their demands (submitted for Wilson's mediation) 'the liberation of Italians, Slavs, Romanians and Czechoslovaks from foreign rule' the Czech Association – the official organ of Czech politics at home – rejected this sharply: 'As in the past, so now and in time to come the Czechs see their future only under the sceptre of the Habsburgs.'

By the beginning of 1917 Masaryk found himself near to surrender: fearing that his wife, imprisoned in Austria, would not survive the war, he considered returning and giving himself up in the hope of seeing her again.

Independence for the wrong reason

Masaryk's despair – and Austria's hopes of a separate peace – were dispelled by the momentous events of 1917: the active participation of the United States of America in the European war, precipitated by the Germans' unrestricted submarine warfare and the Russian revolution. The revolution modified the strategic concepts of the Allies and led them to accept the disintegration of Austria–Hungary into small nation states, in the hope that the governments of these new states would be supported by nationalist political parties and would provide a safer defence against the revolutionary movement spreading from the east than the discredited Habsburg regime.

However, it was another year before these changes became evident. In the meantime Masaryk's campaign was revived by support from the new Provisional Government in Petrograd.

The Czechoslovak National Council established in Russia by Durich in opposition to the identically named organization in France as a continuation of the pro-Russian movement in Czech politics, had been supported by the tsarist regime. The February revolution of 1917 knocked the bottom out of the organization and strengthened the position of democratic factions among the Czechs and Slovaks settled in Russia or arrived there as prisoners of war. Durich was removed from the leadership, and later, at a congress held in Kiev, Masaryk's Czechoslovak National Council in Paris was accepted as the supreme organ of the independence movement.

The ground for this had been prepared by Masaryk's discussions with Professor Milyukov, Foreign Minister in the Russian Provisional Government. The two professors talked about the problems of Central Europe at some length in 1916 during Milyukov's visit to London, and as soon as the new Russian government was formed, Masaryk sent him a telegram which reveals that the leader of the Czech Realistic Party, then in his sixty-seventh year, had been brought to a state of great euphoria by the fall of the tsarist regime. This condition may afflict even very sophisticated Czechs whenever they believe that Russia has turned its great energy towards the achievement of a more democratic and humane way of life.

Distrusting the tsarists, Masaryk had previously denied himself the simple belief that the great Slav power would solve all Czech problems. Now, on 18 March 1917, he wired to Milyukov:

> ... I can say in the name of our entire people that we are at your side ... The solution of Slav problems is now assured ... the reborn Russia will unite the Serbo-Croats with the Slovenes and liberate the Czechs and the Slovaks ... Free Russia with France and Britain, all of which are also great powers in Asia, will solve the old Eastern Question: they will bring about an organic unity of Europe with Asia and Africa. The great eastern republic will join in this policy aiming at a transformation of the world and of mankind.

The enormity of these hopes can be explained only by the need to compensate for the stress which Masaryk had suffered in the failure of his previous efforts. Nor was he alone: those in the midst of the European holocaust, who were next to mountains of dead on the muddy battlefields and fighting off creeping starvation in the big towns, resorted to hopes that a 'brave new world' would result from the Allied victory and that the Russian revolution would bring about a new millennium. Great swings and messianic aspirations characterized the political moods and moves at a time when the war of 1914-18 was coming to its end.

The Russian Provisional Government was in tune with the hopes of the Slav population of Austria–Hungary: within a month of its constitution it came forward in favour of a 'liberated and reunified Poland, partitioning of Austria–Hungary, establishment of an independent Czechoslovak state and the unification of the Serbian territories ...' 'The formation of a Czechoslovak state will erect a barrier against the expansive designs entertained by Germany against the Slav countries,' stated Milyukov in March 1917. This was the first unqualified acceptance of Masaryk's programme by one of the Allied powers.

The euphoria was shortlived. When Masaryk arrived in Petrograd he found Milyukov replaced by Keresnky and the population discontented and tired of war. By the end of May he reported to London that Russia should not be counted on to continue in the war. Acting in association with the French, he agreed with the Provisional Government the formation of a Czechoslovak Army Corps and the transfer of a part of it – about 30,000 men – to France. The collapse of the Russian front, and the Bolshevik revolution on November 7, made the fate of this army uncertain. The immediate danger was its involvement in the civil war. Within two days Masaryk declared the Czechoslovak army's neutrality, and later, after the conclusion of the Brest-Litovsk peace on 3 March 1918, agreed with the Soviet government that the entire Czechoslovak army, over 92,000 strong, should be moved by the trans-Siberian railway to Vladivostok, whence it would be shipped by the Allies to the French battlefront.

The separate peace with the central powers signed in Brest-Litovsk by Trotsky, representing the Soviet government, dispelled the hopes raised in Poles, Czechs, Slovaks, Slovenes, Croats and Serbs by confirming that the Soviet Government accepted the continued existence of Austria–Hungary and a new frontier with Germany. Germany now controlled a territory extending deep into Eastern Europe, engulfing the whole of Poland and the Baltic countries; its influence now reached into Finland and the Ukraine.

As soon as the peace of Brest-Litovsk was signed Masaryk left Russia for the United States. He was received there with the interest due to a man who had spent many months in revolutionary Russia and spoke for the only army on Russian soil determined to continue the war against the Central Powers. But when Masaryk met President Wilson he found him more interested in the possibilities of stemming the advance of the Bolshevik revolution than in the project of an independent Czechoslovakia.

While Masaryk had been in Russia, the Czechoslovak cause had not been doing much better in the west. The French and British armies had suffered great losses without achieving any success on the western front. The Central Powers had broken through the Italian front. The hope of separating Austria–Hungary from Germany by diplomacy seemed more real than the prospect of a military victory. Secret talks between British and Austrian emissaries had been going on since November 1917. On 5 January 1918, Lloyd George stated that the Allied war aims included the breaking of German militarism but not a territorial break-up of the central powers. Three days later this policy was restated by President Wilson in his Fourteen Points. Both Lloyd George and Wilson spoke of the need to grant autonomy to the various nations forming Austria–Hungary, without mentioning independence. The position of Austria–Hungary had been strengthened by military success in Italy and by the collapse of the Russian army. Its continued existence appeared desirable to the Allies at a time when the danger of the Soviet revolution spreading into Central and Western Europe dominated political thinking.

Although Wilson expressed an intention of preserving the territorial integrity of Austria–Hungary, the ideology of his Fourteen Points hastened the end of that Empire. In an attempt to make Allied war aims sound attractive to the Slav peoples, Wilson claimed the 'right of self-determination for all nations'. In London and Paris this was taken at the time as just another of the high-falutin principles which stream out freely whenever an American president speaks to the world. In Central and Eastern Europe, however, Wilson's dictum was believed to mean what it said. The hopes it raised proved an important factor in the events of the second half of 1918.

These developments were precipitated by the rift which appeared between the Allies at the end of 1917. While Britain and the United States remained firm in their determination to preserve Austria–Hungary, France, where Georges Clemenceau had come to power, took a sharp anti-Austrian turn. Italy, now fighting on the Allied side, could be compensated only at the expense of Austria. The establishment of small independent countries allied to France and forming a belt running from the Baltic to the Black and Adriatic Seas, thus separating Germany from Russia, suggested the idea of France as the leading European power and to Clemenceau the prospect of succeeding where Napoleon failed.

But a further deterioration of the Allied position on the French battlefields soon made such grand designs appear very unreal. After the conclusion of peace with the Soviet Government, Germany transferred a great part of its forces from the Russian front to France and on March 21 opened an offensive which broke the Allied lines and was advancing on Paris. On April 2 Austria–Hungary followed with a diplomatic offensive aimed at the isolation of France from its allies. Count Czernin, the Austrian Foreign Minister, insinuated in a public statement that Clemenceau was attempting to arrive at a secret understanding and separate peace with Austria–Hungary. Clemenceau countered by publishing a facsimile of a letter in Emperor Charles's own hand accepting the French claim on the Rhine province of Alsace-Lorraine which Germany had annexed in 1871.

In the uproar that followed it became clear that both Charles and his wife, the Empress Zita, had maintained contact with the enemy behind the back of their government. Germany, by that time bearing the main burden of the war, used this scandal to prepare for the ultimate removal of the Habsburgs and an *Anschluss,* the perennial German aim of integrating Austria into the German Reich. Czernin resigned and the Vienna government was made to conclude with Germany a long-term political and military pact as well as a customs union with the clear prospect of future integration under Berlin's leadership.

A similar closing of the ranks took place on the Allied side. The halting of new German attacks on the French front gave Clemenceau a claim on the leadership of the Alliance: military actions were subordinated to a unified Allied Command under Marshal Foch; in the political field Britain was gradually coming round to the French idea that Austria–Hungary should be broken up. In June 1918 President Wilson stated that 'complete liberation from the Austrian yoke' for all Slav peoples was also the aim of the United States. In August 1918, with British tanks and fresh American units in France, the armies of the central powers were collapsing. The claims of the Czechoslovak independence movement were stronger than ever: the Czechoslovak legions controlled the Volga front and the trans-Siberian railway along its entire length to Vladivostok. The change in Allied war aims enforced by France, the historical accident which obliged the Czechs and Slovaks to hold the railway to be able to get home across Siberia, the weakening of the Habsburg regime *vis-à-vis* Berlin – this all strengthened the position of Masaryk's Czechoslovak National Committee in Paris. Accepted by France as the Provisional Government of Czechoslovakia since June 29, it was now recognized in quick succession by the British Government on

August 9, by the United States on September 18, and by Italy on October 3. On October 14 President Wilson received from Masaryk the Czechoslovak declaration of independence, now known as the Washington Declaration. A fortnight later the new Republic was proclaimed in Prague.

After four years of persistent effort during which they twice believed they had failed, Masaryk and his associates had almost achieved what they set out to do. The dismemberment of Austria–Hungary, at all times a questionable proposition because it upset the European balance of power in favour of Germany and Russia, could perhaps be justified as part of Masaryk's vision of 'free Russia with France and Britain' bringing about an 'organic unity of Europe with Africa and Asia'. For the independence of the small countries in Central and Eastern Europe would make sense only if agreed between the Allies and Russia. It is to Masaryk's credit that he consistently pleaded with the Allies to recognize the Soviet Government and not allow Russia to slip into isolation or alliance with Germany.

In a report written in Tokyo on the way from Russia to America at the request of the United States Government, Masaryk expressed the view that the Bolsheviks would remain in power at least as members of a coalition government, recommended the recognition of the Soviet Government by the Allies, and wrote: 'All the small nations in the East need a strong Russia if they are not to be at the mercy of the Germans and Austrians. The Allies should support Russia at all costs and by all means. Should the Germans succeed in subjugating the East, this would be followed by their domination of the West.'

Unfortunately, Western democratic governments of necessity have their eyes so fixed on the next election that they keep losing sight of the more distant consequences of their policies. Fearing that the Bolshevik revolution, if successful, would inspire revolutionary movements in the West, the Allies embarked in 1918 on a policy of intervention in the civil war in Russia. For this reason they saw in the presence of the Czech legions in Russia and their control of the trans-Siberian railway the greatest asset of the Czechoslovak independence movement.

Such an intervention which was undertaken with hopelessly inadequate means, could hardly halt the Bolsheviks and was bound to antagonize the new Soviet government for decades. Instead of being the child of a grand *entente* joining the West with Russia, as Masaryk hoped, independent Czechoslovakia was to be born out of division between the 'socialist' and the 'capitalist' parts of the world. Indeed, the Allies seemed to hold the absurd belief that they would be enabled to conduct a policy antagonistic to Germany and to Russia at the same time by the existence of a belt of small countries allied to France and separating the two great continental powers.

Established in the wrong circumstances and placed into an impossible situation in 1918, Czechoslovakia was betrayed, again for the wrong reason, in 1938 and cheated of its existence as an independent state by the Yalta Agreement. That things would go this way once the Danube empire disappeared could have been foreseen even in 1918.

Masaryk therefore started to work on the project of a Danubian confederation even before the Washington Declaration. At the beginning of October 1918, émigré groups in the United States formed the Democratic Middle-European Union and elected Masaryk as their chairman. At a congress held in the Independence Hall in Philadelphia they adopted a declaration aimed at the federation of the countries of Central, Eastern and South-Eastern Europe.

The choice of the hall where the Union of the American States had been declared 150 years earlier was a strong hint. But not strong enough to contain the ghosts let loose. The governments of the newly constituted national states did not want any part in a confederation. Like the governments of the big powers, those of the small succession states were engrossed in the day-to-day business of politics and had no mind for statesmanship. They were to be united only much later, first by the German and then by the Russian army.

10 The reluctant heroes

A tourist watching the changing of the Presidential Guard in the time of the First Republic might easily have thought that the country was under a sort of French–Italian–Russian condominium: the three batallions forming the guard regiment did not wear the uniform of the Czechoslovak Army, of which they were a part, but the uniforms of the wartime Allies. The uniforms were, of course, a reminder that almost 130,000 Czechs and Slovaks fought for the country's independence with the French, Italian and Russian armies, in which they formed their own 'legions'. The pageantry also acknowledged the aspirations of the veterans to continue to be the guardian spirits of the country and of its democratic institutions.

The role of the former legionaries in the first decade of the Republic was by no means only symbolic. They formed the backbone of the new Czechoslovak Army and held important positions in public administration and in business. It was natural that the men welcomed home as heroes would expect some show of gratitude – in most cases a pensionable job in government service. Some had political aspirations: others had a flair for business and established organizations of their own, of which the Bank of the Czechoslovak Legions in Prague was the most prominent.

The saga of the legions' 'anabasis', when they fought their way home through the vast expanse of Russia and Siberia, was the country's first heroic epic since the Hussite wars, and as such was fully exploited by the new establishment. This reinforced the influence of the veterans on the internal life and on the foreign policy of the young state. Its early development cannot therefore be fully understood without retracing at least sketchily the legionaries' experiences during the war and in the first post-war years. They brought home with them many of their wartime quarrels and grievances and while this unduly burdened politics with history, it probably preserved the country from the danger which a united military group would present to democratic institutions.

The first legions had been established as part of the French Foreign Legion out of Czech and Slovak prisoners of war and transformed into a separate Czechoslovak Army in 1917 of about 12,000 men. Similar units were later formed in the Italian Army after Italy joined the Allies, and were about twice as numerous (24,000 men) because there were many more Czechs and Slovaks in the Austro–Hungarian armies deployed in the south. These units took part in the battles on the Somme in France and the Piave in Italy. But when the Czechoslovak legions were finally established in Russia they soon over-shadowed those in France and Italy in numbers – 92,000 – and political significance.

In contrast to the French government, which was in need of men for its army and accustomed to enlisting foreigners, the tsarist government was reluctant to enlist them: the Russian army was short not of men but of arms and supplies, and the Czechs, highly skilled by Russian standards, were required in factories. In 1915 the Russian authorities formed special industrial units out of Czech skilled workers among the prisoners of war and resisted attempts by Czech and Slovak residents, who volunteered for military service, to form a separate corps. Instead, the volunteers, calling themselves 'Cesko-slovenská Družina', were split into small units dispersed in the Russian Third Army and employed for intelligence tasks and psychological warfare.

The other reason why the Russian government resisted the formation of a Czechoslovak army was political. If a Czechoslovak state was to be constituted, they intended this should be the work of a Russian army on Czech soil. Even a purely Russian-based movement of Czechs and Slovaks was for this reason suspect, but one which since the end of 1915 had had contact with the Czech Committee in France was quite unacceptable. The Russian Government was cool to this Committee's efforts not only because its chairman Masaryk was critical of the tsarist regime, but primarily because Russia had no desire to help the French gain influence in Central Europe which it regarded as its own zone of interest.

The situation changed radically after the revolution in February 1917. The Provisional Government quickly agreed to the formation of a Czechoslovak Army Corps as part of the Russian Army but organized on a French model.

Masaryk intended to transfer the greatest part of this army to France, away from the revolutionary upheavals of Russia. He could point to an agreement between France and Russia made in 1916 by which France was promised that half a million Russian soldiers would be transferred to the French front. Only 16,000 were in fact sent and in 1917 Masaryk, together with a French representative, agreed with the Provisional Government that 30,000 men of the Czechoslovak army would be transported to France as the next instalment.

At about the same time, as the first transport embarked in Archangel in November 1917, on November 9 (two days after the Bolshevik revolution) Masaryk declared the neutrality of the Czechoslovak army in the civil war and started negotiations with the newly established Soviet government for the transfer of the entire Czechoslovak army to France. The agreement which he reached with the Soviet government released the Czechoslovak legions from the Russian army – then already disintegrating – and recognized them as a part of the French army. At the same time it was agreed that the legions would be transported via Siberia to Vladivostok where they would embark in Allied ships.

While the Provisional Government was still in power the first Czechoslovak brigade took a heroic part in the battle of Zborov and did much to hold back the disintegration of the Russian front. This early distinction won against the armies of the Central Powers helped in the formation of the Czechoslovak corps as long as the Provisional Government was in power but after the Bolshevik revolution on November 7 the aims of the Czechs became confused. The one point on which they were always agreed was that they wanted ultimately to get home. But on the questions of when, how, and in what way, views differed so much that it was not always clear who was friend and who was enemy.

As could be expected, the legions were soon stirred by the clash of three factions. One, representing the continuation of the pro-tsarist groups that initiated the Czechoslovak independence movement in Russia, wanted to fight the Red Army; and indeed one battalion of the legions fought in the end under Kornilov and later under Denikin in the Ukraine. The other extreme was represented by the

Bolsheviks or Bolshevik sympathizers in the legions. They tried to achieve a takeover under the leadership of a soviet of workers and soldiers formed within the Russian branch of the Czechoslovak National Council, but the attempt misfired. Colonel Švec, who is said to have committed suicide in protest against the low morale of his regiment which he attributed to Communist agitation, became in the 1920s an important figure of Czechoslovak political mythology and the hero of an often performed – and hotly contested – play by Josef Kopta.

The strength and influence of the right-wing and left-wing extremists changed from one phase of the Russian civil war to another. The centrist faction, however, which supported Masaryk's policy of non-involvment in Russian affairs, remained strongest at all times, though to get out of Russia it was in the end necessary to fight the Red Army.

Even at the best of times men and even whole ethnic groups can get lost in the Russian empire, and it makes little difference whether it is ruled by tsars or the soviets. But these were turbulent times with no firmly established central power: the starving masses were often hostile to foreigners and the value of human life had been debased by the slaughter at the fronts. A decision was not so much a matter of politics as a matter of keeping body and soul together.

While the homeless army struggled for survival a battle of the gods was taking place in Paris. The French wanted to have the legions transferred to France, with the double intention of getting reinforcements for their front and of building up their future influence in a reconstructed Central Europe. The British government, however, supported by the United States, proposed a number of new alternatives all designed to deploy the Czechoslovak legions against the Bolsheviks. They should either hold Siberia around Omsk, or move to Archangel to secure a base on the North Sea, or, as a third alternative, they should join the White revolutionary force of Ataman Semyonov, operating in Trans-Baikalia.

The leading triumvirate of the Czechoslovak National Council in Paris wavered. It was probably difficult to be entirely unhelpful to the Allies in whose hands lay the future of the country, and Rostislav Štefánik, the Slovak member of the leading triumvirate, was not entirely out of sympathy with the proposals, though he could not make up his mind.

Beneš appreciated that the British proposals were likely to give new international importance to the independence movement but he feared the dangers of the venture in which the legions might be sacrificed and which the Allies were promoting without risking much themselves. Masaryk opposed intervention in Russian internal affairs and firmly resisted the use of the legions for such ends. Though he was far from Paris he made his position quite clear by declaring the legions' neutrality in the civil war before he left Russia. He urged the Allies to cease supporting the White Guards and to recognize the Soviet Government.

The advice was not welcome. The Allies concluded that it would be easier to decide about the Czechs without them, and this method – though it has since become a habit – has never given good results. A meeting of the Supreme Allied Council, held at Abbeville on 2 May 1918, resolved that the legions should be ordered by their French commander, General Janin, to change their plans. The transports east of Omsk should continue to Vladivostok while helping Allied operations in that area. The transports which had not yet reached Omsk should be diverted to Murmansk and Archangel to guard those ports and the railway lines leading to them.

At about the same time (on April 21), though for different reasons, the Soviet government also decided to stop the units moving towards Vladivostok. A month later, faced with Allied intervention, the Soviets went further, decreeing that all Czechoslovak units should be disarmed and disbanded. The representatives of the Russian branch of the Czechoslovak National Council cooperated, and on May 20 ordered the legions to hand over all arms to the local soviets.

The legions, however, were not a Prussian-type military machine accustomed to blind obedience. All volunteers, they called themselves 'brethren' in the Hussite tradition revived by the nineteenth-century national gymnastic association Sokol. The authority of the officers depended on their ability to convince their men that they were being asked to do things likely to help them get home as soon as possible. It was clear to the Czechs that in the midst of this vast country, torn by civil war and plagued by marauding bands of all sorts, the attainment of this aim, even of safety and survival, depended first on conserving their resources and second on not getting lured away from the main force or allowing it to be split into smaller groups.

The Allies' order that the legions should split into two could be justified only by the prospect that each of these groups would be joined by other Allied forces, but this was by no means certain. Moreover, those who transmitted the order to the legions, in the first instance the French mission, committed an unbelievable tactical error by insisting that the men must not be told that the division of the legions was demanded by the Allies. This would have been the only argument likely to persuade the men to obey, for the simple reason that they depended on the Allies for ships to bring them home. As the source of the order was kept dark, the men suspected that the order originated from the Soviet government, whose demands that the legions should give up their arms and disband had been earlier transmitted to them.

There is no better example of how the stupidity of higher military commands can create confusion. The Allies wanted the legions to split to use them against the Red Army; but without proper explanation the proposed operation appeared to be to the advantage of the Red Army, and the legions believed that the order was inspired by the Soviet Government. They were reluctant to accept it, assuming rightly that they would be in a better position to defend themselves against the Bolsheviks if they stuck together. The legions felt they should rid themselves of outside tutelage. An incident which took place in the region of the Urals substantially increased their self-confidence.

The town soviet of Chelyabinsk, where the first congress of the Czechoslovak legions was about to take place, arrested some legionaries involved in a brawl with Hungarian prisoners of war, in the course of which one of the Hungarians was killed. The Czechoslovak transport passing through Chelyabinsk – the men lived for months in the railway wagons – was 8,400 men strong and it demanded the legionaries' release. When the delegations presenting the request was arrested too, the Czech units occupied the town, disarmed the Red Army unit stationed there and rescued the prisoners. The Czech units then returned to their wagons, but remained in a state of war with the town.

The ease with which the Czech units enforced the recognition of their extraterritorial status encouraged the congress to take an uncompromising stand: the diversion of transports to Murmansk and Archangel was refused and the decision adopted to proceed to Vladivostok by imposing on the railway the legions' own law. The order to surrender arms to the soviets was rejected as 'in contradiction to the will of the legions'. The congress went even further: it told the National Council that the army corps on the move would in future have none of its instructions and elected a 'provisional executive committee' as the only authority entitled to issue orders to units on their way to Vladivostok. The authority of this committee was soon concentrated in the hands of three men, one of whom, Captain Rudolf Gajda, was to become one of the few 'political' generals in Czechoslovakia. He ended his career by founding a fascist party in the thirties.

During the summer of 1918 the legions took over the trans-Siberian railway, some 6,000 miles long, and for a time exercised political and economic control over the more important part of Siberia, including Kazan, where the imperial treasury (650 million roubles in gold) fell into their hands. The legions thus became the most important force resisting the Red Army. But before the end of the year they were defeated on the Volga, and were soon overlooked by the Allies. Their main objective – to get home soon – did not fit into any scheme whether of the Bolsheviks, the White Guards, or the Allies. In the end most did get home, and the armed conflict between them and the Red Army was finally closed by an agreement between the Soviet and Czechoslovak Governments in February 1920. The author used to watch the transports arriving at the main station in Prague – then called Wilson's Station in honour of the American president – late into 1921. Individual stragglers kept appearing for some years after that.

The legionaries were returning to a country which had its independence but was threatened by the Hungarians and Poles from the outside and by the Germans from within. There was little peace and even less security. An army had to be organized, and the returning legionaries, particularly those who came early and in good health, had their work cut out for them. They contributed greatly to the transient stability which the country enjoyed after it had settled its post-war problems and before it became threatened by Hitler. When they looked back on the time they spent on the trans-Siberian railway, they were ready to believe in the heroic role they were so reluctant to assume while still in Siberia. In fact the last thing they sought was military glory. They were men ready to fight to get home and to defend their home, and this image is of greater importance than the unreal one projected by their quasi-political nostalgia.

11 Independence movement at home

As the war drew to an end, two sets of forces, external and internal, converged to redraw the map of Central Europe.

The Allies wished to establish a *cordon sanitaire* to seal off western Europe against the revolutionary movements in the east, and had little confidence in the old monarchy which was weakened by defeat. French aspirations to European hegemony by means of a system of alliances with small countries wedged between Germany and the Soviet Union, influenced their conceptions as to how it should be replaced.

The same solution was also preferable, though for other reasons, to the conservative majority of Austria–Hungary – farmers, tradesmen, shopkeepers and small entrepreneurs whose outlook was determined by property, the Catholic Church, and the identification of civilized life with the authority of the civil service – and they found the nationalist radicalism of the separatists more acceptable as a means of releasing the revolutionary pressure built up by wartime suffering than the socialist radicalism of the Communists.

In 1918 there were not many young men left in Europe to continue the slaughter, and in Central Europe the hungry townspeople had little more left to offer in barter to the profiteering peasants who no longer trusted money. They wanted peace and were ready to make peace and sweep away governments which stood in their way, as the Russians had done a year earlier. In Germany and Hungary proper, where the governments were identified with the nationalist and chauvinistic bourgeoisie, the revolt assumed a class character – given a little more time, Karl Liebknecht and Rosa Luxemburg would have succeeded with a Soviet-type revolution in Germany as Bela Kun did in Hungary. In the Slav parts of Austria–Hungary, however, the nationalist bourgeois parties were in opposition to

Vienna no less than the Social Democrats, and were better prepared for action. The revolutionary pressure in the Czech regions and in Slovakia was therefore easily diverted into the channels prepared by the independence movement abroad.

In July 1918, the Czech Association, an umbrella organization of Czech political parties which had consistently pursued a pro-Austrian policy, was replaced by a National Committee which was to act as a domestic counterpart to the Provisional Government abroad in furthering its independence programme.

The committee was headed by Karel Kramář, still antagonistic to Masaryk, but now seeing his hopes for a Romanov prince on the Czech throne waning, Antonín Švehla, leader of the Agrarian Party who was to become later the strongest political personality of the new country, and J. V. Klofáč and František Soukup, both representing the Socialists. The Czech Social Democratic Party was split on the independence issue and did not join the National Committee. Internationalist in theory and with a long record of cooperation with the Austrian Social Democrats in day-to-day politics, the majority of Czech Social Democrats subscribed to the claim for autonomy in ethnic matters but wanted this to be based on contemporary ethnic boundaries and not on historical frontiers. Because of the many small ethnic enclaves and areas with mixed population, this policy was contrary to the idea of nation states.

On the other hand, some viewed social injustice as a greater evil than national injustice. As the revolutionary mood descended on Central Europe in 1918 a faction of Social Democrats led by Bohumír Šmeral (until September 1917 chairman of the party) embraced the programme of social revolution. Šmeral rejected national independence in favour of a revolutionary transformation – social and economic – of the whole of Austria and Germany, a concept in agreement with the Stockholm Congress of the second International in 1917 which called for a peace that would leave the frontiers of the belligerent countries unchanged. During this congress the split in the Czech Social Democratic Party became most apparent. In Stockholm Šmeral and two other leaders of the Social Democratic Party, Huberman and Antonín Němec, met Professor Maxa, a representative of Masaryk's movement. Huberman and Němec agreed to support the independence movement but Šmeral was not to be deflected from his vision of a socialist Austria–Hungary. Apart from the priority he gave to social issues over ethnic autonomy, Šmeral also doubted that a small nation wedged between great neighbours could achieve security in complete independence. Moreover, he feared the risks involved in the attempt to contain a strong German minority within Czechoslovakia: 'How could a Czech state survive with a whole third of its population German?,' he asked, and added the warning: 'Such an attempt at independence could easily become a hazardous experiment putting the existence of the Czech nation at stake.'

Thus in the autumn of 1918, when events on the international scene began moving very fast, Czech politicians were still groping for a line to take. The conservatives were most careful to keep open the possibility of retreat in the event that Austria–Hungary might survive the war. This was a cause of constant anxiety to Masaryk and Beneš, who persistently tried to impress on them that they should not agree to discuss with Vienna the federalization of the empire proposed by the Emperor Charles.

While the Young Czechs, the Catholics and the Agrarians were not losing sight of the offers made by Vienna, the Socialists on the National Committee were pushed towards a greater radicalism by the Social Democrats who remained outside. Finally, on 6 September the National Committee split. The Socialists left, and together with the Social Democrats and the Anarchists formed a new body, the Socialist Council.

The Socialist Council tried to channel discontent at the breakdown of food supplies into revolutionary action. Protest strikes organized for October 14 to stop the transport of locally produced foodstuffs to other parts of the empire were to declare the Czechoslovak republic 'in the name of the working people'. Some proclamations were made in a number of provincial centres but the National Committee, opposed to the idea of a 'socialist republic', prevented any such action taking place in Prague. Most of the provinces remained under the control of authorities loyal to Vienna and the whole attempt misfired. As a result the Socialist Council was brought under the control of the National Committee, and Šmeral, the main protagonist of the 'socialist republic', was expelled from it. On the same day as the feeble attempt at a socialist coup failed at home, Masaryk, Beneš and Štefánik formed in Paris a Provisional Government of the Czechoslovak Republic, thus forestalling by one day the Manifesto proposing federalization of Austria–Hungary, which Emperor Charles signed on October 15.

In the hope of channelling the Czech independence movement abroad to the platform erected by the Emperor's Manifesto, the Austrian government allowed a delegation led by Kramář and Klofáč to proceed to neutral Geneva in order to meet Beneš and agree a common policy between Czech political leaders at home and abroad. However, the talks held on October 28 to 31 were overtaken by events at home.

When the capitulation of Austria–Hungary, contained in an answer to President Wilson's note of October 18, was published on October 28 Prague was swept by anti-Habsburg demonstrations and celebrations of the end of the war. The National Committee first took over the Cereal Institute, the agency in charge of the procurement and distribution of grain and flour. Later in the day, it assumed all civil and military authority and in the evening it proclaimed an independent Czechoslovak state. The first law drafted by Alois Rašín transferred the whole body of Austro–Hungarian law to the new state, so that Austrian law continued to be in force in the Czech and Hungarian law in the Slovak part of the country.

On October 30 Slovak political leaders meeting in Svatý Martin passed a resolution declaring the Slovaks to be part of a single Czechoslovak nation and claiming independence for this nation. The resolution did not mention a Czechoslovak state and no attempt was made to take over power. None the less the St Martin Declaration was later interpreted as the formal accession of Slovakia to the new republic.

October 28 was later declared to be Independence Day, and the events which took place in the last days of October were termed 'revolution'. The revolution was of a very special, Czech, type. No force was used, no blood was spilled, no one was placed under arrest. The porticos of government buildings were slightly damaged by the removal of the Habsburg emblems. A baroque column with the statue of the Virgin Mary on the Old Town Square, where leaders of the Protestant revolt had been executed in 1620 was toppled. Policemen removed the imperial insignia from their caps and continued in service.

Political parties take new positions

The first Czechoslovak government constituted on 14 November 1918, by a merger of the National Committee at home led by Kramář, and the Paris Provisional Government established by Masaryk, was an all-party government, floating on a wave of national euphoria. It promised everything to everyone.

Such an agglomerate could never have existed at any normal time. However, in the aftermath of a great war, the pressure and pace of international and domestic developments in 1918–20 were such that not only was this government soon replaced by a narrower coalition but the entire political scene was changed beyond recognition before the end of 1920.

The right wing split, pushing out of power Kramář, by far the most imposing figure of Czech pre-1918 politics, and relegating him to the leadership of a chauvinistic opposition whose importance finally petered out. At about the same time the extreme left was expelled from the Social Democratic Party and later formed the Communist Party. With the right and left extremists removed from power, the centre reintegrated and produced The Five, a steering committee made up of the leaders of the centrist parties, which from then on for many years ruled the country as an unofficial cabinet, contributing an element of stability to Czechoslovak politics. The development of this specifically Czechoslovak form of government by representatives of five political parties meeting in private was prompted by the experience of the first all-party government which really did not want most of the things which it felt it had to promise to appease stirred public opinion. Kramář's programme tried to please the patriotic intelligentsia by the prospect of more civil service jobs, housewives exasperated by food shortages by promising that profiteering would be punished as the most serious crime, land-hungry farmers as well as the revolutionary left by outlining a policy of nationalization of mines and expropriation of large agricultural estates, mostly owned by the nobility and the Catholic Church.

At that time in Russia the expropriation and distribution of land had transformed a Petrograd putsch into an epoch-making revolution, and agrarian reform soon became the central issue of Czechoslovak domestic politics. The Social Democratic Party demanded confiscation of estates over 50 hectares and committed the crucial mistake of proposing, not distribution of land to the peasants, which would have attracted rural votes, but the formation of large, state-owned farms, which though rational was unattainable at that time.

The Agrarian Party proposed distribution of the expropriated land among medium-size peasant farms and gained by this policy a firm political footing in that stratum of the Czech population which was most realistic in its political thinking, most stable in its allegiance and continually producing men with drive and capable of leadership at all levels of administration and economy.

The National Democrats, Kramář's party and successors to the Young Czechs, who had links with the landowning nobility, proposed that expropriation should leave intact estates up to 1,000 hectares (2,500 acres). The Czech Catholic Party demanded that the limits should be fixed individually between 300 and 700 hectares according to the quality of the land, while the Slovak Catholics opposed any parcelling-out of the Church estates.

The political ascendancy of the Agrarian Party was facilitated by the long absence of Kramář. The Premier was lured away from the domestic political scene which he mastered to the glamour of the peace conference in Versailles, where he was overshadowed by Beneš who had the advantage of wartime cooperation with the Allies in the West. In Kramář's absence power passed to Antonín Švehla, leader of the Agrarian Party, who, as Minister for the Interior and acting Premier, soon revealed himself as a strong man of great political dexterity and statesmanship. A third personality rising at that time to national stature was the reformist leader of the Social Democratic Party, Rudolf Bechyně, but though he was an extremely clever and influential politician he had neither the strength of Švehla nor the

charisma of Masaryk. The inability of the Social Democrats to produce resolute leaders, not only for the top but also for the lower
levels of politics, was probably the main reason why this party, initi-
ally the strongest, always played only second fiddle.

The breakthrough in the old pattern of Czech politics came when
the Social Democrats, pressed by their radical wing, presented their
partners in the government with an ultimatum demanding the passage of the agrarian expropriation law within a fortnight, and that at
the same time, preparatory steps should be taken for the nationalization of mines, foundries and large-scale enterprises. The Social
Democrats also opposed Švehla's plans for a curtailment of civil
liberties in the face of the revolutionary agitation which engulfed the
whole of Central Europe.

In this situation, potentially dangerous for the young state,
Masaryk brought Švehla and Bechyně to direct talks which resulted in
an alliance between the Agrarians and the reformist moderate wing of
the Social Democrats. Švehla agreed to a speedy passage of the laws
introducing the agrarian reform, at the same time making sure that
his party would have the main say in their application. Bechyně
withdrew the demands for nationalization of mines and industry and
agreed to some restrictions on public assemblies – a concession likely
to hit the extreme left wing more than the reformist core of the
party. This compromise between two crafty politicians proved to be
very much in line with the long-term need of the country. It provided a safe majority for a democratic government with support
from both the essentially conservative Agrarians and the essentially
progressive Social Democrats.

In the spring of 1919 the immediate benefits of this political deal
were probably much more evident than its long-term aspects. Slovakia was in the hands of Hungarian Communists and, to the west,
there was considerable revolutionary activity in Bavaria. The last
wartime harvest had been poor and most of the grain was taken
away by the Viennese government before it capitulated. In May,
when the shortages were most acute, demonstrations and protests
throughout the country expressed the people's hardship and understandable disappointment that the end of the war had not brought
the end to starvation. In many places, including Prague, the
demonstrations ended in looting and in some places were channelled
into anti-semitic pogroms.

Although international and domestic conditions combined to favour revolutionary action, the Communists got the upper hand only in
the coalmining district of Kladno, about 30 miles west of Prague,
where administration was for a short time taken over by a workers'
council and some shopkeepers were tried by 'people's tribunals'. The
government avoided using armed force to quell the demonstations,
by pursuing a policy of amicable pacification in which the main role
was played by Social Democratic shop-stewards, supported by government action against overcharging for food and other consumer
supplies.

The demonstrations reached their peak in the last week of May,
only a fortnight before the communal elections in Bohemia and
Moravia, which were held on June 15. This contributed to a great
election victory for the Social Democrats, who received 30 per cent
of all votes. They were followed by the Agrarians with 20 per cent,
the Czech Socialists with 15 per cent, and the Catholics with 10 per
cent; the National Democrats, the party of the then Premier
Kramář, received only 8 per cent of the votes.

These election results confirmed that the Social Democrats and
the Agrarians could form a strong coalition. This was of essential
importance in a country where proportional representation meant
that no single party could achieve a strong majority. Kramář's government resigned, and a new government, appointed on July 8, was
formed by Vlastimil Tusar, a Social Democrat whose role has been
compared with that of Ramsay MacDonald in Britain. His government was a coalition of Social Democrats and Agrarians, led by
Švehla who retained the Ministry of the Interior.

While the centre – reformist Social Democrats and Agrarians –
moved closer together, the left and right wings of Czech politics,
now relieved of responsibility, took up extreme positions.

Kramář, though no longer Premier and defeated in the local elections, continued to lead the Czechoslovak delegation at the Versailles
peace conference, while steadily losing touch with the rapidly changing domestic scene. In the course of the war he had embraced the
vision of a Czech kingdom reborn with a Romanov monarch. During
the peace conference he gladly succumbed to pressure from both
Russian monarchist refugees and the French Government, who were
determined to assist the White armies operating in Russia.

When Kramář returned early in October 1919, he convened a

public meeting in Prague and put to the country his proposal that the Czechoslovak legions, then struggling to get out of Siberia to Vladivostok and back home, should turn and chase the Soviet government from Moscow. He proposed that the legions should join Denikin, whose army was then in control of southern Russia and approaching the capital.

This bombshell was clearly designed to push out of French favour Masaryk and Beneš, who pursued a policy of non-intervention in Russian affairs. The blast, however, turned against Kramář. His proposal was unacceptable to the radical left who were demanding recognition of the Soviet Union and hateful to the families of the men in Siberia. It was scarcely attractive to Kramář's followers, mostly in the business and professional strata, for they were still a little shocked by their audacity in subscribing to independence from the Habsburgs and in no mood to try to save an empire for the Romanovs. In any case the legions were not prepared to recognize any authority which did not support their own war aim, to get home as soon as possible.

In contrast with Masaryk, who never believed intervention could work, Kramář must have been completely deluded about the relative strength of the forces facing each other in Russia; after making his proposal known to the Czech public he left hurriedly for Russia to meet Denikin and hand him a statement on the Russian question issued by the French Ministry of Foreign Affairs, and the draft of a new Russian constitution which he had agreed with Russian émigré leaders in Paris.

Before the year was out, both Denikin in the south and Yudenich in the north were defeated by the Bolsheviks. In Siberia the Czechoslovak legions refused to help Kolchak and handed him over to the Red Army. The Allies finally agreed to the evacuation of the legions from the Soviet Union and on 7 February 1920, the legions signed an armistice with the Red Army which promised no interference with the evacuation. Kramář's plans for a march on Moscow, unpopular from the beginning, met with spectacular failure before they could be forgotten.

Kramář's defeat, first in the local elections and then in his attempt to enter international politics, left the 'Castle Group' around Masaryk in a position of overriding influence on all fundamental policy decisions. In foreign policy this group steered towards a system of

European security supported by both France and the Soviet Union. At home it pursued a moderate course of social reform without undermining entrepreneurial confidence and of civil freedoms, carefully blended with the requirements of defence and of political stability.

The Kramář débâcle also further accelerated the split in the Social Democratic Party. Premier Tusar subsequently expressed his disapproval of Kramář's journey to Denikin but the left wing of his party accused him of having condoned it by his initial silence. The left opposition had already attacked the Social Democratic leaders for taking part in a bourgeois government at the beginning of October, and on 7 December 1919, it formed a separate group, the Marxist Left, which adopted a revolutionary programme.

However, in spite of the general radicalization of Czech politics resulting from shortages and the mounting discontent of the workers, the Marxist Left stayed with the Social Democratic Party and went with it into the general election in the spring of 1920. The Social Democrats obtained 37.4 per cent of all votes, far outstripping the Czech Catholics with 16.4 per cent and the Agrarians with 14.2 per cent. The victory of the left was even greater among the German-speaking population. The German Social Democrats won 43.5 per cent of all German votes while the bloc of German centrist and right-wing parties obtained 8.1 per cent. The remainder of the votes was divided among small parties.

In the summer of 1920 the Red Army advanced in Poland to within 50 miles of the Czech frontier and thus added another explosive element to an already highly inflammable situation. Both extremes of Czechoslovak politics underwent further radicalization and stepped up their attacks on the government, which could be described as an alliance of the reformist wing of the Social Democrats with the Agrarians and the Castle Group. The left wing stirred up a strike movement all over the country and became even more militant when, after the defeat of the Red Army in Poland in August, the Communist International attempted to continue the expansion of Soviet influence by political means.

In September the Social Democratic leadership expelled the Communist faction, which answered by occupying the central office of the party and its main newspaper, *Právo Lidu*. Seeing his party so deeply split, Tusar resigned as Premier on 14 September. He was replaced by Černý, who presided over a caretaker government composed of top civil servants and steered, behind the scenes, by an unofficial Committee of Five which worked closely with President Masaryk. The pro-Soviet wing of the Social Democrats, now feeling very confident, held a separate congress and constituted the Czechoslovak Social Democratic Party (Left), electing Bohumír Šmeral as its chairman. This new party was the future Communist Party.

In the meantime, the right wing of Czech politics led by Kramář had attempted to unseat the Castle Group by frustrating its policy of appeasement and cooperation with the German minority. About two months after the fall of the Tusar Government, the National Democrats occupied a number of German cultural institutions in Prague and the editorial offices of two liberal German newspapers, *Prager Tagblatt* and *Bohemia,* which supported Masaryk's policy. The anti-German demonstrations developed into a pogrom on Jewish shops on the pretext that a number of Prague Jews spoke German and professed German as also did many Jews living in the German districts.

The chauvinistic activities of Czech right-wing extremists led to bloody clashes with the German population and were followed in December by a still more serious subversion from the left. On 9 December Social Democratic leaders took possession of the building which housed the central office and press in accordance with a court eviction order against the Communist faction which had earlier occupied the building. The Communists answered the next day by calling a general strike, which affected a number of industrial centres throughout the country. In the coalmining district of Kladno it attained a revolutionary character: a central revolutionary Committee in which Antonín Zápotocký, the future Communist President, achieved political prominence for the first time, attempted to take over factories, government offices and Lány Castle, country seat of the President. The strike was, however, far from general, and the revolutionary actions were limited to isolated centres and groups. The mass of workers followed the reformist leaders of the Social Democratic parties, Czech, German and Slovak, who had taken a strong line against the strike. With their approval, the Černý government took police action against the revolutionary centres and the strike collapsed after five days.

The defeat of the revolutionary left virtually coincided with the failure of the National Democrats to unseat Masaryk by stirring up trouble with the Germans. The attempt backfired completely: the German Agrarian Party and the German Christian Democrats decided to support the Černý government against the Czech radical nationalists and reached an agreement with the Five.

The political consolidation of Czechoslovakia was achieved by a polarization of forces which gave the centre freedom of action by the neutralization of both left and right extremists, who subsequently suffered a resounding defeat.

Prague government fights for power

Although October 28, the day on which the new independent state was proclaimed in Prague in 1918, is the Czechoslovak Independence Day, it took one year for the government constituted in Prague to assert its authority over the entire country, and one more to make its frontiers reasonably secure. The Czechoslovak government had first to break the separatist movement of the three-million-strong German minority, clear out the Hungarian army from Slovakia together with its puppet soviet, and regain Těšín, which had been claimed by Poland. Military operations ran in parallel with intense diplomatic activity and both were a heavy burden for a new government in a country suffering grave shortages of food and of basic consumer supplies and whose industry had been abruptly deprived of its main markets in the agricultural regions of Austria–Hungary. But the new country had some points of strength. During 1919, the Czech legions were still in control of the trans-Siberian railway and important centres in the Urals. By the time that the legions later ceased to be a potential instrument of Western intervention in Russia, Czechoslovakia was beginning to emerge strategically, economically and politically as the most valuable member of the security system designed by the French.

No sooner was independence proclaimed than German deputies from Bohemia and Moravia met in Vienna and the next day, October 29, issued their counter-proclamation of Deutschboehmen, an independent German *Land* in the territory of north and west Bohemia. The *Land* was to have a parliament, meeting in Liberec (Reichenberg), which also became the seat of its government presided over by Lodgman von Auen. On October 30 the Provisional

Parliament of Austria declared the new *Land* a province of German Austria and assured it of full support against the Prague administration (then still called the National Committee). During the next two weeks Deutschboehmen was joined by further districts with a German majority which integrated into separate provinces: Sudetenland in north-eastern Bohemia, Deutschmaehren in south Moravia and Boehmerwaldgau in south Bohemia on the Austrian and Bavarian border.

Lodgman von Auen, formerly a significant liberal, adopted a pan-Germanic, violently nationalist programme and soon gained the support of the German Social Democrats led by Josef Selinger. Their ambition seemed to be a German Reich including Austria and those parts of Bohemia and Moravia where the German-speaking population was in the majority.

The National Committee in Prague offered the Germans representation on the committee and in parliament, and food supplies for the starving population. The offer was turned down both by Lodgman and by Selinger, who did not want the territory under their control to become part of Czechoslovakia. Their intransigence was a last echo of Germany's attempt to turn defeat by France and Britain into a victory over Austria–Hungary and to create a German Reich including all German-speaking populations in Central Europe.

On 12 November 1918, the Austrian Provisional Parliament proclaimed the Austrian republic and declared it to be 'an integral part of the German republic': at the same time the Austrian Government tried to win support from the Vatican, from the Second (Social Democratic) International and from the United States for its claim that the German part of Bohemia and Moravia should be recognized as part of Austria.

To forestall the emergence of a 'greater Germany' both the Czechs and the Allies had to act swiftly. The Prague Government, formed on November 14 from the National Committee and the Provisional Government in Paris, obtained French backing for military action against the German separatists. A small force consisting of legionaries returned from France and Italy, and volunteers, mostly from Sokol, occupied the German districts without meeting any great resistance. Lodgman and Selinger left the country and the provincial German governments disintegrated.

The high-sounding principles launched by Woodrow Wilson,

during the last stage of the war, were soon to be revealed for what they were: slogans of ideological warfare with no relation to politics. The victory over the German separatists preserved the thousand-year-old political and economic integrity of Bohemia and Moravia but weakened the ideological claim of the new state that it was based on the 'right of self-determination'.

The same argument – a thousand years of common history – which the Czechs used to counter the separatist movement of the Germans was used by the Magyars denying the right of self-determination to the Slovaks: they claimed that Slovakia should remain with Hungary, of which it had been an integral part since the tenth century. The liberal government of Count Karoly proclaimed an Hungarian republic on 12 November and immediately – by an armistice signed in Belgrade – obtained an agreement from the French that Slovakia and other parts of former Hungary should remain under its provisional administration. By the second half of November the Hungarian army controlled Slovakia.

Disruption of food supplies, hoarding of food and other goods caused by political uncertainty, and the resulting distrust of money, proved the best allies of the Czechs in Slovakia, where the Hungarian administration faced serious unrest. Beneš, the Czechoslovak Foreign Minister, got the French to revoke the Belgrade armistice and support Slovakia's accession to the new state, and the Hungarian army was pushed out of Slovakia by 20 January 1919.

The retreat from Slovakia precipitated the fall of the liberal regime of Count Karoly and led to a Communist putsch in Hungary. To be able to present their invasion of Slovakia as an act of 'international solidarity,' the Hungarian Communists formed an international Red regiment, including some Slovak Communists, as part of their army. The proclamation of a Slovak soviet republic followed on June 16. So scarce apparently were Slovak Communists that a Czech, Antonín Janoušek, was elected chairman of the Council of Peoples Commissars set up by the Hungarians in Košice on June 20.

On the same day as the Hungarian Red Army established a Soviet government in eastern Slovakia, the Allies agreed in Paris the final demarcation line between Czechoslovakia and Hungary, leaving the Slovaks in one state with the Czechs and joining with them Ruthemia or Subcarpathian Russia (now part of Soviet Ukraine) as the easternmost tip of Czechoslovakia. The Hungarian soviet government was presented with an Allied ultimatum, the seriousness of which was underlined by the fact that the French officer in command of the Czech army in Slovakia was given dictatorial powers over the civilian population. Under this pressure the Hungarian Red Army, together with the Slovak Communist units and the Slovak Council of People's Commissars, left Eastern Slovakia. The Slovak soviet republic was shortlived.

In Hungary the defeated Communist regime of Bela Kun was replaced by the militaristic, revanchist and anti-semitic regime of Admiral Horthy. Even in June 1920, when the Versailles peace treaty gave a diplomatic seal to the new frontiers, Hungary continued a wide range of activities aimed at a revision of the new map of Central Europe and the return not only of Slovakia but also of Transylvania from Romania and Vojvodina from Yugoslavia.

Early in 1920 a second revisionist centre emerged in Munich. It was led by General Ludendorff and threatened to harness the great potential of Germany in the cause of a monarchic coup that would return power in Central Europe to an alliance of German and Hungarian right-wing extremists.

A third threat to the safety of the new Czechoslovak republic was implicit in the course of events in Poland. The dispute with Poland over the Těšín coalfield was only part of a wider rivalry between Prague and Warsaw: both aspired to be the focal points of the new system of European security. Backed by France but dissuaded by Britain, Poland got involved in April 1920 in a conflict with the Soviet Union which brought the Red Army to the gates of Warsaw in August.

France, later joined by Britain and the United States, pressed the Czechoslovak Government to support the Poles, and the Hungarian army asked for permission to cross Slovakia on the way to the Polish–Soviet front. The threat to Slovakia contained in this request only reinforced the determination of the Prague government to stick to Masaryk's line of non-intervention in Russian affairs. On 19 August 1920, Czechoslovakia declared its neutrality in the war between the Soviet Union and Poland and closed its frontiers with Poland and Hungary.

In the short-term this action could not have appeared well-advised: a few days later the Red Army suffered a decisive defeat on the Warsaw front and at the end of August started to retreat from Poland. However, Masaryk and Beneš pursued a long-term objective. They based the security of the new country on the assumption that both Russia and Germany would continue to exert powerful influences in Central Europe and that these should be somehow harmonized with the new, and from the Czech point of view highly desirable, Western interest.

In 1920 the possibility of simultaneously cultivating friendly relations with both the Soviet Union and Germany appeared real: Ludendorff's Bavarian coup was broken, the danger of a Communist revolution was receding and the Weimar republic appeared the victor in the great internal struggle which followed German defeat. Like Czechoslovakia, Germany had declared its neutrality in the Polish–Soviet conflict.

This longer-term view – which was to prove not long enough – enabled the Czechoslovak Government to brave the displeasure of the French whose support was essential to them. The Czech leaders had a much more intimate knowledge of Russian affairs. They believed that intervention could never be successful and anticipated that sooner or later France would have to join hands with Russia, even a Soviet Russia, in order to hold down Germany to the hardly bearable peace terms imposed by the Versailles treaty. They hoped that in such a European system Czechoslovakia would be the linchpin holding France and Russia together.

However, the Czechoslovak Government's immediate concern in the summer of 1920 was the safety of Slovakia threatened by Hungary. Here their natural allies were Romania and Yugoslavia, both similarly threatened by Hungary in the possession of territories which formerly belonged to her. Czechoslovakia concluded with these two countries treaties of mutual assistance against any Hungarian aggression and thus formed what later became known as the Little *Entente*.

This defensive alliance was later supplemented by attempts at regional economic cooperation but these fell short, both in scope and in territorial spread, of Masaryk's wartime plans for a Central European federation. He had planned to include Poland and Greece, thus forming a continuous belt from the Baltic to the Mediterranean. However, the Little *Entente* served to keep Hungary at bay, and in addition, through a treaty which Czechoslovakia concluded with the

Austrian republic in January 1920, reinforced that country's independence, always potentially endangered by internal or external
movements favouring its *Anschluss* to Germany.

One cannot fail to be impressed that the diplomatic activity of
Czechoslovakia in the second year of its existence did much to steer
Central Europe out of the first post-war crisis in 1920. This activity
had opened with a rapprochement with Austria, surprising perhaps
to outside observers but perfectly natural to Czechs and Austrians,
linked not only by history but also by countless economic and family
ties. It continued in the support of the democratic forces in Germany
struggling against left-wing revolutionaries and right-wing putschists. Czechoslovakia was the first country to establish normal contacts with the Soviet Government in the summer of 1920, in spite of
the fact that the memory of the battles fought by the Czech legions
against the Red Army for control of the trans-Siberian railway was
still fresh. Finally, the Czechoslovak Government organized the
Little *Entente* as the first collective defence of the new frontiers in
Central Europe. Unfortunately the assumption of continued Western
interest in the existence of a belt of countries separating Germany
and Russia, on which this edifice was built, proved to be no more
than shifting sand in less than a score of years.

13   The rise and fall of the Castle

The invisible party

Cut off from Western news since 1914, most Czechs and Slovaks tended to exaggerate the part which Masaryk had played in swinging the Allies in favour of a complete disintegration of Austria–Hungary. At its first meeting, on 14 November 1918, the newly constituted National Assembly of the Republic elected Masaryk as the country's first President. However, the fervently awaited President–Liberator seemed in no hurry to take up office.

He arrived in Prague six weeks later after a leisurely crossing of the Atlantic had given him much-needed time to think about what was to be done – and about his wartime memoirs, *The World Revolution*. The core of this book is a discussion of the spiritual aspect of the conflict between Prussianism and democracy, a conflict which Masaryk saw not only in the war between the Central Powers and the Allies but also within Germany itself – and as Czechs have for so long been mixing with Germans that Lenin called them 'the Prussians among the Slavs' one might even suspect that Masaryk knew that they too suffer from this dichotomy. He also recorded in the book how lucky he often was in not succeeding where success would have brought unsuspected disaster to him and his cause. But the success granted to him – as he believed, by Providence – in greater measure than he ever hoped before 1914, ended in disaster too. This he could not foresee, and so at the age of 69, he embarked on a truly heroic attempt to create an island of democracy in the centre of Europe. The project came to an end when the democratic west colluded with the totalitarian soul of Germany: Masaryk, holding spiritual forces to be more important than power politics and economic interests, had not believed this to be possible.

This ignorance of the facts of life coupled with an unquestioning belief in an ethical code enabled him to become a driving-force in the Czechs' attempt to prove that they could win just by working hard, loving music, and being tolerant and reasonable. Though the proof was not achieved, the attempt probably concluded the process of national renaissance begun at the end of the eighteenth century. By the time Masaryk died in 1935 the Czechs and Slovaks no longer had any doubt about their national aims.

Before the war Masaryk had not been used to much success in politics and even less to public acclaim for his political actions. He certainly did not endear himself to the chauvinist rank and file when he had exposed the Hanka Manuscripts in 1886. He did not improve his record when in 1899 he demanded the retrial of Leopold Hilsner, a Jew sentenced for 'ritual murder'. He was of the race which fights other people's causes, like Zola or Bertrand Russell. In 1909 he fought for Yugoslav patriots sentenced in Zagreb trial; in 1910 and 1911 he used the trial of Friedjung, a liberal journalist, to attack Arenthal's foreign policy. The pre-war Masaryk appeared to be serenely indifferent as to who would get hurt in his quest for truth and justice, and one of the first casualties was his own political career.

Elected to the Viennese parliament on a Young Czech ticket, Masaryk resigned when he disagreed with his party. After the constitution of his own Czech Popular Party (better known as the Realistic Party) in 1900, he kept his seat in the Viennese parliament for the second consecutive term only by courtesy of the Social Democrats, who put his practical interest in social improvement above his ideological opposition to Marxism; they engineered his election by withdrawing their own candidate in his constituency.

This man, who before the war was so patently unsuccessful as a politician, became the spiritual rector of a powerful political clique as soon as he was installed in Prague Castle, which until 1619 was the seat of Czech kings. The Castle group for long retained complete control of Czechoslovakia's foreign relations and was a decisive influence on the country's political and cultural climate. The core of the Castle group was a circle of academics, top civil servants, writers and journalists, who surrounded Masaryk every Friday for a fireside chat, not at the Castle but in the house of Karel Čapek, the playwright, writer and journalist. In a wider sense the Castle was an all-pervasive political club with members who never met, who could belong to any political party or none, and who could be identified only by their support of the somewhat idealistic concept of Czechoslovakia as a paragon of democratic virtues and social justice. The Castle, in fact, was an invisible political party.

Masaryk's personality dominated the Castle group and his influence filtered through into the informal political alliances which the Castle had with the Czech, Slovak and German Social Democrats and the Czech National Socialists. The Castle also had close links with the banks, the Živnostenská Bank in the first place. As a corollary to its efforts to enlist the Soviet Union's support against a revision of the Versailles peace treaty and later against the danger of German aggression, the Castle also repeatedly tried to establish friendly relations with the Czechoslovak Communist Party. These approaches met with a positive response only after France and the Soviet Union had concluded a friendship pact in 1935.

The strength of the Castle in the period of its ascendency was derived from three sources, and, as these gradually dried up, the power of the group declined and with it also the strength of the country to survive. The first of these sources, which diminished after the Locarno conference in 1924, was the link which Masaryk, Beneš and some of their closest associates had with the Allies, with France in particular. In the thirties the Castle's monopoly of foreign policy began to be challenged by the powerful Agrarians.

The second was the facility with which the Castle network could communicate across party-political and departmental barriers and the influence it could exercise through its members simultaneously and unobtrusively in various spheres and at various levels. This ease of communication and influence was severely impaired when the Communist Party came under the complete control of Moscow in 1929 and the large German minority under the equally effective control of Hitler in the thirties.

Finally, there was the tremendous popularity of Masaryk, on whom a large majority of the sober, sceptical, even cynical Czechs pinned their stored-up need to love, so that in the end the Old Gentleman, as he was generally referred to, overshadowed the two who in the nation's consciousness had previously attained the rank of *pater patriae*: Charles IV, the fourteenth-century king who made Prague the centre of the Holy Roman Empire, and František Palacký, the nineteenth-century historian and political leader. When

Masaryk abdicated after a long illness in 1935, the calculating and clever Beneš was unable to fill the gap.

The Castle group claimed merit for the country's independence, and bore the blame when its system of alliances collapsed. Nevertheless, it contributed greatly to the special quality of life which made most Czechoslovaks so proud of their country in the 1918–38 period, and particularly at the time it became a refuge for men like Albert Einstein, Thomas Mann and Hans Kelsen – and thousands of lesser calibre but made of the same stuff. It may therefore be worth analysing in some detail the ideology, domestic politics and bore the blame when its system of alliances collapsed. possible a balance between sympathy for its ethos and regret for its quixotic folly.

Masaryk – the Czech syndrome

However wary one may be of the idea that history is made by great men, it is impossible to discuss the Castle group, and to convey an impression of the political and spiritual climate of Czechoslovakia between the wars, without sketching Masaryk's personality. His life, writings and political activity have been described in an avalanche of books produced in Czechoslovakia by a somewhat sycophantic cult, and abroad by a fascination with the rare phenomenon of a 'philosopher king', to which the fact that this particular philosopher was for a time a professor at the School of Slavonic Studies of London University added further interest in Britain. Most of these writings are more likely to obscure the basic clue to the spell in which he held the country and which had little to do with his philosophical attainments, if indeed there were any. Only a few people were acquainted first-hand with his sociological and political writings and of those who were, many found the philosophy singularly confused, though his non-doctrinaire approach rather added interest to his writings.

Masaryk was not loved because he was a thinker but because, like most of his compatriots, he started life as a poor boy, had courage, sided with the under-dog, spoke plainly, lived simply – and was an extremely handsome old man. Dr Alice Masaryk, his unmarried daughter, who did not grasp the true source of her father's charisma, kept trying to make him behave like a Habsburg monarch, or at least stop him going barefoot at home. She never succeeded. Masaryk retained the manners of his youth, the obstinacy of a peasant and the simplicity of his language. The truth, so far not revealed, is that the great man feared his bossy daughter and conspired with his equerry, to preserve the little pleasures of a simple life in the face of her aspirations to grandeur. Masaryk was much more magisterial in public life: he distributed tasks to ministers as if they were little boys, while treating students as his equals. He was a bad and enthusiastic horseman who would let his mount go where it pleased – but the whole country loved to see him beautifully erect on horseback, and believed him to be in control.

Masaryk's humble origin and simple life-style made it possible for plebeian Czechs and Slovaks to identify themselves with their president and thus appropriate some of his greatness. If this is why they loved him, the reason why they respected him was certainly not because they thought of him as a philosopher. Masaryk never claimed to be one – in fact he was an anti-philosopher, great at finding fault with all philosophical systems which, if they are to be systems, must be founded on one central idea. Neither Catholic doctrine nor Marxism, neither Tolstoy's non-resistance to evil nor Nietzsche's superman found grace in his eyes. He offered also no panacea of his own. Can the human mind grasp reality? Yes, but not entirely. Are events the predetermined results of causes? Yes, but not always; there is also our free will to impose on them ethical rules, but not entirely – Masaryk was humbly aware of an all-pervading Providence.

Like most of his compatriots Masaryk was a pragmatist. He saw a bit of truth in every doctrine, and that each event has many causes. He was all for reason, but one feels somehow that he was more familiar with Providence. Historical and sociological theories, a pretence of knowing the great cycles in which the world and life will continue to move, were not for him. His reason did not allow him to predict for more than a few years ahead. But his belief in Providence was optimistic, making him see mankind as continuously rising from a dark past to an enlightened future along a path of uninterrupted progress.

Much in Masaryk, and in his stimulating impact on Czech

thought and politics, can be explained by the fact that he received higher education only after he had started to train as a blacksmith in a village in southern Moravia, near the Slovak frontier, and that he received this education almost entirely abroad. He met his American wife while they were both studying at the University of Leipzig, and he started his career as lecturer in Vienna. He was thirty-two when he became a professor at the reestablished Czech University in Prague in 1882 and his written Czech was so bad that he had to ask a journalist to polish his writings.

If, on the one hand, long absence abroad made his spelling rusty, it enabled him on the other to see Czech problems in greater perspective and more clearly. He could and did attack the parochialism, the patriotic make-believe, the chauvinistic and anti-semitic moods – because he immediately perceived that the revivalist movement, of Palacký and Havlíček in particular, already provided solid foundations for the nation's modern existence. The self-conscious and provincial petit-bourgeois Prague of 1882 still lacked confidence and looked to Palacký because he made it proud of the past glory of the Czech kingdom. Masaryk lost no time pointing out that not only the past but the intellectual and political achievements of Palacký and Havlíček, and indeed the contemporary achievements of the whole country, were something to be proud of.

This constant soul-searching and emphasis on national achievement is perhaps not immediately understandable to members of great nations with an uninterrupted history of statehood and ethnic identity. Such nations spend no time musing about their existence and still less feel the need to justify it. Dobrovský used German when he wrote the first Czech grammar in the 1820s as an exercise in historical linguistics and a monument to a language still spoken by peasants but, in his view, bound soon to die completely. Palacký wrote his *History of the Czech Nation* first in German, and having found an historical justification for the nation's continued existence, translated his work into Czech.

The need to justify the existence of a separate Czech nation to those who thought that it would be so much more simple and economical for the uneducated classes to accept, and for the educated classes to retain, the already developed German culture, led gradually to the conviction that each nation has to have its special mission, that it must look always to the future and that its every step must be in agreement with its ultimate aim. There was no escape: a new professor of what is now called sociology or anthropology (but what Masaryk preferred to call 'concrete ethics') had to say what he thought about the 'Czech question'. Masaryk's *Czech Question* was published in 1895, to be followed the same year by *Our Present Crisis*. Next year Masaryk published a thick volume on Karel Havlíček, stressing his fight against romanticism in Czech politics. In 1898 followed two books, one on Jan Huss, the other entitled *Palacký's Idea of the Czech Nation*. These long and detailed discussions of the meaning of Czech history and of the aims which could justify the country's continued existence are summed up in *Humanitarian Ideals*, published in 1901.

While preaching 'realism' and denouncing the nationalist romantics, Masaryk outdid them by his ethical romanticism. Nationalism for him is a way to humanity. Claims for justice for one's own nation cannot be based on injustice to or hatred of another. Selfishness is no basis for nationalism. No more is it possible to base claims for social justice on utilitarian or egotistic arguments. 'Unless we have some internal argument for equality, springing from our own souls,' he wrote in his *Social Question*, 'then Marx will be only able to oppose capitalist violence with communist violence.' The kingdom of liberty offered by Engels will not come through violence but through love of humanity.

To Masaryk the special contribution the Czechs could make to humanity was exemplified by the Hussites, who called themselves 'God's warriors' and defended the biblical ethos against a corrupt Church. It was the same Jewish and Christian ethos which was the real, though not the admitted, inspiration of Marx. After the defeat of this tolerant but ethically strict love of humanity displayed by the Hussites the Czech spiritual mission was, according to Masaryk, continued by the Moravian Brethren.

Masaryk's true greatness is in his insistence that man's and nations' happiness depends on love and the observance of a moral code, though even he could not foresee the full horror of Auschwitz, the atomic bomb and environmental pollution, which all result from a purely utilitarian, scientific, technological approach by people stupid enough to believe that business and power can be separated from love and a moral code. He tended to err in the opposite direction, seeming at times to believe that if the whole country would work hard, united by an ethos of love and tolerance, all would be well. To do him justice, it must be remembered that when things began to look bad he said, 'Tábor is our programme,' and this meant a readiness to defend one's truth by the force of arms. However, by that time Huss's dictum 'Truth prevails' already had pride of place on the presidential standard. It is there still, high over Prague Castle, an ironic reminder of recent history.

The tendency to believe in the self-sufficiency of ethics, however, presents only one and ignores the other stream of Czech political thinking, both of which can be traced back to Palacký. In one of his late essays, a sort of political testament, Palacký, who earlier believed he had discovered a priority of spiritual forces in Czech history, wrote that experience had taught him that 'in our country and in our time, what is the truth and the right is no longer dictated by reason but by passion ... which usurped all power ... and will be disciplined only by brutal force'.

This passage was quoted against Masaryk by Josef Kaizl, who held the chair of political economy at Prague University and later became the only Czech minister of importance in the Vienna Government. Kaizl, Kramář and Masaryk started, soon after Masaryk's arrival in Prague, as political allies and formed the 'realist' group of the Young Czech party. While Masaryk left this party in 1893, Kaizl and Kramář moved to its top. In his book *Czech Thoughts* Kaizl presents the other interpretation of Czech history, that the Czech national revival had little in common with the Hussite movement of the fifteenth century and in fact was mainly the work of contemporary Czech Catholic priests; it was just another national movement of which there were many in the first half of the nineteenth century, spiritually and economically in tune with the times. The Czech nation had been revived not by Hussite reminiscences but rather by the gradual social and economic growth of the Czech people. Humanitarian ideals, as far as these could be detected, were an echo of the French revolution and of Western European liberalism, and there was no such thing as a special Czech humanitarianism springing from the Moravian Brethren. The typical Czech tolerance was in fact only liberal indifference, wrote Kaizl, himself a liberal. Having thus pulled down to earth the man who set out to pull down to earth the romantic patriots, Kaizl then spelled out a truth which no small nation likes to hear but of which every small nation is frequently reminded by events: the security of a nation does not depend on its moral justification but on power.

Replying to Kaizl in his *New Europe*, Masaryk thought these views were derived from 'a political materialism typical of official German thinking and politics'. Unfortunately not Masaryk's truth but Kaizl's political materialism prevailed and this was to be the tragedy of the Castle and of Czechoslovakia – twice in recent history.

It is impossible to be a statesman without a proper appreciation of power, for states are mainly about power, and by this definition Masaryk was not a statesman. For a long time, almost to the outbreak of the First World War, like Palacký and Havlíček before him and Šmeral in his time, Masaryk viewed Austria–Hungary as the only world in which the Czechs could make their contribution, by helping to transform it into a modern, federal state. Then the great opportunity seduced him into confusing the affinity which existed between the Western democracies and the Czechs in their way of life and in the cultural and spiritual sphere with a community of political interests, which in the case of the United States and Britain simply did not exist, and in the case of France existed only as a temporary expedient. However, even this error which disqualified him as a statesman helped to bring one step further the emancipation of the Czechs from the German and Russian cultural influence and to free the Slovaks from Hungarian apron strings. Thus, by placing contemporary achievements before historical reminiscences and humanitarian ideals before selfish and purely utilitarian aims, and by making his compatriots feel the greater space of the world beyond Europe, Masaryk can be seen as the last great figure of the national revival, who helped his country if not to freedom then at least to a discovery of its own very specific identity.

In command – but only just

Masaryk and later Beneš, and the Castle group as a whole, remained in a leading position throughout the twenty years of the Czechoslovak republic, but it was by no means a dominant one. On the conrary, it was at times most precarious. In this the opponents of the Castle often enjoyed the advantage provided by a party-political

organization. President Masaryk, though close to the Social Democrats, was supposed to stand above the parties, and Beneš's position
in the Czechoslovak National Socialist Party was sometimes highly
problematic.

The Castle could balance this disadvantage by the more dispersed
and intangible, but essentially national, loyalty which it enjoyed. In
the absence of other traditions of statehood, Masaryk, the real as
well as the mythical man, and the intellectual élite surrounding him,
provided an easily understandable personification of the country's
aims and struggles. The intellectualism of this leadership, combined
with the emphasis on the humble origins of its chief protagonists, did
much to secure for the Castle the allegiance of the professional
workers, central and local government officials, teachers, tradesmen
and small businessmen. It boosted their self-confidence at a time
when their social and economic status seemed threatened by the
nouveaux riches of expanding large-scale industry and banks. Such
was the emphasis laid in the schools on the poor boy who achieved
greatness that it became a popular jibe among schoolboys to say:
'He made good although his father sent him to university.'

The Castle also, of course, had its share of hostility, and in this,
personal and political motives were inextricably mixed. The die-
hard chauvinists remembered the pre-war Masaryk as a denigrator
of cherished patriotic illusions and a defender of the Jews. The pre-
war Czech politicians felt slighted by the eminence enjoyed by
Beneš as Minister of Foreign Affairs; his name had not even been
mentioned in public before 1914.

It was also inevitable that dynamic young men who were not yet
established in 1918 and therefore had nothing to lose by taking part
in the adventure of building a new administration rose fast and after
some years provoked the envy of those who were old enough to claim
pre-war merit. Some of the legionaries, particularly those whose war
record was better than their aptitude for a peacetime career, felt that
while they had liberated the country, Masaryk and Beneš had stolen
their thunder. Some central posts had to be reserved for the Slovaks,
leading to the disappointment of Czech candidates, while the initial
need to fill the gap in Slovakia by Czech teachers and officials, later
led to dissatisfaction among a new generation of Slovak graduates.
In short, the 'salon of the rejected candidates' was a powerful anti-
Castle lobby.

Personal grievances were blended with political and ideological objections. Curiously, the fundamental question whether it was wise to have helped the disintegration of the Habsburg Empire was never raised in public. So intoxicating was formal independence that the idea that the price paid for it might be a forfeit of real freedom began to dawn on the wider public only when the Nazi occupation of 1939 was topped by the Soviet occupation of 1968.

There were other objections. The Agrarians did not like the idea of economic integration with the agricultural partners in the Little *Entente*, which Masaryk saw as a possible substitute for the Habsburg Empire. They would have preferred a closer link with predominantly industrial Germany. The Catholics objected to the secular, anti-clerical concept of the State and also to the inherent Protestantism of Masaryk with his emphasis on Jan Huss and Commenius.

In Slovakia, where the village priest was still supreme and the Catholic Church the only real power, the political aspects came more into the fore. In Bohemia and Moravia, where even those Catholics who resisted the general climate of religious indifference did not like to see the Church mixed up in politics, the objections against the Castle assumed a more ideological character. The Catholic intellectuals argued, not without some justification, that national traditions sprang not only from the Reformation but also from the Catholic baroque period and that grammar schools, run by the monastic orders, and the village priests had played an important role in the national revival.

However, the disappointed chauvinists, the Agrarians and the Catholics, were no more than political or ideological adversaries always ready to make a political deal and even become temporary allies of the Castle. The Castle's real and determined enemies were the Communists, the Fascists and the Nazis, who realized that its anti-totalitarianism was not just a policy that could be changed but the basis of its ideological and political identity.

The gradual submission of the Czech Communists to Moscow is traced in the next chapter. Between 1929 and 1935, when the Soviet Union agreed a friendship pact with France, the Communists continued to harass the Castle, accusing it of fascist leanings. This did not cut much ice, but the Communists, acting on a Comintern thesis that Czechoslovak imperialism threatened Germany, tried in those years systematically to undermine the morale of the army and thus weaken the Castle's hand in its efforts to salvage the vanishing support of the Allies. In this way Communists prepared the ground for the Nazis to whom they passed the anti-Beneš banner in 1935. After the conclusion of the friendship pact between France and the Soviet Union, the Czech Communists discovered that Hitler was their enemy too. They even gave their votes to Beneš in the presidential election of 1935 held when Masaryk abdicated after a long illness. Then the Seventh Congress of the Comintern checked them for having gone too far.

The Czech Fascist movement had a longer record of anti-Castle activity than either the Communists or the Nazis but it was without foreign support and its following was almost insignificant when compared with the other two totalitarian movements. Several small fascist groups were constituted in Czechoslovakia soon after Mussolini's takeover in Italy in 1922, and they appeared in public during anti-communist demonstrations after the assassination of Rašin, the Minister of Finance, by a Communist. Almost forgotten, the Czech Fascist movement attempted to catch the public eye again during the election campaign of 1925, and on this occasion it was already directed against the Castle. Thus far it had been supported exclusively by a small radical fringe made up mostly of disappointed adventurers. It gained more solid political and financial support in 1926 when an election defeat and political impotence in the face of the powerful Agrarians led to differences within Karel Kramář's National Democratic Party. At about this time General Rudolf Gajda, Chief of the General Staff, assumed the leadership of the Czech National Fascist Community and started to prepare a putsch. At about the same time Jiří Stříbrný, a clever politician and demagogue, who had so far played second fiddle in the National Socialist Party, made an attempt to oust Beneš from its leadership and change its course into right-wing radicalism.

The Castle acted swiftly and decisively. Gajda was sent on leave before he could make a putsch and was later retired in disgrace. Stříbrný was expelled from his party. The conservative wing of the National Democrats, dominated by industrial and financial interests, gradually got the upper hand over the right-wing extremists and moved closer to the Castle.

Deserted by the National Democrats, the Fascists sought support from the right wing of the Agrarian Party and before the general elections in 1929 merged with Stříbrný, who controlled the tabloid press, in a league against the proportional electoral system with party lists of candidates – in Czechoslovakia electors voted not for the individual candidates but for political parties which presented national lists of candidates.

Even in this alliance the Fascists were rejected by the electorate. The usefulness of a nationalist and totalitarian government could perhaps be argued in Italy and Germany by those who wanted expansion by war, but to the Czechs it was abundantly clear that it would make no sense in a small country of fourteen million of which one third were ethnic minorities. Gajda, already sentenced to a two-month prison term in 1931, got involved in 1933 in a ridiculous plot to overthrow the Government hatched by an insignificant garrison commander. Soon after, he was discarded as useless by his more influential political supporters. Not so Stříbrný, who was at the same time accused of corruption and taking bribes in a trial to which the Castle press gave great publicity. He was acquitted, and his value to the right wing was enhanced.

The National Democrats reached for him when in anticipation of the 1935 general elections they made a last attempt to recover mass support. The National Democrats, with Stříbrný's League, and the National Front (an agglomerate of small fascist groups) formed a political group under the name National Unification. The formation of this group is sometimes attributed to the influence and financial support of Jaroslav Preis, the powerful chairman of the Živnostenská Bank, who shortly before had visited Hitler's Germany and was favourably impressed by what he had seen. However, even these funds, if true, did not secure the group an election success. The National Unification obtained only 5.6 per cent of the total vote, compared with the 4.9 per cent secured by the National Democrats alone in the previous elections of 1929. Gajda, who first entered the National Unification as vice-chairman but then parted with it, obtained for his National Fascist Community only 2 per cent of the total vote. The 1935 elections made it very clear that the Czech Fascists and right-wing radicals were an insignificant irritant when compared with the pressure to which the Castle and the Republic were exposed, first from the Communists and then from Germany.

Although the Castle could deal effectively with Fascist elements, and indeed its moral superiority in the eyes of the population gained as the true nature of Fascism became evident in Italy and Germany, its influence on internal and economic affairs had declined. This decline reached its lowest point in 1925 when an election defeat of the Social Democrats followed closely on the setback which the Castle's foreign policy suffered in Locarno, where the Allies joined hands with Germany for the first time after 1914.

By this time a number of factors which made the Castle so strong in the first years of the Republic had disappeared. Conservative elements no longer felt the need of a liberal and socially progressive shield against the post-war revolutionary wave inspired by the Bolshevik revolution. The alliance negotiated by Masaryk between the Social Democrats and the Agrarians came to an end. Initiative on the home front passed to an Agrarian and Catholic bloc. In 1926 the Agrarians agreed to state salaries for Catholic priests – this helped the Castle in its dealings with the Vatican – in exchange for a replacement of sliding tariffs by fixed import tariffs for the main agricultural products. This protectionist trade policy jeopardized Beneš's efforts to establish closer links with Romania and Yugoslavia. In the same year the National Democrats joined the Government, which from then on was known as the Gentlemen's Coalition. This swing to the right in Czechoslovakia was not an isolated development; it could at the same time be observed throughout Europe. The conservative coalition tried to oust Beneš from the Foreign Ministry; he was held in that position only by the great personal authority of Masaryk.

The Gentlemen's Coalition adopted a number of unpopular measures which weakened somewhat the highly advanced system of social security introduced by the Social Democrats and also retarded agricultural reform. Even so, it was a very confident government: because of its conservative character it secured a higher degree of participation by the Slovaks, whose principal representative was Milan Hodža, an Agrarian who was later to hold the office of premier during the Munich crisis, and it was the first government to secure the participation of the German minority, which was represented by two ministers. Presided over by Antonín Švehla, the leader of the Czech Agrarians, it remained in office until 1929 and firmly established the Agrarian Party as the dominant force in domestic affairs.

The Gentlemen's Coalition, oriented at home on a restriction of social-security expenditure and abroad on closer cooperation with Streseman's conservatively democratic Germany, could not survive the impact of economic crisis and the economic and political upheaval in Germany. In 1929 it was superseded by a wider coalition under František Udržal, an Agrarian politician. A further decline in the National Democrats, the secession of the Slovak Catholic party, and the weakening of the German democratic parties had by this time undermined the political strength of the Agrarian–Catholic bloc. The Udržal Government represented a shift to the left and marked the beginning of a return of the Castle to the leading position in home politics. The Udržal Government was a transitional formation trying to alleviate the worst social consequences of catastrophic unemployment, sever contacts with Germany and revert to a foreign policy based on the French Alliance and a revival of the Little *Entente*.

The next government, formed in 1932 under another Agrarian, Malypetr, by the same political parties but with new personalities, adopted a completely new programme, in which the hand of the Castle was clearly evident. It was based on a Social Democrat policy which Masaryk had helped to formulate in 1928 and a National Socialist programme largely drafted by Beneš in 1931. The Malypetr Government represented a turn from complete liberalism to a New Deal type of dirigism in the economy and the use of restrictive legislation in defence of democracy. As an answer to Hitler's takeover in Germany, Parliament approved a series of laws enabling the dissolution of anti-democratic political parties, press censorship, and prosecution for anti-state activity. In 1934 the National Democrats left the Government, leaving the Castle in a still stonger position. The returning tide reached its highwater mark the next year with the election of Beneš as President in accordance with a recommendation made by Masaryk when he abdicated for reasons of ill-health.

The authority of the Castle, and of Beneš personally, was challenged again in 1936, this time on a fundamental issue. Milan Hodža, the Slovak Agrarian, and his group left the Castle bloc and in 1937 quickly gained a standing both in home and foreign affairs. With British support, Hodža attempted to form a new defensive alliance against Hitler with Austria and Hungary – nothing less than an attempt to reconstitute, in a way, the Austro–Hungarian Empire. Hodža also tried to reach agreement with the German minority, by this time already strongly influenced by Hitler. Unfortunately his moves came too late for in 1938 Hitler occupied Austria.

Beneš again became supreme. But the authority conceded to him in this last phase of the First Republic was the authority conceded to any ship's captain in a storm even if he is to blame for having taken the ship on a dangerous journey. In this particular storm Beneš, and with him the entire Castle group, were swept from the bridge as soon as the ship of state was wrecked by the Munich agreement of the Four Powers.

Šmeral plays for time

In the course of 1921 the left factions of the Social Democrats –
Slovaks and Germans first, and finally the Czechs too – accepted the
twenty-one conditions of the Communist International, and merged
into a single Communist Party, the Czechoslovak Section of the
Communist International or Comintern. These famous 'Twenty-
One Conditions' which the Moscow-controlled Comintern has laid
down for affiliated national parties were designed to transfer the
complete control over the policies and choice of national leadership
into the hands of Soviet party bosses. However, the way from a
promise of obedience to total subordination of the Czechoslovak
Party to Moscow was arduous – it took ten years to travel and led to
a disintegration of the Left.

The Czech Social Democrats (and this applied no less to their left
faction) were steeped in the reformist traditions of Austro–Marxism
– their party had been formed in 1878 as a division of the Austrian
Social Democratic Party. Their main political objectives were first
the achievement of general and equal franchise and then the strongest possible parliamentary representation of workers' interests. In the
years preceding the 1914–18 war the Social Democrats were the
strongest of the Czech political parties.

As a condition of being admitted into the Comintern, the Czech
left-wing Social Democrats were required to accept the political and
conspiratorial methods which Lenin developed in fighting tsarism as
well as the repressive methods which the Bolsheviks inherited from
their defeated foes when taking over the rule of a vast empire. By
contrast the Czechs had done fairly well during the preceding fifty
years by using parliament, the press association and economic power

against the Vienna Government. The whole country found the Russian methods – whether tsarist or Communist – abhorrent and the
advocates of a 'bolshevization' of the Czech Party could not argue, as
Communists in some other countries could, that it was necessary to
defend the labour movement against the strong-arm methods of the
employers.

The Czech Communists therefore fought a series of rearguard
actions against the Comintern. The transformation of their party
from a political organization, representing the interests of its members or wooing the favour of the electorate, into a foreign agency
organizing local support for the policies of the Soviet Union, was a
painful and protracted process. It took the form of an internal
struggle between the essentially Czech, more reformist and more
democratic right and centre factions on the one side and the left
faction on the other. Consisting mainly of German and Hungarian
'professional revolutionaries', as they liked to call themselves, the
left faction was entirely dedicated to the cause of the Soviet Union
and of the Comintern. The first four Congresses of the Czechoslovak
Communist Party are the milestones on the road to total submission
to Moscow which was sealed at the Fifth Congress in 1929.

Throughout the struggle Moscow's primary objective was to replace leaders who rose from the ranks and enjoyed the confidence of
the workers with Party officials appointed by the Comintern and
entirely dependent for their positions and income on its support. The
history of the loss of the Czech Party's independence is consequently
also the story of the decline of Bohumír Šmeral who, as even his
adversaries agreed, was the greatest political personality produced
by the Czech labour movement. It was his fate to become the first
Czech Reluctant Communist, a species which multiplied as time
marched on.

Dr Šmeral, a great tribune of the people and until 1917 leader of
the Czechoslovak Social Democratic Party, was in 1921 still suffering from the damage he had done his prestige by opposing the disintegration of Austria–Hungary. He had insisted that the insecurity
of a small, independent state with a strong German minority could
gravely jeopardize the future of the Czechs. While other Social
Democratic leaders decided to ride the nationalist wave, Šmeral remained unrepentant in his belief that it would have been better to
have had a socialist Austria–Hungary. Decried as a traitor and ostra-

cized by patriots, he was soon to become suspected of Czech patriotism by the Comintern.

Like Havlíček and Masaryk before him, Šmeral was struck by the incompatibility of Russian and Czech political thinking – and the danger implied in this for the Czechs – during a visit to Russia. Heřman Taussig, a member of the first Central Committee of the Communist Party of Czechoslovakia, who was with Šmeral in Moscow in 1920, told the author (when they met in the Pankrác prison in 1953) that Šmeral was not only disillusioned but also very alarmed by the way the Russian Communists behaved when in power. This was the reason why he played for time when in the spring of 1921 Moscow Communists pressed his party, then called the Social Democrats (Left), to accept all the obligations of a member of the Comintern. Although he returned from Moscow with a brief to establish the Communist Party and stated publicly that he was a Communist, his interpretation of the term continued to be very Czech.

As editor of *Rudé Právo*, the newspaper of the Marxist Left and later of the Communist Party, Šmeral claimed for the Czech Communists the right to be guided by local conditions and not blindly to follow the Russian example. Even more telling is his demand that the Party should not depend on Russian money. With Marx, he differed from Lenin in claiming that a revolutionary party should be backed by an 'overwhelming majority'. 'It would be madness,' wrote Šmeral, 'to push someone out of the Party because he holds different views. Such a tendency does not lead to a natural selection of the best leaders but to a constant deterioration of leadership and will in the end lead to obscurantism.'

It is not surprising that Moscow, as Zinoviev told Karl Kreibich, the leader of the German Communists in Czechoslovakia, did not trust Šmeral. Kreibich was only one of the internationalists whom Moscow used in its campaign against Šmeral and those of the Czech Left with a different view of Communism. Prominent in the anti-Šmeral phalanx were Hungarian Communists employed in Moscow as Comintern experts for Central Europe. These Communist exiles took up an impeccable internationalist attitude and professed total indifference to the national, ethnic interests of their country. Yet one suspects that the ardour with which they denigrated reformist, or in their parlance 'opportunist', Šmeralism was, at least partly and perhaps subconsciously, driven by a sort of frustrated patriotism. Both the German and the Hungarian Communists were smarting under a double defeat, of their countries first and then of their attempted revolutions afterwards. The German Communists consoled themselves with the hope that Germany, the cradle of Marxism and of the nationally organized labour movement, would become the spearhead of the world revolution. The Hungarian Communists again could hardly have erased from their memory that in the preceding year, while still in power in Hungary, they were pushed out of Slovakia by the Czechs.

These Comintern experts and confidants of Moscow were supported in Prague by former Czech Anarchists, a small group which exchanged their former rejection of all authority for a belief in the 'dictatorship of the proletariat' and the strict centralist discipline demanded by the Comintern. One of their leading men, Emanuel Vajtauer (who ended by collaborating with the Nazis during the 1939–45 Occupation), demanded that the leadership of the Czechoslovak Communist Party should be supervised by a committee composed of foreign Communists. The wish was to be fulfilled.

Much like the Hungarian and German Communists, the former Czech Anarchists boasted complete national indifference. The Czech nation should be only 'manure on the field which will produce a new race, according to Thy doctrine, O Moscow!', wrote Stanislav Kostka Neumann, who as a youthful patriot spent a year in prison – albeit with all the facilities for literary pursuits – for conspiring against the Vienna Government. Now he prostrated himself before the superior wisdom of the Comintern to become, later, the Party's leading poet and propagandist.

Šmeral, however, was in no hurry. In contrast with the volatile Anarchists and the fanatic German and Hungarian Communists he was slow to embrace new ideas, for he was more interested in their practical use than in their abstract beauty. Hard pressed by Moscow, he proposed that the Twenty-One Conditions stipulating obedience to the Comintern should be accepted in principle but that their application by the Czech Party should be postponed.

At the first Constituting Party Congress, on 14 May 1921, which was to merge the German with the Czech and Slovak Communists, Šmeral, presenting the main report, still insisted on his concept of a democratic party dependent on the electorate and striving for mass membership. But the following debate showed that the left wing was on the offensive, the Czech Anarchists and German Communists leading the attack against Šmeral. In the end the vote was 562 for joining the Comintern and Šmeral was not among the seven who opposed the application. He voted for it, sealing the beginning of his own downfall. Soon he was removed from the editorship of *Rudé Právo* and the paper turned against him. At the next congress of the Comintern in Moscow in June 1921 Bukharin branded Šmeral as an 'opportunist' – an ugly word invented by Lenin for Social Democrats – and Radek accused him, probably correctly, of never really wanting to join the Comintern. The Czech delegation to this Comintern congress was split, and one of its members who attacked Šmeral in Moscow was Rudolf Slánský, then speaking for the Communist Youth. Šmeral's fall was slow compared with that of Slánský thirty years later.

Between 1921 and 1929 the Czechoslovak Communist Party incessantly discussed two alternative policies. Some wanted it to be a party with a mass membership fighting for the day-to-day interests of the workers, primarily by parliamentary means and militant trade unionism. To others nothing mattered except the advent of the world revolution; they believed that 'the worse are the workers now, the nearer is the revolution'.

At the beginning of this period there seemed to be still some justification for Šmeral's hope that time would work for his concept of Communism, for it coincided with Lenin's liberal New Economic Policy and his acceptance that world revolution was not yet round the corner. While Šmeral was branded as an 'opportunist' by Soviet ideologists, he could also draw some hope from the fact that at the Third Congress of the Comintern Lenin appeared to have come round to his view that revolution should be prepared by winning over the majority of the working class, and that the Soviet Union was preparing to normalize its relations with the capitalist world.

In the spring of the following year, however, Lenin withdrew from political life and was replaced by Stalin. The New Economic Policy was terminated and the first heads (those of the SRs, the Russian Social Revolutionaries) began to roll. In the autumn of 1922 the Executive of the Comintern instructed all its national sections, including that of Czechoslovakia, to demand the formation of governments of workers and peasants, and to prepare for revolution.

The Czechoslovak Communist Party adopted the new Comintern line as a slogan suitable for attracting radical elements but without any illusions that it could be translated into practical policies. The Czech workers were interested in better wages and working conditions and expected their representatives to care. The peasants, with whom every worker was closely connected through family ties, were not dispossessed *muzhiks* but small farmers who, if anything, overestimated the importance of private property and abhorred all types of socialism. Finally there were the leaders and political organizers. Like Šmeral, they were moulded in their youth by the reformist Social Democratic Party and this, more than the revolutionary slogans, was reflected in their actions.

The Fifth Congress of the Comintern, with Zinoviev in the chair, found ample reasons for dissatisfaction with Czech Communism. The Congress demanded that it should take action against 'right-wing tendencies and views' in its midst and start on the course of a real bolshevization. It provided also a definition of the 'united workers' front', which was unlikely to endear this Communist proposal to members of other Czechoslovak socialist parties, used to thinking for themselves. 'The tactic of the United Front', stated the Comintern, 'was and will remain a tactic of the revolutionary strategic manoeuvre of the Communist *avant-garde* in its fight against the treacherous leaders of the counter-revolutionary Social Democrats.' The 'workers' government', it declared was synonymous with the dictatorship of the proletariat.

Not only the Czech but also the German Communists in the Czechoslovak Party felt let down. In Moravia and Bohemia at least, democracy was viewed as the ultimate good and dictatorship was a dirty word. Communism was to breed a better race of men and the Czechs found it hard to stomach that this could be achieved by treachery, pretending friendship to the Social Democrats while considering them 'counter-revolutionary traitors'. The Comintern was obliged to mobilize a new left opposition, this time within the Communist Party. It used groups of ambitious young men whose past was not tainted by reformist experience. One of these groups, located in the Karlín district of Prague, already had direct contacts with the Party Secretariat and soon became the focal point of Comintern-inspired opposition. It included men destined to play an important role in the history of their country: Klement Gottwald, Rudolf Slánský, and Václav Kopecký, the 'Karlín Boys'.

The rise of the Karlín Boys

In 1924 Stalin's moves against political rivals within the Party presented a striking contrast to the evident internal and external consolidation of the democratic regime in Czechoslovakia and made very difficult the task which the Comintern was facing there. As a result, the Comintern had to develop ingenious tactics to keep the Czechoslovak Party, its largest section, under control. Their main feature was the promotion of successive opposition factions which depended on Comintern support of ousting the leadership of the day – only to suffer the same fate as soon as they became too established and independent.

Human rights and the acceptance of a diversity of views were in 1924 still very much part of the Czech Communists' political view; 'bolshevization', with all the sinister meaning the word acquired under Stalin, was not really palatable to the Left, and still less to the wider Czech public. This could probably have been talked away with the argument 'it can never happen here'. But the Czech Communist leaders knew that the proposed policy of stirring up trouble, and street battles with the police, in the hope of advancing the cause of distant world revolution would not be favoured by the realistic, relatively well educated and by no means desperate workers who wanted immediate advantages and a share in the economic boom. In the eyes of the Czech Communists 'bolshevization' had the supreme fault of being impracticable.

Nor were they as isolated as in 1921. Kreibich, the leader of the Germans in the Czechoslovak Communist Party, who in 1921 had led the attack against Šmeral, was now, in 1924, attacked with him and Antonín Zápotocký by the sentinels of the Comintern; in fact, as the most outspoken opponent of the radicalization demanded by Zinoviev, he was the main target. 'So expel me, if you think I am an enemy!', Kreibich shouted at the Comintern delegates during the Second Congress of the Czechoslovak Party.

On the other side, the Comintern faction was strengthened by three members of the Executive Committee of the Czechoslovak Party, Doležal, Neurath and Verčik, who placed themselves at its head and demanded that the Party should be 'bolshevized' by the elimination of the remaining members of the Executive Committee.

Šmeral, probably in the hope that he would be able to continue 'accepting in principle but postponing the application', registered his disagreement with the policy ordered by the Comintern, but promised obedience. As a result, when the Second Congress of the Czechoslovak Communist Party opened in November 1924 there were not two but three factions, the opposition against the Comintern being split between Šmeral's centre and the intransigent Right.

This gave the Comintern a certain possibility of manoeuvre which it used most successfully. Instead of supporting all the demands of its supporters, it assumed the role of peacemaker and mediator through its delegation headed by Manuilsky. Manuilsky persuaded Šmeral's centrist faction that it was not the Comintern's intention to eliminate them but only to strengthen the left at the cost of the right wing. The two separate lists of candidates for the Central Committee, already presented to the Congress, were withdrawn and the Comintern delegation negotiated a coalition of its own left faction with the centrists; in the new Central Committee elected from a single list, the Comintern supporters had eighteen seats against fourteen held by the supporters of the previous leadership. Šmeral, stepping down from the leadership of the Party, declared: 'The responsibility passes to the opposition.'

In fact, the Czech Communists had in 1921 promised obedience but remained free to keep or reject this promise. In 1924 the Comintern for the first time secured a majority on the Central Committee for its nominees. However, the Czech Communists were not yet altogether silenced. Operating in a country with a free press and exposed to the competition of other political parties, the group put in charge by the Comintern could not altogether ignore the demands of the workers.

Political realities began to have a sobering effect on them almost immediately. In the first heat of left radicalism after the Second Congress, the new executive attempted to organize in the spring of 1925 the first purely Communist strike, in the coalmines and chemical factories of Ostrava. The Red trade unions completely failed in this: the strike, opposed by Social Democratic trade unions, was broken after a week, and brought the strikers no benefits. Even more serious was that the Red trade unions proved unable to protect those who took part in the strike from persecution by employers.

The Party leadership, now headed by Joseph Haken, gave the zigzag party line one of its turns to the right and started intensive cooperation with Social Democratic trade unions. This policy, as well as the integration of the Independent Socialist Workers' Party – former anarcho-Communists who had earlier joined and then left the Czech National Socialists – was approved at the Third Congress, held towards the end of 1925. As a result the Party gained in the next parliamentary elections, held in the autumn of 1925, 13.2 per cent of all votes, second only to the Agrarians.

However, in February 1926 the radical members of the Politbureau attempted a new 'revolutionary' action, this time in Prague. They called for a protest march against the high price of consumer goods, but the demonstration misfired because workers were not interested. The radical left accused the 'reformist' Secretary of the Prague Communist Organization, Václav Bubník, of sabotaging the planned action in order to justify a 'reformist' coup in the Party and bring Šmeral back to power. The left radicals, holding the Politbureau's majority, demanded Bubník's expulsion in order to gain control of the important Prague organization. This time Šmeral hit back, though it was to be for the last time. The meeting called to expel Bubník was presented with an audit report by Heřman Taussig (who had been with Šmeral on his first eye-opening visit to Moscow), accusing two left members of the Politbureau, Julius Verčík and Ernoe Seidler – both representing Slovak organizations – of taking bribes from industrialists and of embezzlement of Party funds. Bubník's expulsion was not approved and the meeting ended in the defeat of the Politbureau.

The issue was later settled in Moscow. It seems that Stalin realized the weakness of the Comintern group in the Czechoslovak Party and concluded that it was too soon to try to push out the 'opportunists'. In any case, he accepted a compromise solution: Šmeral agreed to acknowledge that Verčík and Seidler were cleared of the accusations on condition that they resigned from the Politbureau. It was his last political victory, and a costly one: the next man chosen by the Moscow group to represent the Slovaks in the Politbureau was Klement Gottwald, who by 1929 succeeded in ousting Šmeral from political life completely.

In 1926 the task of revolutionizing the workers, difficult at any time and even more difficult since the onset of an economic boom, was made almost impossible by the Comintern's further demands and dogmas. Not only were the Communist leaders required to tell the workers not to think about wages but only about world revolution; they were supposed to convince the peasants, who knew about collectivization in the Soviet Union, that once in power they would give them more land than they had received from the reform. In a country rightly or wrongly proud of its new statehood they had to insist that the German separatists were right. To crown it, at a time when Czechoslovak industry was experiencing an unprecedented upswing and expanding into new fields including automobile and aircraft construction and chemical production, the Fourth Congress of the Party held in March 1927 was obliged to accept the absurd assertion, formulated by the Seventh Plenary Session of the Comintern Executive, that industry in Czechoslovakia was being systematically liquidated at the behest of imperialist powers and that the country was reverting to an agricultural economy.

Not all members of the Party leadership could be made to repeat blindly whatever the Comintern decreed; Šmeral and Kreibich had to be removed from the Czechoslovak scene by a transfer to Moscow – Šmeral was also for a time sent to China as a Comintern observer. But even those left wingers who had led the 1924 revolt against them, Doležal and Neurath, had to be removed from influence. The Comintern reached for members of the ultra-left opposition of the years 1921–2 and had them elected to the Central Committee of the Party. At the same time the real power of the Central Committee was curbed and the running of the Party machine concentrated in the hands of a small secretariat headed by B. Jílek.

The result was that workers lost confidence in the Party and interest in the activities of the secretariat. The secretariat in turn was becoming more and more exasperated by the impossible task of organizing 'revolutionary, illegal activity', while rejecting criticism from Right and Left as heresy against the Comintern policy. So the Jílek leadership itself ceased to be of any political value to Comintern. The majority of the Party organizations demanded a more realistic policy and greater attention to the immediate interests of the workers. Moscow was faced with the danger that the Party would slip back into the reformist or 'opportunist' stream represented by Šmeral. Again the only possibility open to the Comintern was to organize its own opposition against the 'ultra-left' Jílek group.

Their new opposition was formed by the 'Karlín Boys' led by Klement Gottwald and including Rudolf Slánský and Josef Krosnář – later to become the leading triumvirate after the Communist take-over in 1948, as well as Václav Kopecký and Pavel Reiman.

The same stick used in 1926 against Bubník, a misfired demonstration, was raised again against Jílek in 1928. An attempt to stage in Prague a 'Red Day', and to bring workers into the streets to demonstrate against the police prohibition of a Communist gymnastic festival, failed completely and no workers turned out, though many Party members were brought for the event from the provinces.

The Karlín Boys made an issue of this failure and then widened their criticism to encompass the whole 'bureaucratic' management of the Party by Jílek. The first step towards the transfer of power into the hands of this group was taken at the Sixth Comintern Congress held in Moscow in 1928. The Czechoslovak delegation was split between the Jílek supporters who had the majority and the supporters of Gottwald's opposition. To bolster them up, the Comintern Executive gave voting power to three Czech students at the Moscow Party School and accepted as a representative document a memorandum agreed by a group of Prague Communists and brought to Moscow by Kopecký, a prominent member of the Karlín group which split only when Kopecký became, in 1950, Slánský's chief accuser when he was awaiting his trial in prison.

After thus creating two seemingly equivalent and mutually opposed Czechoslovak delegations, the Comintern sat in judgement over the Czech Party. The members of the tribunal were Bela Kun, the deposed leader of the Hungarian Soviet Republic of 1920–21; the Finnish Communist Otto Kuusinen; and Sergei I. Gusev, a Russian of Lenin's old guard, who presided. This commission drafted an open letter to the Czechoslovak Party condemning the Jílek leadership which, while suffered by the Czech Communists so far, had no other real support than that of the Comintern. As a result the Jílek group in Moscow immediately disintegrated and after returning to Prague left the initiative almost completely to Gottwald, the new Moscow favourite.

The Party 'discussion' ordered by the Comintern was designed to indoctrinate the membership with the views expressed in the open letter, but succeeded in this only partially so that the Comintern felt obliged to persuade Gottwald to postpone the holding of the Fifth Congress, which a Comintern delegation arrived to organize.

Helped by this delegation, Gottwald, already a member of the Politbureau, could together with his friends assume control of the Party Secretariat and in this way see to it that the regional conferences would send delegates favourable to his cause. The main resistance came not so much from the 'opportunists', who were passive, but from the Trotskyists, who still retained some fighting spirit.

At the last moment the carefully constructed edifice of the Karlín Boys was almost wrecked by their attempt to show that they really were capable of stirring the workers into revolutionary activity. Braving the opinion not only of Social Democratic trade unions but also of Communist ones, they called a political strike of textile workers on 7 February 1929. Only a few responded to the call and even they gave up on 12 February. As a failure the textile strike of the Karlín Boys was no less resounding than the Jílek's Red Day, so that on a count of 'revolutionary actions' the two groups were even.

A few days after the collapse of the strike the Fifth Congress of the Party met. Gottwald and his friends were exposed to sharp attack for this blunder, both from the 'reformist' wing, formerly led by Šmeral, and the Neurath group which had helped to topple him in 1925; and from the Jílek group which removed Neurath. But the Karlín Boys prepared the congress and presented the reports, and they declared themselves elected as the new leadership of the Party. They labelled Šmeralism as the worst form of opportunism, declared Neurath Trotskyist. The ultra-left Jílek group were described as the 'main protagonists of right-wing tendencies.'

According to the programme adopted by this Congress, the main task of the Party in the future was to be the defence of the Soviet Union against the danger of an imperialist war and the preparation of the Party for revolution. The Czech Social Democrats were labelled 'social-fascists' and Masaryk's Castle group, standing rather left of centre, was defined as the focal point of fascist putschists.

It all sounded utterly mad, not only to the opponents of Communism but to Communists themselves, and when the new leadership attempted a purge of 'opportunists', Red trade unions seceded and expelled the few implanted representatives of the Karlín Boys from their Central Office. Jílek, Neurath, and twenty-six other Communist M.P.s refused to recognize the authority of the Fifth Party Congress and formed a new party of Independent Communists. Almost the entire Communist press turned against the Karlín Boys. Intellectuals and writers who had done so much for the Communist cause started to leave the Party; leading the exodus were four big literary personalities of the time, writers Ivan Olbracht and Vladislav Vančura and poets Josef Hora and Jaroslav Seifert, as well as such bigoted Communists as S. K. Neumann, Marie Majerová, and Helena Malířová.

By the end of 1929, on the eve of the great economic crisis which was to hit Czechoslovakia more severely than any other country in Europe, Moscow had achieved its end. Its nominees, Klement Gottwald, Jan Šverma, Josef Krosnář, Václav Kopecký, controlled the Party machinery. The price paid was a complete isolation of this Party from the Czech labour movement and the Czech intellectuals.

The elements of weakness

The early history of the Czechoslovak Communist movement, which was born on the revolutionary wave of 1920, reached its peak in 1925 and disintegrated in 1929 with a massive exodus of Party members, the disillusionment of sympathizers and the isolation of the Moscow-sponsored leadership, presents a pattern which was to be repeated once more after the Second World War.

Neither Moscow nor the Czechoslovak Communists could profit much from such developments, and not only outside observers but even those who had their part in the events often seemed puzzled and searched for the underlying causes which made things as no one wanted them.

Any analysis has to start with recognizing that these events resulted from the interplay of two sides, Russian and Czech. The Russian motives are relatively easier to understand.

As the first revolutionary wave of the post-war years receded and the Soviet Communists settled to the task of consolidating their power at home without waiting for a world revolution, they began to view the Communist parties in other countries as a political weapon which could be used in defence of the Soviet State. Paradoxically this meant handing over to these parties the belief in the early advent of world revolution which they themselves had discarded. As a belief in salvation and eternal life can help people to be reconciled with poverty and suffering during their temporal existence, so the Soviets hoped that the prospect of early revolution would stop Western Communists from trying to get for the workers the best possible deal and ultimately identifying their interests with the interests of the country of which they were a part. From the Soviet point of view foreign Communists' main value was as a potential fifth column in case the West decided to embark on a new war against Russia.

Though the Soviet objective was sound, the tactics used against the Czechoslovak Communists were not. Soviet political methods were geared to a population still largely illiterate and in any case deprived of alternative sources of information. Moreover it was a population used to respecting authority. The first great mistake of the Soviets was to ask their Prague representatives to behave as if the Czechoslovak workers were *muzhiks*.

The second mistake was to demand absolute conformity with Soviet aims. If it had been allowed to sweeten the Moscow objectives with at least a small proportion of Czechoslovak aims, the Czechoslovak Communist Party would probably have achieved a greater cohesion. Instead of crippling the Party into complete obedience a more tolerant approach by Moscow could have gained it a useful and effective ally.

It is much more difficult to discover the underlying elements of weakness which made the Czechoslovak Communists cooperate with Moscow in this self-defeating game. There must have been reasons which led them to submit to foreign dictates, to suffer the ignominy of transparently fraudulent political tricks, to profess beliefs contradicting their own experience and to pursue policies which lost them the confidence of the workers.

One reason, and probably the most important one, can be seen in the relative classlessness of Czech society which makes it remarkably easy for radical politicians of all types to lose contact with the mass of their supporters: they are tempted to substitute political hot-house plants for field crops which take more time but yield a bigger harvest. In contrast to the England described by Karl Marx in *Capital*, or the Russia where some of his revolutionary ideas were applied, there were no barriers and little differences between the owners of capital and the workers in Bohemia and Moravia. They all started at the same school and spoke the same kind of Czech or German. Many workers and miners had also a small agricultural holding and even those who lived in big towns had rural roots and relatives in the villages whom they helped at harvest time and from whom they could expect help if food became scarce. The artisan mentality, the pride and feeling of independence based on skill, were still very much alive and in fact most small entrepreneurs and tradesmen started as workers or employees. The parents or grandparents of doctors, lawyers, higher civil servants and clergymen were peasants, tradesmen, workers.

All this made it extremely difficult for the 'professional revolutionaries' to convince their followers that in order to improve the world they would have to destroy a social class opposing them. If they got as far as thinking in terms of a class struggle they saw themselves opposed by their brothers, cousins, schoolmates, and though envy abounded, the hatred necessary for fratricidal strife was lacking. To have their fair share, better wages and shorter hours, the same security in illness and old age as more fortunate relatives, that, certainly, they wanted. If the Communists had more grandiose ideas let them do what they could, but it was not really their business. This lack of interest in the workers allowed their leaders to slip into a world of political dreams.

The second factor which contributed to a certain air of weightlessness in the Czech Communist movement was the disproportionately important role assumed in it by writers, poets, artists and intellectuals in general. The left-wing intelligentsia is, of course, not a specifically Czech phenomenon, but the importance of literature to politics is. At the crucial time of the national revival, in the first half of the nineteenth century, the aristocracy was irretrievably Germanized or otherwise identified with the Habsburg regime and could not provide the country with effective political leaders. The bourgeoisie was not yet mature enough for political activity. On the local scale the teacher and the parish priest, on the national scale the writer and poet, acted as substitutes for a non-existent political leadership.

Theatres, and National Theatre in particular, were not places of entertainment but temples for patriotic rituals, mostly in operatic form. The Czechs never embraced the aristocratic notion that art should entertain and amuse, and still less the bourgeois notion that it is an end in itself. For three generations the glory of art had been in its patriotically political function. Communist writers and artists easily accepted the requirement that they had to serve the Party.

This in itself is not sufficient to explain the extreme volatility of Czech writers who like S. K. Neumann exchanged patriotism for anarchism and that for a masochistic prostration before the whims of Moscow, against which they revolted only to recant later. Those who lived long enough went through many such turns. One suspects that the alternating fits of revolt and obedience were prompted by one and the same feeling, of guilt and helplessness produced by the acceptance of a political role contrary to their literary and artistic aims. This clash produced a conflict for which they were not equipped and which overstrained them.

The Czech Communist movement, however, did not consist only of workers with bourgeois aspirations and writers and artists precariously and guiltily perched on political clouds. It counted also many politically mature members who had no illusions about the realities of power politics and still suicidally retreated step by step before Moscow's demands. The same type of Czechs who were reluctant monarchists under the Habsburgs – and among them were Palacký and Masaryk, each of them called Pater Patriae during his lifetime – became reluctant Communists in the first ten years of Czechoslovakia and again after 1945.

The political development of Bohumír Šmeral, the tragic hero of this chapter from Czech history, provides an explanation of this phenomenon. To Šmeral the need for outside support against the engulfing danger of Germany was the paramount consideration. He believed in the need to preserve Austria–Hungary; when it distintegrated before it could be transformed into a socialist republic he was left only with the hope that some sort of support for the Czechs could be obtained from the international Communist movement.

Šmeral played for time, holding back Moscow's advance to the domination of his Party until about 1925. Until then Czechoslovakia had the backing of the Allies and in particular of France. After 1924, when the conference at Locarno gave a new direction to the

European policy of the Great Powers, this support waned. France and Britain set out on a course which led to Munich and to leaving Czechoslovakia at the mercy of Germany. Šmeral must have known what Karl Marx wrote in 1848: 'An historical misfortune places the Czechs on the side of the Russians, on the side of despotism against revolution . . .'. Still he saw no other way out.

The Upper Land of Hungary

In the ninth century (around 835) one of the first political centres of
the western Slavs was established in Slovakia by Prince Pribina,
ruler of Nitra, now a provincial town north-east of Bratislava. It
moved further west when this principality was integrated with the
Great Moravian Empire. Pribina sought refuge with the Franks, and
in 847 Louis the German installed him as ruler of a province adjoin-
ing Lake Balaton. The same problem, whether to integrate with the
Czechs or seek support for independence in Germany, came up again
after eleven centuries. Through the vicissitudes of history the national development of the Slovaks was interrupted for almost a thousand years, so that in spite of their early start they were the last of
the Slavs to achieve an ethnic identity of their own.

Pannonia, on the present territory of Slovakia and Hungary, was
torn from the Great Moravian Empire by the Magyars who arrived
from the east in the first decade of the tenth century and exterminated or drove out the Slav tribes from the lowlands; there they
settled, and ruled over the Slovak highlands until 1918. Slovakia
became the Upper Land of historical Hungary, which consisted of a
core inhabited by the Magyars – modern Hungary – and peripheral
regions inhabited by Slavs.

The history of Slovakia cannot therefore be treated separately
from that of Hungary. However, relations between Czechs and
Slovaks, so important for the history of the Czechoslovak Republic,
can hardly be explained without reference to the main differences in
their historical experience. When the two ethnic groups rejoined after
a thousand years of separation, each was living in a different historical time. In 1918, the Slovak economy, institutions and cultural

achievements were in that rudimentary state from which the Czechs had made a new start at the beginning of the nineteenth century.

Whatever progress to nationhood the Slovaks had made thus far, it left them with a traumatic experience, for they were few, poor and harshly ruled by the Hungarians, who themselves clung far too much to their feudal past and kept their country out of the mainstream of economic and social development. The deprivations experienced under the Hungarians made the Slovaks compulsive seekers of political advantage and suspicious that the Czechs wanted to rule them as the Hungarians did. Even patriotic Slovaks were conditioned by education in Hungarian schools and in a way resented the Czechs even more because they were unashamedly plebeian meritocrats. They could see service to the aristocratic and haughty Hungarians as a matter of accepted class distinction. By contrast, the claims of the egalitarian Czechs that leadership required expertise seemed an affront to Slovak national pride.

Compared with this great difference in way of life, outlook and general level of civilization, the language difference seemed insignificant – many insisted then, and some still do, that there are not two languages but only two dialects of one and the same language. Paradoxically, this language problem, a subject of controversy among the Slovaks themselves, consumed much of the energy needed for more important facets of Slovak national development.

The root of these competing problems, the Slovaks' retarded development towards nationhood and the question mark over their language, can be traced back to the seventeenth century. When Commenius, Bishop of the Moravian Brethren, arrived in Slovakia (in Sarišsky Potok) in 1650, Slovakia was not a territorial, and still less a political entity within Hungary – it was all that remained of Hungary at that time since its lowlands were occupied by the Turks. The Turkish frontier was then still being pushed northwards, and some ten years later cut through what is now southern Slovakia. Slovakia was overcrowded with Magyar barons, gentry and burghers who sought refuge from the Turks, and they as well as the army units defending the frontier lived off the land. The plight of the Slovak serfs tilling the land was proportionate to the high demand for agricultural produce, though they could and often did escape to the Turks or to the no-man's-land between the opposed armies and form marauding bands.

The concentration of Hungarian refugees made Slovakia the centre of Hungarian political, social and cultural life. Commenius wrote four of his educational works there and made the local Calvinist college in Sarišsky Potok the foremost Protestant school in Hungary. It was a Latin school and the four books Commenius wrote were in Latin. But the Moravian Brethren who emigrated to Slovakia to escape Catholic persecution brought with them their Kralická Bible. Its language (which differs from contemporary Czech rather less than Shakespeare's English from that of the BBC), written with the modern phonetic orthography introduced by Jan Huss, became the literary language of the Slovaks, who called it *bibličtina*, 'the Bible language'.

The *bibličtina* and the Czech culture of the Slovak Protestants attained their full importance in the national development only after the Turks were driven out of the lowlands and after the last big uprising of the Hungarian nobility against the Habsburgs. When the Magyars returned south to their fertile lowlands, which soon again became the political and social centre of Hungary, the peasant population which remained, the Slovaks, gained greater space for national development.

This development was hampered by poor economic conditions. When Turks, Habsburg armies and Hungarian nobles had gone, Slovakia was devastated and depopulated in much the same way as Bohemia and Moravia had been after the Thirty Years War, so that demands on the Slovak serfs increased. Though mining and metal smelting became an important industry in the eighteenth century – and probably more advanced technologically than anywhere else at that time – there were no manufacturing industries and the Slovak population remained divided between Hungarian-speaking lords and their officials and the Slovak serfs, with no bourgeoisie between them.

This had important political consequences in the second half of the eighteenth century. While in Bohemia and Moravia the bourgeoisie – both Czech and German – joined hands with the reforming Habsburg regime and strengthened its hand against the reactionary aristocracy, the Hungarian lords had the field to themselves. They successfully resisted Viennese centralism and thus prepared the ground for the dualistic concept of the Austro–Hungarian Empire, confirmed a century later. By rejecting all the reforms of Joseph II, except the abolition of serfdom, the Hungarian aristocracy prevented the development of industry and of a bourgeoisie such as that which assumed political leadership in Austria and in the Czech crown lands.

Even the abolition of serfdom did not bring the same benefits to the Slovak highlands as to Bohemia and Moravia where the peasants had fertile land of their own and industry offered alternative employment to the surplus of the rural population. The Slovaks remained dependent on the feudal domains. They worked in winter in the local forests and were hired in summer as gangs of cheap labour to help with export crops in the Hungarian lowlands. The terrible conditions in the exploited Slovak villages attracted wider attention only when eastern Slovakia was shaken by a great peasant uprising in 1831.

Even this upheaval did not lead to the formulation of an anti-feudal programme, because there was no one to formulate one. By this time the small country gentry, which was the main force opposing the attempts of Joseph II to replace the aristocratic administration of Hungary by a centrally-controlled civil service, had lost its political importance. The anti-Habsburg banner was taken over by the middle-stratum aristocrat who combined a feudal ideology of Hungarian autonomy with a liberal and nationalistic programme reflecting the contemporary efforts of the western bourgeoisie. The economic liberalism of this programme viewed Slovakia as a reservoir of cheap labour, while its fuedal nationalism led to the initiation of a rigorous policy of forceful magyarization.

For these reasons the defensive character of Slovak nationalism, the feeling of being threatened, has always been very prominent, and when Prague instead of Budapest became the seat of the central government departments after 1918, the force of these emotions was redirected. This complicated Slovak relations with the Czechs still further. In the early nineteenth century the Protestant Slovaks, using the Czech bible and bible language, were drawn to the (mainly Catholic) Czechs – Kollár, Šafařík and other prominent revivalists strove for a 'Czechoslovak' literature. By contrast, the Catholic Slovaks, mainly in western Slovakia, found Czech Catholicism much too liberal and Czech society and political programmes much too secular, and they followed the ideas of Anton Bernolák, who in 1790, opposed the idea of a single Czechoslovak nation and in a series of linguistic works tried to develop a separate Slovak literary language.

The balance was tilted in favour of a separate Slovak literary language by the second generation of the Slovak Protestant intelligentsia, whose leading personality was L'udovít Štúr. The main argument was that it should be made as easy as possible for the Slovak villagers to overcome illiteracy – though this very argument later led to several local Slovak dialects competing for acceptance as the literary language. The other, not so well publicized reason, was the wish not to antagonize further the Budapest Government which regarded links with the Czechs as a possible danger for Hungarian autonomy and likely to provide Vienna with a new political lever. These apprehensions of the Hungarian Government became evident when Slovak leaders, meeting in Turčiansky Svätý Martin in 1861, agreed a Memorandum of the Slovak Nation. It claimed that the Slovaks were a separate nation and should have equal rights with the Magyars. When the Slovak leaders petitioned the Emperor for a *Privilegium* sanctioning these ideas, Budapest declared this step unconstitutional.

The movement started by the 1861 Memorandum had no success. In the 1872 elections only three Slovak deputies were elected to the Budapest parliament; in 1874 the last three Slovak grammar schools were closed by the Government; in 1875 the Matica Slovenská, the only Slovak national institution with a patriotic education and publishing programme, was dissolved and its assets confiscated because, as the Minister of the Interior K. Tisza said, there was no Slovak nation. All this was taking place at a time when the Czechs were successfully building a dense network of secondary and technical schools and crowning this, in 1882, by splitting the Charles–Ferdinand University in Prague and restoring their half of it as a Czech national university. While Czech literature and science advanced to a stage at which they were ready to absorb the best achieved elsewhere and add to it, the banner of Slovak patriotism was carried by a score of parish priests and teachers, Catholic and Protestant, harassed by their superiors in Budapest.

This, of course, made election prospects on a Slovak ticket very unlikely. The Slovak National Party, which since 1870 had been publishing a newspaper three times a week, decided in 1884 not to participate in elections and continued this form of protest in the elections of 1887 and 1892. When it finally took part in the election of 1901 it gained four seats in Budapest.

The turn of the century saw the formation of several Slovak political nuclei and the emergence of names that were to play an important role in the future Czechoslovak Republic. *Hlas*, a literary and political magazine, began to appear in 1898. V. Šrobár, who was in touch with Masaryk, steered it along a liberal course, promoting economic and cultural contacts with the Czechs. But both Protestant and Catholic leaders turned against *Hlas* because by Slovak standards it was much too 'progressive'.

In 1905 Milan Hodža, a leading personality in the Slovak Agrarian political group formed a few years earlier, was elected to parliament, with the help of Serbian and Croat votes. Five years later he started to pin his hopes on Archduke Franz Ferdinand, the heir-apparent, who was known for his anti-Hungarian bias, while some of the Slovak political Catholics led by Andrei Hlinka started to co-operate with the Budapest Government. At about this time cooperation with the Czechs, opposed by the Catholic party, received a new impetus from Czech industrial and financial enterprise beginning to discover Slovakia. After 1908 economic and cultural cooperation between Czechs and Slovaks was discussed every year at conferences held in Luhačovice, and these prepared the ground for the inclusion of Czech–Slovak cooperation in the programme formulated by Slovak politicians in Budapest in 1914, which demanded federalization of both parts of the Austro–Hungarian monarchy. This meeting, held on the eve of the First World War, decided to establish a Slovak National Council on which all Slovak political parties were to be represented – and also the Social Democrats, who since 1897 had also had a Slovak magazine, published in Budapest by František Tupý, a Czech boilermaker from Slaný.

Junior partners

Unlike the Czechs, the Slovaks were not led into the promised land of independence by a new man. Milan Rostislav Štefánik, the promising young Slovak astronomer with a flair for politics, did not return with Masaryk and Beneš. The aircraft bringing him home in 1919 crashed near Bratislava. He soon became a legend – but Slovakia badly needed a leader.

The absence of secondary schools and the stagnation of political life under Hungarian rule resulted in only a handful of Slovak politicians being available for the new state administration, and even these few were deeply divided. Those favouring cooperation with the Czechs were grouped around *Hlas* and led by Vavro Šrobár, who after his studies in Prague maintained contact with Masaryk. Near to this group stood Milan Hodža, the able and ambitious leader of the recently established Slovak Agrarian Party. They were opposed by Catholic conservatives who until 1918 cooperated with the Budapest regime in which the Catholic hierarchy had a great part. The leader of this party, called the Slovak Popular Party, was Andrei Hlinka, a priest. Somewhere in the centre between these two wings were the conservatives of the original Slovak National Party, but in 1918 they were rather closer to the pro-Czech Hlasists who started as an opposition group of this party.

Such disunity on the fundamental issue – whether the Slovaks would be better off with the Czechs or with the Hungarians – further weakened the unstable structure of Slovak politics. The Slovak political parties were greenhouse plants without the subsoil of an electorate aware of its interests. Slovak villagers, struggling against the harshness of nature and of society, were completely controlled by the parish priest. Their hopes were pinned on a better life after death, or perhaps after emigration to America, but certainly not on the politicians in Martin or Bratislava, whose programmes they could not understand.

Except for the few who completed their education at the Czech University in Prague, the educated Slovaks of 1918 all came out of Hungarian schools and quite often did not know what they were, Slovaks or Magyars. They were bilingual, and many could be swayed one way or the other by political developments. The young men of 1968 who were successfully demanding the duplication of all central government departments in Slovakia, to provide more careers for Slovak graduates, found it hard to believe that before 1918 out of the 13,400 officials in Slovakia only 53 stated their nationality as Slovak, as did only 33 out of the 1,133 public notaries who held a key position in administration. Of the 660 secondary school teachers only ten claimed to be of Slovak nationality.

After the Hungarian Red Army was driven out of Slovakia it was clearly better to be a partner of the Czechs than a member of the Hungarian minority, and many turned their coats accordingly.

The Hungarian Government, which for centuries had been deny-ing the existence of a Slovak nation, recognized in the early 1920s that pro-Hungarian Slovaks might be a more effective ally than the small genuinely Hungarian minority and started to support Slovak nationalism in its confrontation with Czechoslovakism. This situa-tion gave rise to the Czech jibe that Slovak is the language Slovaks use when talking to Czechs, the implication being that between themselves they speak Hungarian.

Besides the starving villages and the rootless intelligentsia, how-ever, there was yet another body of Slovak opinion – though not in Slovakia: millions of Slovak emigrants who had made good in the United States retained a lively interest in their old country. While Czech emigration during the nineteenth and early twentieth cen-turies had been on a very small scale, there was a massive exodus of the poor of Slovakia. The Slovak emigrants, if lucky, learned to read and write in the single-form village school and thus escaped magyar-ization at a secondary school. They did not doubt that they were Slovaks. To overcome the religious division of Slovak clubs in the United States, they formed a Slovak Association in Pittsburgh in 1890. This was followed in 1907 by a League of Slovak Clubs to support the Slovaks at home.

During the 1914–18 war these American Slovaks took upon them-selves a sort of political guardianship for their compatriots at home and supported Masaryk in his campaign for an independent Czechoslovakia. On 30 May 1918 representatives of Slovak and Czech organizations in the United States signed with Masaryk the Pittsburgh Agreement approving the idea of an independent republic formed jointly by Czechs and Slovaks in which the Slovaks would have their own parliament and administration. It was this agreement which the Slovak autonomists led by Andrei Hlinka later invoked against Prague.

A week before this agreement was signed in Pittsburgh, a secret meeting of the Slovak National Party and representatives of other Slovak factions, held in Turčiansky Svätý Martin, made a declara-tion in favour of Czechoslovak independence. They met there again two days after the republic was proclaimed in Prague on October 28 and made another declaration, later interpreted as Slovak accession to the new republic. But no record was preserved and in 1928 some Slovak autonomists came up with the claim that in Martin, Slovakia acceded to the Czechoslovak Republic for a trial period of ten years only.

Whatever were the intentions of those endorsing the declarations of Pittsburgh and Martin, their mandate to speak for Slovakia was highly questionable. The declarations in fact remained without any immediate political effect: Slovakia was integrated into the Czecho-slovak Republic – and the Hungarian Army pushed out – only on the strength of the Versailles Peace Treaty. In August 1919 Andrei Hlinka was in Paris to argue the case for Slovak autonomy before the Peace Conference, but it was the Czech Army which drove out the Hungarians and the Czechs were left a free hand to establish a new administration.

In the wake of the advancing Czech army, the Prague Govern-ment gave full powers to Vavro Šrobár, the most prominent among the Slovak politicians who before the war had adopted a Czecho-slovak programme. There is no doubt that Prague feared that the Slovak National Council, constituted by the Slovak political parties in the last days of the war, would only create further complications at a time when Hungary was a soviet republic and the Red Army was advancing deep into Poland. The Slovak National Council was therefore first left without any power and in January 1919 was dis-solved. Šrobár ruled Slovakia as plenipotentiary of the Prague Gov-ernment, supported by the Hlasists, the Slovak Social Democrats and, to a certain extent, also by Milan Hodža, the Slovak Agrarian. He was strongly opposed by Hlinka's Catholic party.

When food and fuel scarcities resulted in unrest and strikes by farm workers, Šrobár's regime, involved in fighting Communist sub-version coming across the border from Hungary, could not handle the situation. In the spring of 1920 Šrobár's National and Agrarian Party suffered a defeat, obtaining only twelve seats, the same as Hlinka's Popular Party, while the Social Democrats, with 23 seats, became the strongest party in Slovakia. Šrobár was replaced as plenipotentiary by the Social Democratic leader Ivan Dérer, but he too was unable to handle the situation and resorted to martial law in the summer of 1920.

In contrast with Bohemia and Moravia, where the moderate and centrist influence of Masaryk and of the Castle in general was in those years supreme, in Slovakia all political parties were radical: even the Slovak Social Democrats of 1920 were much nearer to

Communism than their Czech fellows. It was the danger of left radicalism which drove the two Slovak right-wing parties into co-operation with the Czechs. The National and Agrarian Party led by Šrobár and Hodža formed a joint parliamentary club with Antonín Švehla and his Czech Agrarians; and the two Catholic parties, Hlinka's Popular Party and the Czech Popular Party led by Šrámek, also a priest, linked hands.

In the autumn of that year (on 15 September 1920) Vlastimil Tusar's Government – a coalition of Social Democrats and Agrarians – fell and Hlinka came to a far reaching agreement with Černý's caretaker government. The Catholic Church was returned to a position of great influence in the educational system of Slovakia and in exchange Hlinka supported the Czechoslovak Government against the ex-Emperor Karl's attempt to return to the Hungarian throne in 1921. In April of that year Hlinka solemnly signed the Czechoslovak Constitution and the deputies of his party made a declaration in favour of Czechoslovak unity.

This Czech–Slovak *rapprochement* did not last long. In October Beneš succeeded Černý as Premier and in November Hlinka broke with the Czech Catholics. However, the slight shift to the left in the Prague Government was not the only reason. In those post-war years the political situation in Central Europe was changing with kaleidoscopic ease. By the end of 1921 Soviet rule in Hungary was replaced by the Fascist and pro-Catholic regime of Admiral Horthy, who was ready to support a Slovak autonomist programme in the hope of its leading to a reintegration of Slovakia with Hungary. This change in Hungarian policy towards Slovakia led to the emergence of Professor Vojtěch Tuka (who had so far passed for a Hungarian) as the ideologist in Hlinka's party of Slovak autonomy.

In 1921 this programme was still quite impractical simply because there were not enough Slovaks who could and wanted to make it work, but the situation was rapidly changing in favour of the Slovak autonomists and the Czechs were rather slow in keeping step with this change. Immediately after the war there was no other choice than to replace Hungarian teachers and officials by Czechs. After a few years a new Slovak intelligentsia was graduating from the schools opened and run by the Czechs, and resented their continued presence. The small number of posts open at the higher levels of administration could be filled with Slovaks right at the beginning;

the problem lay with the relatively large number of Czechs in the lower ranks where they were even more visible to the public. Many of the Czechs, who enjoyed the high social status accorded in Slovakia even to petty officials, were not keen to return home where the best jobs were already occupied and competition was much more severe.

Another objective reason for discontent was the immediate economic effect of integration with the economically more advanced Czech crown lands. Severance of the links with Hungary was bad for the Slovak forest industry and for the seasonal workers who relied on money earned on the Hungarian grain farms. Moreover, the weaker and sparse Slovak manufacturing industry was exposed to the surplus capacity of a much more advanced Czech industry which after losing the Great Austro-Hungarian market was readjusting, concentrating its resources and fighting hard for survival. The deflationary policy of the Prague Government, of which a credit squeeze was part, meant that there was no money for making use of the opportunities which Slovakia offered.

Continuation of support from Hungary and justified domestic discontent were the background to Hlinka's next move: in January 1922 he presented in parliament Tuka's proposal for Slovak autonomy. In the past the Slovak political Catholics had agreed well with their coreligionists in Hungary. Even now the real motives of the Slovak Catholic clergy were not so much ethnic and nationalist but confessional. The Slovak Catholics feared the decidedly anti-clerical nature of Czech politics, the progressive attitude of the Castle and the Protestant elements in its ideology.

This concern of the Catholic priests should not obscure the fact that the idea of autonomy appealed also to many non-Catholics. When Hlinka broke with the Czech Catholic Party the members of the former Slovak National Party, feeling pushed into the background by the Agrarians with whom their party had integrated, decided to separate from them on an autonomist programme. Being mainly Protestant, they could not join Hlinka and formed a new Slovak National Party. This party was not as pro-Hungarian as that of Hlinka, but the two autonomist parties cooperated as a powerful opposition. After the secession of the autonomists, Šrobár's and Hodža's party virtually became a purely Agrarian party and remained closely linked with the Czech Agrarians.

This political constellation had disastrous consequences. The

Czech Agrarians represented the small and medium farmers who wanted high prices for bread grains and did not care if the subsidy came from a levy on imported feeding stuffs. With very little arable land, however, Slovak agriculture depended on animal husbandry for its development. Without imported feeding stuffs it was reduced to sheep grazing.

The policy of dear feeding stuffs thus prevented a diversification into dairy farming and perpetuated Slovakia's economic dependence on forestry. As a result, when in 1926 the Czech Agrarians pushed through protection tariffs and Hungary answered with a 'tariff war', Slovakia suffered even more. The impossibility of exporting timber down the Slovak rivers to Hungary meant unemployment in the forest districts. The Slovak Agrarians, who should have opposed the Czech Agrarians at every step, were little more than their Slovak agents. The Czechs appeared to rule the state-owned forests. They did not exploit the Slovak villagers as their Hungarian predecessors had done; they just had no jobs for them. Predictably, the Slovaks did not see this as the right direction of progress.

This unsatisfactory state of the economy contrasted with the real progress achieved with massive Czech aid in the administration of justice, in the health and social services, and above all in the field of education. In 1918 there were only 276 Slovak primary schools, staffed by only 390 teachers. They were attended by about 30,000 children, while some 220,000 children from Slovak-speaking homes had to attend Magyar-language schools. The Czechs sent to Slovakia 1,400 teachers and by 1927 the number of Slovak primary schools increased tenfold, to 2,655, and were attended by 277,800 children. The number of Slovak teachers' colleges was increased from three to thirteen, so that by 1927 the number of teachers in Slovak primary schools could be increased to 4,354. In that year the number of Slovak grammar schools (gymnasia) reached thirty-nine – there were none in 1918 – and there was a large number of technical colleges modelled on the highly successful Czech schools preparing technicians and production managers for industry. Finally, the Slovak university, opened in 1919 with great difficulty as no more than ten Slovak candidates could be found for senior teaching posts, by 1927 had fifty-five professors and 185 lecturers.

In this way the Czechs did for the Slovak revival what Joseph II's educational reforms had done for them at the turn of the nineteenth century. The schools they opened, often with the help of Czech teachers, were turning out a new, genuinely Slovak, generation. These young people still possessed the drive which their parents had had to have to keep alive but were better educated and looked for opportunities for an easier life. Unfortunately, the opportunities were not there. They saw the economic plight of Slovakia as a direct result of Czech policies – though these were no worse than those of any other *laissez faire* market economy towards its underdeveloped regions – and also that the Czech Agrarians were trying to ward off the political consequences of their economic policies by election bribery and blackmail.

The autonomist programme promised to put all that right and they turned to it, gladly overlooking the fact that the priests used a sort of religious blackmail no better than that employed by the Agrarians. They needed some hope and so they overlooked also the fascist tendencies inherent in the autonomist party. This development in the Slovak domestic political scene was very much in step with changes in the wider European scene, where the first publicly visible signs appeared of a future agreement between Britain and France on one side and Germany and Italy on the other for a revision of the peace treaties which had established Czechoslovakia.

In 1927 Hungarian pressure for the revision of the Trianon Treaty reached its highest point when Lord Rothermere's press's support of its cause was somewhat overestimated by the Budapest Government. At the same time Prague made a move to narrow the gap separating it from the autonomists by a rather timid administrative reform. The autonomists were not satisfied and Tuka joined in the campaign unleashed by Budapest and Lord Rothermere's press. Meanwhile Father Josef Tiso, another astute autonomist, became one of Hlinka's principal assistants.

In 1929 Tuka, the pro-Hungarian ideologue of Slovak autonomy, was sentenced for espionage and subversion. When he was pardoned in 1937 he was still an autonomist but pro-German. The boom brought by Czech armament factories moved to Slovakia for strategic reasons in the 1930s came too late to improve Slovak feelings.

Both the Czechs' cultural contribution and their economic neglect made the Slovaks mature fast. When in 1938 France and Britain agreed to give Hitler a free hand in Czechoslovakia there was no longer any doubt as to the ethnic identity of the Slovaks as a separate nation, historically, politically, socially and perhaps even linguistically. Out of Hitler's grace the stage was set for the tragedy of the Slovak state.

Ruthenia

Besides Czechs, Slovaks and Germans the 1918–39 Czechoslovakia included also Ruthenians who were undecided between themselves whether they were Ukrainians or Russians. The official name of the region in this period was 'Subcarpathian Russia'. Both the Ruthenians and the very numerous orthodox Jewish population were still living in the Middle Ages.

Much of what was said about the economic neglect and party-political manipulation of the electorate in Slovakia applied in even more drastic terms to Ruthenia, which was part of Hungary before it was attached to Czechoslovakia in 1918. At that time it was guaranteed autonomy but this never materialized. The Czech officials, teachers, doctors and social welfare workers achieved little in face of the economic adversities, resulting from neglect under Hungarian rule. These hardships were further aggravated by the sudden separation from Hungary which at least was a market for timber from the Carpathian forests where men would work in winter while in summer they could hope for employment on the fields of the Hungarian plain. Though extremely badly paid this work had at least kept the population above starvation level. The subsequent trade war between Czechoslovakia and Hungary was a further catastrophe for an already destitute population.

The extreme poverty of the underdeveloped region combined with the lack of national consciousness to deprive the Czech educational contribution of much of its local effect: those who graduated from the new schools looked for employment and settled in the western parts of the republic. A large part of the young Jewish generation was emancipated from the medieval orthodoxy only to emigrate to Palestine.

The links unexpectedly established between Ruthenians on the one side and Slovaks and Czechs on the other in 1918 were cut with the same suddenness in 1939 when Ruthenia returned for a short time to Hungary, to be annexed by the Soviet Union in 1945.

16 An economy at the mercy of bankers

A difficult heritage

The twenty years of the first Czechoslovak Republic coincided with
a really difficult period for the Western market economy, with which
the new country was inextricably interlocked by trade, investments
and politics. The toll of young men taken by the war made it difficult to recover quickly from shortages, and in Central Europe these
meant outright starvation in the towns. The separation of Russia
from Europe and the tumultuous inflation into which Germany tried
to escape from the consequences of defeat made the situation even
worse. When finally the world recovered, the prosperity was of short
duration and was abruptly ended in 1929 by the Wall Street crash,
heralding the Great Depression. This lasted so long, and was so
severe and so nonsensical, that many people began to wonder
whether the capitalist system would be able to survive.

In addition to these general problems of the world economy,
Czechoslovakia had its special problems. It was torn out of the
'common market' of Austria–Hungary and inherited from it a transport system centred on Vienna – unsuitable for a country stretching
700 miles east–west – and its share of war debts. Those responsible
for the management of its economy had no easy task but it can
hardly be claimed on their behalf that they did the best they could.
First a merciless deflation imposed by banking interests, and later
agrarian protection tariffs made industry suffer – the export industry
located mainly in German regions more than the rest – and retarded
the development of Slovakia.

Unsuitable economic policies coming on top of an industrial structure developed for a different market resulted in economic depres-
sions of extraordinary severity. In a country with a population of

around fourteen million the number of unemployed was 450,000 in 1923 and after a brief boom, 840,000 in 1933. Including family dependants a full third of the country's population was without earnings in that year. Most of the benefit from industrial restructuring and technological advance was thus dissipated by bad management of the economy. Indeed, the only reassuring message to be derived from the economic history of Czechoslovakia between the two wars is that an ingenious and hardworking people can survive the most staggering blunders of successive governments. But the Czechs achieved more than mere survival. Though real wages were by 1938 still only about half of those in Britain, the pattern of industry was improved and its infra-structure developed. Expansion of educational facilities and the social security system made Czechoslovakia a welfare state far ahead of its time.

With 13.6 million inhabitants on 140,000 square kilometres, the new Czechoslovak Republic inherited about one quarter of the population of the Austro–Hungarian monarchy and one fifth of its territory but some two thirds of its industrial capacity, almost all located in Bohemia, Moravia and Silesia. Cut off from its original market, almost half of this industrial capacity was now dependent on export and with it about 40 per cent of the new country's national income.

The German population, over three million strong, was settled mainly in belts along the Bohemian frontiers and in ethnic enclaves such as Brno and Jihlava. These regions had a high concentration of light industry, mainly textile, glass and ceramic, consisting largely of small enterprises depending on the cheap labour of cottagers for their ability to compete on foreign markets. Any economic policy likely to make life difficult for export-oriented light industry was therefore also a policy bearing heavily on the German districts. The Czech parts of Bohemia, Moravia and Silesia had a greater area of fertile agricultural land and their industry was better assorted, including coalmining, basic industries, and several large engineering groups.

The percentage of population dependent on industry was 40 in the west and only 17 in the east of the country. The economic development of Slovakia, with a population of about four million, was in 1918 about 70 years behind the western part of the country. A mountainous country, it depended mainly on sheep-grazing, forestry, and timber exports, though the lowland along the border with Hungary was a fertile, grain-producing region. The severance from the Hungarian plains into which all of Slovakia is drained was detrimental to the timber trade and deprived the Slovaks of seasonal work on Hungarian farms at harvest time. An even greater problem was that Slovakia lacked the industrial skills, the capital and a consumer market to compete with Czech industry at a time when the Czechs were trying hard to replace lost markets.

About a third of the population lived in towns of more than 5,000 inhabitants but only seven towns had a population greater than 50,000. Prague, the capital city, had 677,000 inhabitants in 1921, and was growing much faster than other cities, reaching almost a million by 1938. The western part of the country was on the whole urbanized but in a pleasant way which did not lead to the social and cultural disintegration of communities. In Slovakia the towns were farther apart, but both there and in the west the town communities preserved architecturally and socially a pattern evolved over several centuries – many still have an intact seventeenth-century core and some preserve much evidence of their prosperity in the fourteenth century.

The occupational distribution of the population deceptively presents a picture of a good balance between agriculture and industry. In 1921 of the total of 5.57 million gainfully employed 39.6 per cent worked in agriculture and 33.8 per cent in industry; by 1930 both proportions had levelled out at just under 35 per cent. (For agriculture this represented an acceleration of a downward trend but for industry merely recovery to the 1910 relative level of employment.) This apparent balance was a good thing in times of unemployment for with mixed agricultural production those living on the land did not need to starve however bad the state of the economy. But the cost to the economy is evident from the fact that 28 per cent of all farms had less than a hectare (2.25 acres) of agricultural land and 42.7 per cent between one and five hectares (12.5 acres). Only 1 per cent of farms had more than 50 hectares (125 acres).

In the post-war period the output of Czechoslovak industry was less than 80 per cent of the level achieved in 1913. It began to rise in 1923, reached the pre-war level in 1924, overstepped it by 40 per cent by 1929, and fell to almost the post-war low towards the end of the great recession in 1933, to surge back almost to its 1929 peak in

1937. In these twenty years its structure underwent an important change in favour of engineering and the mass production of certain consumer goods.

The power of the Czech banks

Monetary developments in the Czechoslovakia of the 1918–38 period are an indispensable clue to the understanding of its history. In the damage they caused to the country and to the good name of its democratic institutions, Czech bankers, though keeping discreetly in the background, virtually matched the political generals who plagued other countries. Instead of palace coups and putsches, monetary operations and credit management were the principal political weapons in Czechoslovakia.

Initial post-war inflation was answered by a brutal attempt to restore pre-war values. Though this deflationist policy succeeded only by half, its cost was massive unemployment and a loss of foreign markets. It was superseded by a period of stabilization leading to the acceptance of the gold standard, which had to be abandoned quickly in face of the Great Depression and the need to reintroduce exchange control. Trading done simultaneously on the basis of free convertibility with the West and of clearing accounts with Germany and the countries of Eastern Europe drained Czechoslovak hard-currency earnings to the clearing countries. Technicalities of currency and credit management formed an effective screen obscuring not only to the man in the street but also to many leaders of public opinion the progress of the two major Czech banking groups, one headed by the Živnostenská Bank and the other by the Prague Credit Bank allied with the Agrarian Bank. They first took over Austrian and (foreign) German industrial holdings and then fought each other for control of locally owned industry.

The banks, primarily the Živnostenská Bank, controlled the Ministry of Finance, which in the early years was in fact a ministry of economy incorporating the central monetary institute, and also retained a hold over the Czechoslovak National Bank when this was established in 1926. The banks at least shared with the Government the direction of foreign trade policy through a special department in the Ministry of Foreign Affairs, whose head was always closely linked with Dr Preiss, Živnobanka's chairman and one of the most powerful men in the country.

The two other important banks also had close links with the power centres of the country, the Castle and the Agrarian Party, but the partnership was in each case of a different nature. The Agrarian politicians and party workers had farming backgrounds and practical experience of business and finance; they could hold their own in partnership with the bankers. It was quite the opposite with the Castle group led by humanists, intellectuals and trade unionists oriented on foreign policy matters and, in domestic affairs, on education and social security; they tended to look down on businessmen but were awed by 'financial experts' and for most of the time gave the impression of following them without knowing why or where. In a modern industrial society even the 'philosopher king' needs some knowledge of banking and finance.

The political power of the Czech banks followed from the fact that in 1918 they were the best organized sector of the economy. There were twenty-seven commercial banks and a large network of small cooperative banks and savings banks on whose deposits – five times as big as their own – the commercial banks could draw. Further, there were mortgage banks, and regional banks in public ownership for financing local-government operations. Finally, and this was a special feature of Czechoslovak finance, the private and public institutes for health and pension insurance disposed of large funds: in 1935, for example, their total assets were 16,700 million Czechoslovak crowns (Kc) compared with the Kc41,000 million of all commercial banks. The political influence of the bankers grew with the progressive concentration of banking: by 1937 six commercial banks represented 56.3 per cent of the aggregate share capital of all banks and held almost half of all deposits.

The leading banks formed two groups. The stronger, led by Živnobanka, included the Boehmische Escompt Bank (Bebka) which had an important stake in heavy industry, and the Agrarian Bank partially controlling the Länderbank, a mixed Czech–German institute with interests in the sugar industry. The other group was led by the Pražska Úvěrní Bank (Pragobanka) and included the Boehmische Union Bank and the Anglo–Czechoslovak Bank. Živnobanka, the Agrarian Bank and Pragobanka had purely Czech

management, Bebka and the Union Bank German management, and
the Länderbank mixed Czech–German management.

The Great Deflation

In contrast to its well organized banking interests, the Republic did
not in the beginning have any monetary establishment of its own.
During the first four months of Czechoslovakia, notes of the Austro–
Hungarian Bank in Vienna continued to be the legal tender. To the
Kc35,000 million in circulation in October 1918 this bank constantly added more and more notes to finance governmental expenditure in Austria and Hungary, so that the anti-inflation policies of the
Prague Government, pursued for a considerable time without separating the circulation, resulted in a great influx of the debased
money, not only because it could buy more in Czechoslovakia immediately, but also because revaluation was anticipated. The only
step taken by the Government in those months was to prohibit credit
against the security of Austro–Hungarian war loans and their acceptance in payment of taxes on the territory of the Republic.

The volume of money in circulation in Czechoslovakia, including
banknotes, cash certificates and giro balances, reached Kc10,000
million, much too much for the needs of the economy, and was a
measure of the real assets which the Goverment allowed to pass into
foreign hands in exchange for a constantly falling currency. In the
end the Czech banks were refusing to accept deposits for which they
had no use, and the need to separate the currency was generally
recognized as the most urgent task in the economic field.

The delay in separating the currency, though probably due to lack
of self-confidence, was explained by technical reasons: there was no
press equipped for the printing of banknotes. The influx of devalued
money was detrimental to the economy but fitted well with Živnobanka's plan for revaluation and brought large profits to this as well
as to other banks.

The Austro–Hungarian crown was by that time offered in Zurich
at a quarter of its 1914 value and the plan of the Živnobanka's
chairman, Dr Preiss, adopted by the Finance Minister, Alois Rašín,
was to pull the Czechoslovak portion of the old currency, as the new

Czechoslovak crown, back to its pre-war parity in relation to the Swiss franc.

This policy made easier the 'nostrification' (transfer under local control) of banking and industrial enterprise operating on the territory of Czechoslovakia and owned by Austrian or Hungarian capital. Such institutions and enterprises were required by law to become incorporated as independent entities in Czechoslovakia, and as they could no longer be financed from abroad many were taken over by the Živnobanka and other Czechoslovak banks.

Separation of the Czech currency was decreed in February 1919. It was combined with a withdrawal from circulation of half the money in private hands and carried out by a very clumsy technique. The frontiers were closed for a week to transfers of banknotes and in the meantime banks overstamped half of banknotes presented to them by any caller and exchanged the other half for non-transferable one-per-cent bonds issued by the Government for this purpose.

Notes held by banks or needed by industrial enterprises for wages were exempt. Out of a total of Kc7,157 million presented, only Kc5,149 million were in private hands and of the Kc2,452 million retained Kc815 million were later released in response to political pressures and claims of hardship. In the end banknotes in circulation were reduced not by a half but by only a fifth, according to official records. In reality the proportion was smaller still, for two reasons: Kč1 and Kč2 notes, not subject to stamping, continued to be smuggled into Czechoslovakia and the stamps affixed to higher values were easy to falsify.

Small shopkeepers, legally obliged to continue sales during the week in which the operation took place, were hit hardest. Property owners and industrialists were better off, though industry immediately became dependent on bank credit. All banks profited but Živnobanka the most, both directly and indirectly through subsequent takeovers.

All business enterprises were required to draw up balance sheets and private persons to make a return of their assets to the date of 'stamping' in preparation for a property tax which was to level out the injustices of the measure. This tax, designed to produce funds for the repayment of the bonds issued in exchange for banknotes, was enacted eleven months later in January 1920. The amount of paperwork resulting from this measure paralysed tax-collecting offices and caused long delays in assessing and collecting current taxes. When the Government finally succeeded in deflating prices, wages and incomes, the taxes based on the higher-income figures of the previous period were unbearable. Many tax payers were insolvent and a special law had to be passed to write off tax arrears totalling thousands of millions.

The reduction of money in circulation did not succeed in raising substantially the exchange rate of the Czechoslovak crown. Heavy imports of food and raw materials necessary in the first post-war years pressed the exchange rate to its lowest point of Sfr0.05 for Kc1 in February 1920. This stimulated exports, which in the following year achieved a Kc5,000 million surplus over imports with the result that the exchange rate recovered to Sfr0.13, to fall again to Sfr0.10 in the autumn of 1921 when Karl of Habsburg was attempting a come-back in Hungary. At about the same time the Government succeeded in bringing the budget and finances of local government into balance, and the first post-war boom began.

This was the signal for the Živnobanka group to put new pressure on the Government in favour of further raising the exchange rate of the Czechoslovak crown. Živnobanka now followed twin objectives: greater profitability for the import-dependent heavy industry in its group; and a weakening of the export-dependent companies, controlled by the Pragobank group or privately owned, mainly by German industrialists. Although there was a substantial export surplus, the Government took costly loans in London and New York to be able to intervene on the exchange market even more effectively, and succeeded in pushing up the exchange rate to Sfr0.19 by September 1922. It was estimated at the time that an economically justified rate – corresponding to the relation of Czechoslovak domestic prices to world prices – would have been about Sfr0.10 to the Kc. The artificially high rate collapsed before Christmas but after exhausting all its foreign exchange reserves, the Government continued to support the exchange rate at Sfr0.15 at great cost, with the help of short-term borrowing abroad.

The cost of the foreign credit was, of course, only the smaller part of the loss from the operation. A bigger loss resulted from the influx of hot money before the exchange rate was raised. The greatest disaster of all, however, was inflicted on the domestic economy. The exchange rate held 50 per cent above its natural level made imports cheap and depressed domestic prices by 30 per cent. This sudden fall in the price level was a severe blow to all enterprises which had invested on credit or held stocks of material or products bought on credit at higher prices and now could not produce the money necessary for repayments. They were the first victims, and if not exceptionally strong or resilient they were driven into bankruptcy or taken over by the bank to which they owed money. The second wave of bankruptcies came when the export industries found it impossible to compete on foreign markets at the new high exchange rate. After the large surplus the year before, the balance of trade suddenly developed a wide gap which the Government tried to close first from its reserves and then with the help of foreign credits. At the same time the wilfully-caused depression led to massive unemployment, and in 1923 the number of people out of work reached about 450,000.

The avalanche of bankruptcies put pressure on the weaker banks, and depositors panicked. Mass withdrawals threatened the entire banking system and the Government saw itself obliged to save the remaining banks. A special fund to help banks in difficulties into which both the Government and the less severely hit banks contributed was set up. In another form of government subsidy banks' current-account balances with the Viennese Postal Savings Office (Giro) were classified as war loans.

Unemployment, writing-off of tax arrears, the rescue of banks, all resulted in a grave fiscal crisis. The Government felt obliged to accept a United States loan on very hard terms, receiving 89 dollars for 100-dollar debentures bearing a 5½ per cent interest and repayable with 5 per cent premium. To get this loan it had to accept responsibility for the repayment of a portion of the Austro–Hungarian war debt.

As a result of deflation the country suffered from unemployment, restriction of production, loss of foreign markets. Support of the exchange rate consumed Government reserves and obliged it to incur burdensome debts. Hot-money speculators who bought the Czechoslovak crown when it was cheap had to be repaid in hard currencies with up to 50 per cent premium. The economy was left dislocated and disorganized. It appeared that the young state would not survive.

Much industrial ownership passed into the hands of the commercial banks, and the banks therefore claimed that the deflation was a healthy process, eliminating unsound enterprises. Dr Karel Engliš of the Pragobank, the leading Czech economist of the time, himself commented: 'It is not easy to say where is the line dividing the unsound enterprise from the healthy one; one can imagine that the exchange rate could be pushed to a point where no enterprise at all would pass as healthy.'

Stabilization and the Great Depression

In October 1926 the National Democrats, the party of the Živnobanka, were pushed out of the Government coalition. In the new Government of other Czech and German conservative parties the Ministry of Finance was taken over by Dr Engliš. In terms of the banks' power struggle this meant that the Agrarians, who had held almost from the beginning the Ministry of Defence and had established a hold over the armaments industry, could now perfect their alliance with the Pragobank and the Anglobank whose export-oriented industrial groups had been badly shaken by the deflation and were threatened by the Živnobanka.

The new Minister of Finance's first move was to lower the interest rate and thus facilitate the servicing of bank loans which were becoming more burdensome with falling prices. Cheap credit was also indispensable for the export industry.

The next step was to take monetary policy out of day-to-day politics by the establishment, in 1926, of the Czechoslovak National Bank and by writing the stabilization of the exchange rate at Sfr0.15 into its charter. Finally a tax reform passed in 1927 reduced the tax burden on industry not only by lowering taxes but also by introducing 'stabilization balance-sheets' converting past results to the new price and foreign exchange level. The state debt stopped increasing after 1926; gradually it was converted into bonds with a lower interest rate, and in 1928 the burdensome United States loan of 1925 was converted to a domestic loan.

The output of Czechoslovak industry, which had reached its prewar level only in 1924, entered a period of rapid growth, stimulated first by domestic demand in connection with the modernization and re-equipment of industry and later by export. The upswing of exports was made possible by stabilization of the exchange rate at a time when Czechoslovak industry became ready to add capital goods to the traditional export products of light industry and to increase exports of armaments while expanding its activities into more distant markets.

The boom, however, was of short duration. In 1929, when Czechoslovak industrial output had risen to 140 per cent of its pre-war level, Wall Street crashed and the Great Depression came. The National Democrats had meanwhile returned to the Government and the deflationists' influence was again rising, with the result that Czechoslovakia adopted the gold standard in 1929, at a time when the price of gold was rising and some countries were already giving up the gold parity of their currencies in order to save themselves from the deflationary consequences. At a time when both Britain and the United States freed their currencies from gold the Czechoslovak currency remained linked to it, though the escape of monetary gold and capital from the country was prevented by an exchange control. This had to be reintroduced, after only three years of exchange freedom, to curb imports, stimulated by the high exchange rate, at a time when exports fell from Kc20,000 million in 1929 to Kc6,000 million in 1933. This deflationary policy aggravated the consequences of the world-wide depression to such a degree that in 1933 industrial output fell to 60 per cent of its pre-war level and unemployment reached the enormous figure of 920,000, almost a third of all employed in industry and trade in 1930.

Adherence to the gold standard when others were leaving it was the main aggravating factor in problems of Czechoslovak trade with the West – in 1932 exports to Britain fell by 70 per cent and those to Scandinavian countries by 59 per cent. On top of this a further increase in agricultural tariffs in 1930 brought almost to a standstill trade with Poland, Hungary, Romania and Yugoslavia. Hungary, so far the main supplier of agricultural products and the main buyer of Czechoslovak timber and textile products, retaliated and the ensuing tariff war reduced mutual trade to between 15 and 20 per cent of its previous level.

This was a terrible blow to Slovakia and Ruthenia where most of the population depended on employment in forestry and the timber industry. The closing of the Hungarian frontier to Czechoslovak textile exports and a temporary suspension of these and other consumer goods exports to the other agricultural countries of eastern and south-eastern Europe hit in the first place the German population, who had by far the greatest stake in the textile, ceramic and glass industries. (The textile industry was not only the leading export industry but also had greater weight in the domestic economy than any other industry. The reduction of textile exports to a quarter of the 1925-8 average was equivalent to a 50 per cent cut in this industry's total output – and this was still further reduced by a sharp fall in domestic sales when the large army of unemployed almost completely stopped buying textile products.)

Exports to the states which succeeded Austria–Hungary – Czech industry's traditional market – receded after the introduction of agricultural tariffs in 1926 but continued to be paid for by convertible currencies as long as these countries could export elsewhere or could obtain foreign credits. The Great Depression put a stop to this possibility and trade could continue only on the basis of clearing accounts established by the central banks of these countries. The clearing accounts soon created new and unsuspected problems for the Czechoslovak export industry.

The recession and the deflationary policy caused a fall in domestic prices which did not much help exports to countries which devalued in relation to gold but kept up and even stimulated exports to countries from which payment could be expected through clearing at the old parity. In 1934 Czechoslovakia devalued in relation to gold by one sixth, and though this helped exports to the area of convertible currencies, the effect on trade with the clearing countries was disastrous: Czechoslovakia accumulated high clearing balances and the devaluation of its currency made imports from the debtor countries one sixth more expensive. By now imports were also being restricted by import licensing and the clearing balances in south-eastern Europe froze up.

In 1935 trade was gradually revived by allowing barter business but this did not greatly assist in the repayment of accumulated clearing balances. Companies with large amounts frozen in the clearing accounts became dependent on the banks from which they had accepted export credits. Although the difficulties of the export industry had been caused by the monetary and trade policies of the Government, nothing was done to help them, and a wave of takeovers by

Živnobanka and other banks followed. Only when these takeovers were completed did the Government establish the Reeskontní a Lombardní Ústav, a credit institute which provided finance against frozen clearing assets. However, by that time this re-financing device benefited mainly the banks who had in the meantime taken over many insolvent exporters.

This concluded the wave of takeovers following the Great Depression, the third and last by Czech banks; the first in the early 1920s was connected with the 'nostrification' of Austrian and Hungarian interests, the second with deflation in 1924–5. There was yet another takeover wave at the time of Munich in 1938. But this time the Živnostenská Bank was no longer acting on its own account but as an agent of the German banks.

From the aggregate figures for the 1932–6 period it can be seen that the import surplus in trade with the area of freely convertible currencies, amounting to Kc345 million, was less than a fifth of the Czechoslovak export surplus with the clearing countries, amounting to Kc1,913 million. The total of frozen clearing balances reached in 1936 was Kc2,170 million. Raw materials were bought in the West for convertible currencies and processed for export to countries where payments remained frozen on clearing accounts.

During the first fifteen years the credit squeeze had been an almost permanent feature of and a corollary to the policy of the banks, whose main objective was not to lend money but to acquire equity and control of industrial companies. Throughout the Great Depression a public debate raged between the two leading Czech economists Josef Macek and Karel Engliš. Macek, a Social Democrat of unorthodox views, demanded Keynesian public spending to combat unemployment and claimed that to provide the Government with spending power the National Bank should operate on the market in support of Government obligations. Engliš opposed this with arguments of classical economic theory which came in handy for the narrowly conceived interests of the export industry fearing that a spending spree and higher employment would push up prices and wages.

Engliš was overruled when the rising influence of the Agrarian Party enabled it to cooperate with large-scale industry in measures designed primarily to expand the domestic market for food, building construction and armaments and to protect this market against imports. The new power bloc obliged him to accept both support of Government borrowing by operations on the market and a second devaluation. Lending to banks against Government paper (in addition to rediscounting of private bills, mainly in connection with export credits frozen up on unbalanced clearing accounts) and dealing with this on the market became the task of the Reeskontní a Lombardní Ústav, established in 1934. The second devaluation – by 16 per cent – took place in 1936 mainly at the insistence of the Agrarian Party which wanted to make imports of agricultural products dearer. Though it was opposed by Engliš it was in fact also indispensable to the Czechoslovak export industry confronted on foreign markets with a wave of export-oriented devaluations.

Organized market support for Government borrowing and the 1936 devaluation brought to an end a deflationary policy which for fifteen years had held up economic growth and technological advance. Fearing competition, Czechoslovak industry, kept in a state of financial starvation, had turned to cartels and compulsory syndicatization so that it could by-pass the high exchange rate by export subsidies. The best known example of this was the export of sugar at a fraction of the domestic price, which the sugar cartel kept at a level high enough to compensate for the loss on exported sugar. With the exception of three years preceding the Great Depression, this restrictionist policy depended on exchange control, and on import licensing. Inefficient industry and trade were protected against newcomers by production and sales quotas imposed by cartels and syndicates with the support of the Government.

Reversal of this policy, accomplished between 1934 and 1936, took place in anticipation of another world war which seemed unavoidable in view of Hitler's aggressive expansion. The course of action which the Czech bankers ridiculed as impossible and irresponsible when claimed on behalf of the starving unemployed became suddenly acceptable when needed for the construction of fortifications and the re-equipment and expansion of the armaments industry and the allied basic and metalworking industries.

At the same time the lower exchange rate, together with a revival of the world economy and the expansion of barter trading with the clearing countries, helped to expand exports. But even here the benefits were to a considerable extent frustrated by the shadow German aggression cast ahead of its progress. Under-invoicing of exports and overpaying of imports, prompted by fear of the uncertain future, led to a substantial escape of capital. Foreign-exchange earnings also were heavily taxed by the build-up of strategic reserves of food, fuel and raw materials, as well as a stocking-up by private enterprise, stimulated by both the expectation of war and the rise in commodity prices. All these activities in the end only increased the booty of the German occupants.

The twenty years were not long enough for the achievement of a sounder balance of forces in the economy, although banking, which in 1918 was the only sector sufficiently organized to be able to use political means for its ends, was towards the end of this period challenged by the Agrarians who seemed to be far on the way to outsmarting the Živnobanka in the game of combining business and politics.

There were other, less obvious but more fundamental, changes taking place in the Czechoslovak economy which were gradually shifting the banks' control of industry from the macroeconomic to the microeconomic sphere, from the manipulation of the currency to the supervision of managements of industrial companies belonging to a bank's group.

These changes could be discerned in all sectors of the economy. In the credit sector a rapid growth of deposits in savings and cooperative banks made the Government and industry less dependent on the commercial banks. Protectionist trade policy led to a financial recovery in the agricultural sector. Large-scale industry, expanding abroad and employing large complements of organized labour, could not be ignored by the Government and could make its voice heard outside the board meetings dominated by bankers. Moreover, since the Great Depression the economy was becoming more and more dirigistic and this meant that the roles of the Government and Parliament – and their responsibility – were visible and that politicians could no longer hide behind the fetish of a high exchange rate.

Agriculture: disintegration by land reform and integration by depression

The natural and climatic conditions of Czechoslovakia call for a mixed and capital-intensive agriculture. Cultivated in the best possible way, the land could probably have provided all the food needed, but so far it had never done so – partly because of economic and technological factors not conducive to this and partly because much of the capacity was taken up by the production of industrial and export crops. The resulting food deficit was met by imports of bread grains, animal feeding stuffs, fats and meat, though the composition of this import basket varied greatly.

During the 1918–38 period 95 per cent of all land was cultivated: about a third was covered by plantations of conifers making Czechoslovakia one of Europe's foremost exporters of timber. Almost half of the cultivated land was ploughed, about one tenth was grassland for haymaking, and less than one tenth pasture. According to figures for 1930, about 60 per cent of ploughland was used for the cultivation of cereals, 17 per cent for sugarbeet and potatoes, 16.5 per cent for fodder, and the rest for specialized industrial crops and vegetables.

In the twenties Czechoslovakia was a net importer of bread grains, Europe's second-biggest exporter of sugar, after Germany, the world's most important supplier of malt and hops. In 1927, for example, agricultural imports totalled Kc4,440 million and exports Kc1,715 million. During the thirties the adverse situation on the world markets for sugar, barley, malt and oats led to a change in favour of bread grains. The Czechoslovak grain monopoly established in 1934 kept the price of bread grains well above the world market price, and as a result imports of wheat and wheat flour which in 1930 had still amounted to 290,000 and 190,000 tons respectively gradually dwindled, and by 1938 Czechoslovakia was a net exporter of wheat. Cultivation of wheat expanded not only at the expense of sugarbeet and barley but also of fodder crops. At about the same time imports of meat were curtailed in favour of imports of fats.

Sugar factories and breweries were run as industrial enterprises separate from agriculture, and so were about half of all alcohol distilleries; the other half formed part of agricultural enterprises either as distilleries on larger estates or as cooperative distilleries.

As in all other respects, the difference in the agriculture of the Czech lands and that of Slovakia (and even more so of Ruthenia) was so big that combined data and an overall discussion of their problems hardly make any sense. In the west the proportion of the population dependent fully or partly on agriculture diminished from 40 to 35 per cent between 1921 and 1930, when it still amounted to

60 per cent in Slovakia and Ruthenia. The consequences of agricultural overpopulation were multiplied by the extreme backwardness of agriculture in the east of the republic. In Bohemia and Moravia the preponderance of small and medium farms was compensated for by relatively advanced agricultural education and a network of cooperatives modelled on those of Denmark. The cooperatives served procurement of supplies and marketing of products, and a dense network of agricultural cooperative banks helped with financing production, and holding of stocks.

While the Czech scene was dominated by the medium stratum of shrewd, money-oriented farmers, in Slovakia the peasants still lived in the shadow of the feudal estate and their technology was about the level passed by the Czech lands in the middle of the nineteenth century. In Ruthenia agriculture was even more backward: medieval methods of production were not yet completely eliminated. In addition to backward production methods, lack of finance and absence of cooperative marketing, Slovakia and Ruthenia were far away from industrial regions and badly connected with them by roads and railways. Bohemia and Moravia bordered industrial Germany and Austria; Slovakia and Ruthenia were surrounded by Poland, Romania and Hungary, all countries exporting agricultural produce.

The differences between east and west of the country were matched by fundamental differences in the problems and interests of small and large farms. About a quarter of all farms in Czechoslovakia cultivated less than a hectare (2.25 acres) of land and this meant that a quarter of the population recorded as agricultural in fact relied only partly on agriculture for a living. These were the so-called 'metal-peasants', that is foundrymen and metalworkers who cultivated their little plots at weekends. A similar category were construction workers whose wives looked after the small farm, mostly alone. These small plots were, of course, of great assistance in time of unemployment. According to the 1930 census, that is after some of the expropriated aristocratic estates were distributed, still 43 per cent of all farms cultivated between two and five hectares, totalling only 14 per cent of all agricultural land. Less than 30 per cent of all farms cultivated between 10 and 50 hectares and over 40 per cent of all land was cultivated by farmers with more than 50 hectares who represented only 1 per cent of the agricultural population.

The agricultural reform which had such great political importance in the early years of the Republic did not amount to a radical re-distribution of agricultural property. Like the nostrification of banks and industrial property, it eliminated the influence mainly of German and Hungarian aristocratic landowners. The compensation they received for expropriated land enabled them to turn to industry or to re-equip their other estates. On the other hand, the price demanded from those allotted expropriated land caused an increase in agricultural indebtedness, which became heavier to bear with deflation and quite intolerable during the Great Depression. Many farmers went bankrupt and had to sell out. The most spectacular effect of the reform was in the political field, by boosting the electoral results of the Agrarian Party.

The land reform was a big political issue not only because of the peasants' hunger for land but also because it was seen as a means of weakening important enemies of the new Republic. The 150 largest estates totalled 1.46 million hectares, a tenth of the country's area. The Schwarzenberg family alone had agricultural and forestry estates totalling 248,000 hectares in south Bohemia, all under excellent management and very profitable. For the aristocratic families, the Catholic Church and the Habsburgs, the large estates were a source of economic power, and this power was hostile to the constitution of an independent Czechoslovakia, to its secular, republican character and to its domination by banks.

The landowning aristocracy was not entirely without Czech friends. Some of them, like Josef Pekař, an historian of Catholic and extremely conservative bias, came into the open immediately, claiming the economic advantage of large estates and defending the old Czech aristocracy and constitutional revivalists among the foreign families which had received land confiscated by the Habsburgs after their victory over the Czech Protestants in 1620. The argument used by Pekař in favour of the claims of children of Archduke Franz Ferdinand, the heir apparent assassinated in 1914, was based on more recent history: the supreme merit of Franz Ferdinand in Pekař's eyes was that he was an 'uncompromising reactionary' and a delcared anti-semite, comparing favourably with the other Habsburg faction represented by the earlier deceased Crown Prince Rudolph, whom Pekař accused of a tendency towards 'Jewish democratism'. Other friends and potential allies of the aristocrats remained in the

background, and proved much more useful to them than Pekař
with his innuendoes, by tuning down the law, and the extent and
pace of its application.

Even among those who agreed that the large estates should be
expropriated, there was basic disagreement about what should be
done with the land. The Social Democrats, the strongest party in the
first years of the republic, wanted to preserve the economic advantages of the large estates and nationalize them intact. This
economically sound idea pleased neither landowners nor peasants.
The Agrarian Party's proposal that land should be allocated to peasants won for the party the rural electorate, pleased the banks to
whom the peasants had to turn for money, and in addition produced
a large number of 'residual estates' for allocation to the Agrarians'
prominent supporters and friends – or as bribes to potential enemies.

The law passed in 1919 applied to all estates with more than
150 hectares of agricultural land or more than 250 hectares in total
area. There were 1,913 such estates with a total of 4 million hectares
of land: more than a quarter of the country's area was subject to
redistribution. In reality, things were not so drastic. In most cases
the law was used only to press the landowners to sell or lease the
land. More than half of the land to which the law could be applied
was exempted for various reasons or left in the possession of the
original owners for a further twenty to thirty years. Out of the 1.8
million hectares actually expropriated only 790,000 were allocated
to small farmers; about the same area was integrated with state
forests allocated to towns and communities or transformed into state
farms. There were 2,291 'residual estates' allocated mostly as political favours, comprising 226,000 hectares (usually the best land) and
the cores of the estates with buildings and equipment.

The land reform reduced the number of the tiny farms with less
than two hectares, added to the number of farms in the fifty to 100
hectares category and so slowed down the polarization of the rural
community between the practically landless peasant and the well-to-
do medium farmer. Those who acquired expropriated land on credit
had a debt totalling over Kc3,000 million. The reform probably
reduced the efficiency and productivity of Czechoslovak agriculture.
Its main achievements were the removal of aristocratic and Social
Democratic influence from rural areas and the establishment of the
Agrarian Party as the strongest political force in the country.

The first ten years after the war were a time of relative agricultural prosperity when Czechoslovak farmers could rationalize their production and re-equip and improve their living standards. This process was greatly assisted by an expansion of agricultural cooperatives. The number of cooperative credit banks, the oldest form of cooperatives initiated in the second half of the nineteenth century, increased from 4,478 in 1918 to 5,326 in 1927 and 6,075 in 1937. Other types of cooperatives concerned with procurement, marketing, rural power stations, agricultural machinery, alcohol distillation and cattle-breeding experienced an even faster expansion, from 2,088 in 1918 to 4,156 in 1927 and 5,437 in 1937.

Associations of cooperatives were financially strong trading and banking organizations, some with important industrial groups of their own. A central organization established in 1921 and dominated by the Agrarian Party embraced 90 per cent of all agricultural cooperatives and became an important basis for the grain monopoly and other dirigistic measures provoked by the Great Depression. The depression not only lasted longer in agriculture than in industry but was also accompanied by a deeper fall in prices. The index of agricultural prices fell during 1929–34 by 42 per cent, compared with a 33 per cent fall in industrial prices.

The Czechoslovak Grain Company formed in 1934 as a state monopoly for trading in grain, flour and animal feeding stuffs raised prices of wheat by 15 per cent and those of rye – used for bread in Czechoslovakia – barley and oats between 54 and 74 per cent by 1935. This led to an increase in the production of bread grains, formerly imported, beyond the point of self-sufficiency. The surplus was stockpiled, some was exported to Germany at dumping prices and the rest made unfit for human consumption and resold as fodder. Another monopolistic formation of that time, the Syndicate for Marketing of Animals and Animal Products, influenced the domestic market mainly by regulating imports.

Though the depression affected the profitability of agriculture more deeply than that of industry, the agricultural population had at least always enough to eat and for that reason was better off than the 850,000 unemployed in industry. On the other hand the economic consequences of the depression lasted longer in agriculture. Machinery and equipment was depleted, amelioration work suffered, fields were exhausted by a 50 per cent reduction in the application of fertilizers. Cattle herds were reduced and their quality lowered, particularly on small farms where dairy cows were used for traction. The total indebtedness of agriculture increased to between Kc25,000 million and Kc30,000 million and was relatively greater in small holdings under five hectares.

The total number of forced sales of mortgaged land (including non-agricultural land) increased in 1934 to 300,000 compared with a yearly average of 84,000 in 1925–7. The Great Depression thus accelerated the social polarization of rural areas which had been slowed down by the land reform. It contributed to the integration of agricultural property and the elimination of the least viable peasant holdings.

Still, the impact of the depression was cushioned by stepping up protectionist measures: first the import tariffs were introduced in 1926, increased in 1930 and finally the grain monopoly was introduced in 1934. The decisive role of the Agrarian Party assured to agriculture advantages dearly paid for by industry.

Industry

The events of 1918 changed nothing of the fact that two thirds of the industrial capacity of the former Austro-Hungarian monarchy was located in the Czech crown lands while the population of the domestic market for this industry was from one day to the next reduced by about three quarters. In terms of purchasing power the loss was substantially greater because the lost three quarters of the market included the industrialized Austria and the high-consumption centres of Vienna, Budapest and the important port of Trieste.

Czech industry could no longer hope to regain its leading position in traditional markets when soon after the war the agricultural succession states began to develop their own industry behind new tariff frontiers. This process received new impetus when the protectionist policy of the Agrarian Party provoked retaliations by Hungary (until then the most important export market for Czechoslovak timber and textiles) and to a lesser degree also by the other agricultural countries of Eastern Europe. The most urgent need of industry was to concentrate, to restructure, and to reach wider export markets.

These three objectives were pursued with uneven success: the concentration of Czechoslovak industry proceeded fast; its restructuring only haltingly; in the conquest of foreign markets it succeeded significantly only in two industries which enjoyed specially favourable conditions – armaments and footwear.

The initial phase of concentration was linked with the transfer of ownership from banks and groups based in Vienna and Budapest to mainly Czech banks by the combined effect of the nostrification law and the revaluation of the Czechoslovak currency after its separation. French, Swiss and British interests had some participation in Czech banks, particularly in the Länderbank, the Czech Escontbank and the Czech Unionbank. British shareholders had a majority in the Anglo-Czechoslovak Bank.

Foreign participation in the major industrial groups was concentrated mainly in the iron and steel industry. Almost the entire output of pig iron and over three quarters of steel and rolled materials were produced by three companies which also had an important share in the mining of coking coal. Vítkovice Iron Works, the largest of the three and one of the world's principal exporters of large castings, was owned by the Viennese Rothschilds who in 1937 sold it to Alliance Assurance of London. Three quarters of the equity in Báňská a Hutní (Mining and Foundry), a producer of high-grade steels, was owned by French, British and United States companies. In the third, the Prague Iron Company, 27 per cent of the equity was owned by shareholders in Germany.

Chomutov Tube Works was controlled by the German Mannesmann Werke. Schneider-Creusot, the French heavy engineering group, had a majority interest in Skoda Works, the largest engineering and armaments enterprise. Large electrical engineering industry was linked with German companies, mainly A.E.G. and Siemens-Halske, but also with Philips and British and United States interests. I.C.I. and Solvey (Belgian), as well as French and German companies, had a stake in the chemical industry, and the Schicht margarine and soap factories were part of the Unilever group.

Throughout the period 1918–38, Czech banks increased their control of industry by the acquisition of equity. This concentration was supplemented by cartel agreements, both domestic and international, and in later years by government-sponsored syndicalization. Take-over activity assumed a new and ominous significance in the last years before Munich: the shape of things to come could be guessed when French and British companies started selling their interests to German banks, and the ominous significance of this was confirmed when German banks, using Czechoslovak banks as their agents, began buying up Jewish-owned industry heralding thus the approach of the Munich agreement.

Compared with industry in the Czech lands, Slovak industry was at a disadvantage for several reasons. The return to peacetime economic conditions in Slovakia started only after the Hungarian Red Army had been pushed out in 1920 – and an agreement concerning the nostrification of enterprise owned by Hungarian residents was concluded with Hungary only in 1927. By 1924, of fifty-one enterprises to which the nostrification law applied only three had established their headquarters in Slovakia. The process was much faster in the Czech part of the country where a similar agreement with Austria had been in force since 1920. Altogether 235 industrial enterprises and seventeen companies operating local railways transferred their headquarters to Czechoslovakia.

Because of Slovakia's very low industrial density, the isolation of Slovakian enterprises from their links across the new borders could not easily be overcome. Industrial development was also held back by the low purchasing power of the local market, the scarcity of capital, and bad and costly transport to the western part of the newly formed country. On top of this many technicians, railway personnel and administrators emigrated from Slovakia to Hungary, so that in business, transport and public administration it was often a question of a fresh start. The result of all this was not only the much slower development of new industry but even the emigration of some existing enterprises, particularly textile, to Hungary. Only towards the end of the twenty years did the building of armaments factories in Slovakia and a nucleus of chemical and petrochemical industry in Bratislava bring new hopes for the future.

The textile industry of Bohemia and Moravia was also pruned during the first post-war years of some of its machinery which was used for equipping new factories in the other succession states, but the effect of this was not as negative as in Slovakia. While economically obsolete factories were being dismantled new factories were being opened and some at least of the textile factories were re-equipped with more advanced machinery. Re-equipment was facilitated by the 1920–21 slump in world prices of raw materials and further accelerated by the overvaluation of the new currency which favoured imports of machinery and raw materials while between one fifth and one half of investment costs could be claimed as a tax allowance.

The re-equipment of the textile, glass, china and furniture industries aimed at increasing the proportion of high-grade products saleable in the western markets. The greatest investment activity, however, was directed towards the expansion of engineering (particularly in the field of machine tools and automotive and aircraft production) and of the leatherworking industry.

Pre-1914 engineering included mainly sugar factories and distilleries as well as certain heavy engineering products of Vítkovice and Skoda. Exports of armaments greatly expanded after 1918 – partly, of course, because the capacities used for the former Austro–Hungarian army became available for the national armies of the succession states. Later on, Czechoslovakia began exporting armaments factories, particularly for small arms. Vítkovice, Skoda, Mining and Foundry Company, Brno Armament Works and Českomoravská Kolben a Daněk (C.K.D.) were the main exporters of capital goods and the main investors abroad. In the later years of the republic they were in this respect overshadowed by Bata, whose shoe factories started mushrooming throughout the world and formed important clusters in Britain, Canada, Brazil and India.

The growth of the world's largest footwear group within the span of twenty years is one of the most interesting chapters of the economic history of Czechoslovakia and throws a sharp light on the wealth of skill and entrepreneurial talent which was not given the same scope in other fields. The growth of Bata was made possible by an accumulation of capital during the war and resulting independence from the banks, and was further stimulated in the post-war years by a hungry domestic market for which little was left over during the war after the satisfaction of military needs. Moreover, the Government's monetary policy made imported leather cheap.

By its virtue of central location, Bata was a more truly Czechoslovak enterprise than any other: Zlín (now Gottwaldov) is in eastern Moravia, almost on the Slovakian frontier. It was modelled on large-scale industry in the United States and in this way paralleled in the economic field the political and ideological affinity of the new regime with democratic, liberal and meritocratic America.

Tomáš Baťa, the founder of this great enterprise which influenced the national climate not only through its economic impact but also through its spirit, admired by some and detested by many, started before the war as a small manufacturer mainly producing cloth slippers. During the 1914–18 war he became one of the principal suppliers of boots to the imperial army.

Zlín, at that time a small provincial town, is situated in the centre of a hilly region which suffered from agricultural overpopulation. There was practically no limit to the cheap labour which Bata could draw from the surrounding villages. The novel approach leading to his explosive growth consisted in refraining from doing the obvious, namely using cheap labour instead of investing in machinery and profiting from the relatively high price of footwear dictated by the prevalence of small-scale enterprise. Contrary to the management philosophy of the day, Bata decided to combine the advantage of cheap labour with the utmost mechanization of production and advanced management methods and to cut prices drastically, selling through his own newly formed chain of retail shops – the first chain in the country. He sold at a fraction of the prices asked by other manufacturers and thus opened up a vast untapped market, first at home and then abroad. Offering a good-value utility product, he aimed at the customers who had before walked barefoot.

The main features of Tomáš Baťa's character were an absence of prejudice and a great ability to learn, not only systematically but also from chance encounters: he once paid a sizeable sum of money to the author's father because, he said, 'his conversation gave me a certain idea' – he never disclosed what it was. He also encouraged his employees to learn from experience. His 'young men', the management trainees, started by spending time as machine hands in the production departments and then had to work their way up as shop assistants.

Baťa was also a stubborn man and in the end paid for it with his life when he overruled his pilot's objections and made him take off in weather too bad for his small executive aircraft. But although domineering, he based the organization of his enterprise on a far-reaching devolution of decision-making and decentralization of profit accounts. Each department head operated his unit as a separate accounting enterprise and his personal account was credited with the profits and debited with the losses of the department. And the employees could and did spend most of what they earned in Bata's shops and on the company's houses.

However, Bata Works revealed to the Czechs and Slovaks not only the great possibilities inherent in the industrial mode of production but also some of the ugly aspects of the industrial mode of life. Bata's employees were better paid than their neighbours, had the benefits of belonging to an expanding enterprise, were either well housed in Zlín or brought from the countryside by factory coach. But they paid for all this by having the rhythm of their life dictated by the conveyor belt and by a certain loss of freedom.

Arriving in Zlín, even entering any of the retail shops, one became immediately aware of the intensive indoctrination to which employees were exposed. Baťa's slogans, facing the workers from the walls and on streamers, and repeated by the house press and factory loudspeakers, were concerned with everything, from service to the customer to the personal behaviour of a model young man. The model young man was to marry early and buy and furnish a house on credit provided by the works, thus bonding his attachment to the employer. Baťa's sister was in charge of a department which freely spied on the private lives of employees and if two young people on the payroll were discovered dating they were likely to be summoned and told to marry or quit. Radical political views were not favoured by the management either, and independent trade unions were unthinkable under the conditions prevailing in Zlín, where the town hall was just another department of Bata headquarters.

The totalitarian aspect of the Bata works was rightly criticized, though the reasons prompting the critics differed greatly. The small shoemakers who were put out of business first were later joined by small-scale manufacturers who had the choice of selling to Bata or closing down. Trade unionists saw in Zlín a dangerous precedent which might ultimately put labour at the mercy of employers; and liberal intellectuals were alarmed at the wider implications of the hard pursuit of profit, the lack of grace in a life where rich village traditions and art were being replaced by ugly slogans on the walls. They also feared the political aspirations which they believed they sensed in Tomáš Baťa's younger brother who took over after the founder's death.

But the most vociferous critics of the Bata system were the Communists: Baťa was doing what they planned to do themselves. When they took over in 1948 the slogans, the trade unions subservient to management, and the spying became general. Unfortunately, the Czechoslovak Communists were obliged by Moscow to scrap their first system of industrial accounting, modelled on the Bata system of departmental profit centres, and so in a way they turned the whole country into a Bataland from which only the productivity and profitability of the Bata system was banished.

An egalitarian culture

In the 1918–38 period Czechoslovakia differed from most countries
by an exceptionally wide spread of cultural activities. Gymnastics
and sports, reading, theatre-going and good music were enjoyed not
by the few but by a very large part of the entire population. The
egalitarian system of general education instituted under Joseph II
enabled the nineteenth-century patriots to make Czech books available to the widest possible readerhip and enrol the greatest number
in patriotic gymnastic organizations. This development was intensified after 1918 by the new establishment which President Masaryk
impregnated with life-long interest in education. The more conventional literary output, of course, had the widest impact, for
broadcasting, the cinema and commercialized sport only began to
encroach on traditional entertainments during the thirties. On the
whole the quality of life offered much to all who had a steady job,
even if it provided only a modest income. The only aspect of life for
which the cultural standard could not compensate was the insecurity and hardship generated by the two protracted periods of unemployment.

The homogeneous society was largely the product of a system of
uniform state schools for all children up to the age of eleven. School
attendance was obligatory from six to fourteen years of age but
differentiation, in which talent and interest played a greater role
than income, started after the first five years of the primary school.
There was no streaming but one or two pupils of each class were
often left behind to repeat the whole year with younger children. In
isolated villages the local school would cover the entire obligatory
period from six to fourteen but in bigger centres all children not

enrolled in grammar schools moved into a high school after passing out of the fifth class of the primary school. In 1934–5 in a population of about 14.5 million there were 2.4 million children attending primary and high schools. In 13,672 schools the teaching was in Czech or Slovak, in 4,408 German, in 856 Hungarian, in 602 Ukrainian and in 167 Polish. Children who did very well at the primary (or high) school could sit for an entrance examination to one of the 695 technical colleges preparing for lower managerial levels in industry and agriculture. In 1934–5 the number of students enrolled was 90,000.

Those who wanted to remain at school till eighteen or nineteen, and passed an entrance examination, could go, at the age of eleven, to a grammar school, of which there were three types. A Gymnasium (8 years) prepared for university; a Realka (7 years) led to technical university. The third type was a Real-Gymnasium (8 years), halfway between the two basic types. These secondary schools continued the tradition of the monastic 'Latin' schools, though all were now state schools, with uniform curricula of three types all leading to 'matriculation'. In 1934–5 there were 345 such secondary schools with 136,000 students of whom some dropped out after the first four years at the age of fourteen, often to transfer to a technical college. Most continued for the full seven or eight years. Since the secondary schools were the gateway to university and thus to leading positions in the civil service and large-scale business, their distribution according to language was of political importance: in 247 of the secondary schools teaching was either Czech or Slovak, in 83 it was German, in 8 Ukrainian, in 6 Hungarian and in 1 Polish.

There were a Czech and a German university in Prague, both originating from the Charles University founded in 1348 and taken over by the Jesuits after 1620; a Czech university in Brno; and a Slovak university in Bratislava. Prague and Brno each had two technical universities, one Czech and the other German, and there were three other university-level schools, one for art, another for music and a third for drama, all located in Prague.

All primary and high schools were completely free, and a large number of pupils obtained free textbooks and other material help. Fees required from students at secondary schools, technical colleges and universities were relatively low when compared to incomes (all schools were non-residential), but even so students who made good progress could have the fees waived provided their parents' income did not exceed a certain limit. The same criterion applied to the allocation of rooms in university hostels to students whose parents did not live in one of the university towns.

Gymnastics, including some sport, were usually allocated only two hours weekly at Czechoslovak primary and secondary schools and were not really a part of university life. Most of these activities took place outside school. By 1935 Sokol, the patriotic organization of gymnasts formed on the model of the German gymnastic associations, the 'Turnervereins' in the second half of the nineteenth century, had 760,000 members from the age of six upward, and halls and sports grounds in nearly every village. A similar Catholic organization, Orel, numbered 160,000, while the Social Democratic Workers' Gymnastic Unions had 142,000 members. The Communist Federation of Workers' Gymnastic Unions had a somewhat smaller membership. All these organizations periodically held national festivals; those of Sokol were occasions for pilgrimage to Prague not only from all over the country but also by Czechs living abroad, including many Americans of Czech and Slovak descent.

One of the consequences of a uniform educational system was that people of all classes and occupations spoke the same language and such small differences in pronunciation and dialect as existed were purely regional. Another was that by the age of fourteen everyone was familiar with the landmarks of his country's history and literature, as well as with an outline of European geography and history, and received an introduction into the sciences. Such comprehensive general education not only provided for adaptability to changing industrial skills but was also a good basis for appreciating books. Many people acquired a reading habit before they left school (always provided with a lending library) and still more could turn to books at a later stage in life.

Writers and poets spearheading literary development tended, of course, to appeal only to an intellectual élite; Franz Kafka certainly was not for everyone. The brothers Karel and Josef Čapek had a large readership but spoke mainly to the better-educated stratum, while Jaroslav Hašek, author of *The Good Soldier Švejk*, had popular appeal. Schoolchildren usually started with *The Grandmother*, the classic by Božena Nemcová, and the historical novels of Alois Jirásek, which were well written and some of which had a considerable charm. Translations of Karl May's books on Red Indians and of Jules Verne's science-fiction, both vehicles for a high code of honour, were next on the list. The older generation delighted in sentimental and cruel historical novels by Třebizský, and in rural districts preferred authors were Jan Vrba and J. S. Baar, the latter a parish priest in one of the Chod villages near Domažlice where most of his novels are located. Another writer of the lighter genre was J. S. Maria, the pen-name of a provincial judge who delighted in writing scandalous novels about living personalities only slightly disguised.

Humour stood very high on everyone's list, starting with Jan Neruda's *Small Town Stories* and continuing with *The Good Soldier Švejk*, all the tragi-comic works of Karel Poláček, and finally the memoirs of Eskymo Welzl, a Czech who became an Eskimo chieftain (recognizing the sovereignty of both the United States and the Soviet Union in order to get double medical supplies). His rambling reminiscences full of racy popular humour were written down by Rudolf Těsnohlidek, whose other books provided the libretti to Janáček's operas. When Těsnohlidek died Eduard Golombek and Jaroslav Valenta continued filling Welzl's glass and writing down his memoirs.

Czech literature of the twenties and thirties can hardly be understood without realizing the important place occupied by the translation of prose, poetry and plays, which during this period developed into a great art of its own. Otakar Fischer, professor of German literature at the Charles University, was probably the greatest of all Prague translators, and that comes very nearly to the assertion that he was unsurpassed anywhere else. Completely bilingual, the great germanists of the Prague University, Fischer, Arnošt Kraus and Pavel Eisner were highly perceptive of the unique onomatopaeic quality of the Czech language which is capable of sounds of extreme hardness as in 'tvrz' (a fortress) and of airy loftiness when using for 'temple' the long soft sound of 'chrám'. *Tvrz a Chrám* is the title of a book by Eisner, a German Jew in love with the Czech language.

Otakar Fischer, who educated a generation of Prague germanists, produced a new translation of the works of Goethe, and Karel Čapek was one of the many who translated modern French poetry. Translations from English contemporary literature filled entire editions.

Several publishers forming the financial backbone of the literary expansion also have their place in Czech literary history. Some of them had political links. Melantrich, for example, belonged to the National Socialists, Beneš's party. Borový was closely associated with the small but intellectually significant, liberal Labour Party headed by Adolf Stránsky and another Castle party. Topič was an old-established private publisher, very selective, with a tradition of fine production. Aventinum, by contrast, was a new and courageous venture of Storch-Marien, a publisher whose literary ambitions unfortunately exceeded the potential of the small market. It was he who published the first books of the Čapeks and encouraged a whole generation of young writers – and painters, for whom he provided a gallery. He started an excellent and lively literary magazine on the model of the French *Marianne*, and had a great success with his Standard Library of contemporary English novels; but he lost all his money when he started a long and expensive series of such works as *Geography of the World*. He ended after the war as an assistant in a second-hand bookshop in Prague. Orbis was a government controlled publishing house which specialized in textbooks and officially-sponsored publications. Florian was a small country publisher of rare and esoteric books – he was the first to publish Kafka; at the other end of the scale was Kočí, a large house producing cheap books.

An important feature of the Czechoslovak scene between the two wars – and one which made it very different from the Anglo-Saxon world – was the absence of a dividing line between literature and journalism. Some of the best Czech writers of the past, Neruda and Havlíček, for example, had seen themselves primarily as journalists and contributed much to the development of *Národní Listy*, by 1918 a great national newspaper. Unfortunately, though many excellent writers remained on its staff, including the poet Victor Dyk, the paper suffered by being attached to Kramář's increasingly embittered nationalist opposition to the Castle.

The distinction of literary excellence gradually passed to *Lidové Noviny*, originally published in Brno by Adolf Stranský and later transferred to Borový in Prague. Eduard Bass, the paper's editor, and a distingushed writer and wit, gathered round him some of the best writers of the period. Karel Čapek, Karel Poláček, Rudolf Těsnohlidek, Ferdinand Peroutka were all staff members for many years, and leading academics, sociologists, economists and art critics were regular contributors.

Of the other two national newspapers of quality, *Prager Presse*, a German-language daily, was sponsored by the Ministry of Foreign Affairs and reflected its views. It had an outstanding literary supplement where many authors who fell into disgrace with the Nazis found refuge. The other German newspaper of distinction was *Prager Tagblatt*, the only independent newspaper apart from the Czech *Politika*. *Politika*, the main vehicle for classified advertisements, was dull, local, and conservative in outlook. *Prager Tagblatt* had extensive foreign affairs coverage and quite a number of Jewish journalists on its staff. It was liberal in outlook and much concerned with economics and business.

Some of the dailies also had separate evening papers, of which the most widely read was the *Večerní České Slovo*. But when Jiří Stříbrný moved to the extreme right and started to publish an evening paper full of scandals and sensations the Left answered with a parody published under the name *Přišerný Večerník* (The Ghostly Evening News).

No picture of Czechoslovak life in 1918–39 can be complete without brief reference to its theatre and music. Commercial theatres were the exception. At the centre the National Theatre operated on a Government grant and showed a wide repertory of plays and operas on three stages: in the National Theatre proper, in the old Theatre of the Estates, and in the Chamber Theatre. The Vinohradské was financed by the city of Prague; an excellent German Theatre, also subsidized by the Government, had a second stage in the Kleine Bühne. Of the smaller theatres, those lasting long enough to establish theatrical traditions of their own included that of an excellent comedian and entertainer, Václav Burian, and the Communist *avant-garde* theatre of E. F. Burian. At the Liberated Theatre Jiří Voskovec and Jan Werich, authors of a long series of intellectual musical reviews in which they played, sang and quarrelled as two inseparable clowns, were the darlings of the left-wing youth and became the embodiment of a witty and courageous stand against the advance of Fascism and Nazism. There were also between ten and fifteen provincial theatres, some with ensembles of their own and others relying on visiting troupes.

Jaroslav Ježek, who wrote and conducted the music of Voskovec and Werich, was a great master of traditional jazz, but most composers followed in the steps of the nineteenth-century Czech musicians. The line from Dvořák leads to Josef Suk and Vitězslav Novák; Janáček made music still within the conventional compass, though only just. More advanced forms and experiments are connected with the names of Alois Hába, Bedřich Vycpálek and Karel Reiner.

There were three great conductors, Karel Talich, who shaped the Czech Philharmonic Orchestra, Karel Ančerl, the musical director of the National Theatre, and Georg Szell, of the German Theatre. Karel Kubelík, the violinist (father of Rafael Kubelík, the conductor), and Jarmila Novotná, later prima donna of the Metropolitan Opera in New York, are only two names out of many outstanding singers and performers of the period.

There were excellent choirs, notably the Prague and the Moravian Teachers' choirs. But more important, in this period the Czechs and Slovaks were still a singing people.

The terror of the utilitarian society

During the last fifty years of the Habsburg monarchy Czech politicians were engaged in obtaining concessions from Vienna step by step; it was left mainly to writers and artists to keep the flame of a more radical nationalist spirit alive. The establishment of independence in 1918 relieved them of this self-imposed duty. The 'resurrection' of the Czech nation now seemed complete and Masaryk believed, at the time he wrote his *Czech Question*, that the world expected from the reborn nation an important message. If the Czechs did not deliver that message they would soon be forgotten again, and Masaryk had probably not been alone in fearing this. However, things when they happen always differ from expectations: the message when delivered did not concern the problems of small nations but the much more fundamental problem of man's survival in an industrial society; far from being eagerly received the prophecy passed unnoticed and its significance began to be grasped only after the Czechs were sold down the river, first to Hitler and then to Stalin, the two extreme protagonists of a utilitarian society.

Another unexpected development was that the Czech renaissance also deeply affected the German population, so that the Prague German writers were nearer to Czech thought than to the main stream of contemporary German literature. Indeed, there was a single bilingual literary movement in the western parts of the country in the twenties and thirties. Slovak literature, on the contrary, was linguistically near to the Czech but very different in spirit because it was the product of a different historical stage. Czech and Slovak were at that time officially held to be but two dialects of a single language. But throughout the 1918–38 period Slovak writers remained apart and the influence of Russian literature was as strong on them then as it had been on Czech writing before 1848. The Russian problems of an intelligentsia emerging from a rural and feudal substratum had an affinity with the situation the Slovaks experienced after 1918. In Bohemia and Moravia the common experience of alienation and bureaucratic rule, provided by fast industrialization, seemed to overshadow the divisiveness of language. Since all educated Czechs of that period read German, and most of the German writers living among them read and spoke Czech, even the literary influences which reached the two groups from outside did not differ very much.

This bilingual literary culture was the product of a relatively recent development. Only a hundred years earlier the German writers of Bohemia had the advantage of an accomplished literary language while the Czechs had the impetus of the cultural minority trying to revive the forgotten literary glory attained in the sixteenth century. By 1918 the Czech language was once again a perfect tool for literary expression, but this time the Germans were a cultural minority and displayed the alertness which goes with it.

The ethnic profile of the Prague-centred literary output would not be complete without reference to the contribution made by Jewish writers, either German or Czech, whose distinction as a separate group became necessary with the advent of Nazism. The Jews, who had lived in Bohemia and Moravia since the tenth century and were released from the ghettos at the end of the eighteenth century, contributed to both cultures of the country.

In the nineteenth century the Jews of Bohemia and Moravia began to be integrated with the Czech and the German communities. Some were drawn to the great cultural centre of late nineteenth-century Vienna, and like Sigmund Freud and Gustav Mahler reached their fame there, never to return. Some of the greatest Czech writers were of Jewish origin, including Richard Weiner,

Ignat Herrmann, Vojtěch Rakous, Karel Poláček, Otaker Fischer, Pavel Eisner, Hostovský, Josef Orten and Hanuš Bonn. These regarded themselves as Czechs and until the rise of Nazism were little aware of their Jewishness. Those writing in German, including Franz Kafka, Max Brod, Franz Werfel, Utitz, and Egon Ervin Kisch, were in a different position: even before Hitler, the antisemitism within the German community of Prague made the integration of Jews problematic, and afterwards impossible.

Jews belonging to the German cultural circle of Prague were a minority in a double sense and this perhaps more than anything explains the extraordinary sensitivity which they displayed. In Franz Kafka they were the first to express, in a surrealistic form, the anguish of modern man. But it was not long before – in the early twenties – the same theme of the small man facing a soulless power was treated in Czech and in a quite different style (and with a greater contemporary impact) by Jaroslav Hašek, in *The Good Soldier Švejk*. Soon afterwards the nightmare of the utilitarian society took the form of science-fiction drama like Karel Čapek's *R.U.R.* (Reason's Universal Robots) and his *Life of the Insects*.

These three, and many others, wrote about a non-hero, the small man, a plebeian individual in a classless society. Czech society is reflected in its literature as composed of small farmers, craftsmen, shopkeepers and petty officials. Bankers and industrialists gained social importance only after 1918. There was too little time for writers to take account of this new social factor. The instinctive exclusion of the 'upper-middle-class' – if such a British term can be applied at all – from Czech society can be seen in the frequent use of German names for any of its members in Czech novels or plays. Tomáš Baťa, the entrepreneur extraordinary, was an exception, a solitary giant, rather than a social type. Only František Langer in his play *Angels Among Us* included a scene in which he is confronted with a small shoemaker deprived of his livelihood by the expansion of Bata's factories. A banker and a captain of industry make a not altogether convincing appearance in Karel Čapek's novel—*The Factory for the Absolute* the Czech meritocracy did not have time to gain literary recognition.

Kafka's Mr K. is quite obviously the small man, one of the many well-educated young officials with a law degree and a sensitive conscience and without aspiration to power or wealth. He is gradually crushed by the feeling of guilt produced by a split in personality typical of bureaucrats: as a cog in the social machine he has to treat his fellow creatures as objects while identifying with them as a private individual. As a lawyer on the staff of a social security and insurance corporation, Franz Kafka signed František Kafka and used to pay lawyers out of his own pocket to fight claims which in his official capacity he had had to reject.

The conflict between bureaucratic machinery and the conscience was treated differently by Jaroslav Hašek, whose way of life was pub-crawling. His Švejk has no need of conscience because he cannot decide anything anyway, and cannot afford the luxury of truthfulness and decency if he wants to survive. The foul-mouthed joviality of Švejk, who says 'Yessir' to his officers and kicks them in the pants every time they turn away, contrasts sharply with the suspense of Mr K.'s ghostly trial. But there is less hope in Hašek's nihilism than in Kafka's soul-searching, and the ready acceptance of Švejk as a national prototype was a terrifying experience.

By their metaphoric quality both Kafka and Hašek have a greater emotional impact than Karel Čapek but it is his play *R.U.R.* which provides an explicit statement of the problem. With a lucidity that in the hands of a lesser playwright would be bound to kill all dramatic effect, the problem treated by Kafka and Hašek is defined in *R.U.R.* as the irreconcilable contradiction between life and the utilitarian industrial society. Mr Rossum (the name sounds to a Czech like 'Mr Reason') produces robots better equipped for their tasks than the human beings they resemble entirely but for the inability to feel pain, fear and love. When worn out and no longer useful as labour they are scrapped like motor cars, like some twenty years later the Jews in Auschwitz. But nature has its revenge: in the world of plenty created by the robots the idle humans cease to have children and, applying the same criterion of utility, the robots revolt and exterminate the humans as no longer useful; only the kind-hearted architect of Rossum's factory is spared, and is employed by the robots to rediscover the secret formula by which they can be reproduced. He does not succeed, but the sensation of pain built into a couple of experimental robots as an accident-prevention device leads them to love and makes them human. Thus in the midst of a decaying utilitarian industrial civilization, new life is created by pain and love.

The pastime of doomsday-watching was not known in the twenties when Čapek wrote *R.U.R.*; nor nuclear energy, which figures in his other novels, or the media and public-relations effect, depicted in his *War with the Salamanders*. The evils of social power-structures were recognized but it was not yet evident that the good they do is self-defeating. Kafka, Hašek and Čapek, and to a lesser degree many other writers in Bohemia and Moravia, detected the modern malaise with remarkable foresight. Čapek's first novel, *The Krakatit*, is about a young engineer knocked out by his own atomic super-explosive into a coma in which he proceeds through erotic and anguished dreams to God. Another novel, *The Factory for the Absolute*, is about nuclear reactors generating in people saintly and fanatical attitudes causing society to disintegrate. But towards the end, when the Nazi threat was imminent, Čapek turned from distant to nearer dangers: in *White Disease* a humanitarian Jewish physician refuses to treat the Dictator unless he gives up war; in *Mother* a deeply pacifist war-widow ends by sending her last surviving son to defend his country.

Karel Čapek worked closely with his brother Josef, a writer of philosophical inclinations, but primarily a painter of brightly coloured canvases peopled by children and women. His geometric, often triangular, compositions bear the mark of Cubism without losing any human warmth and truth. Karel Čapek, though principally a writer, journalist and dramatist, was also an accomplished and witty illustrator of his travelogues (the *Letters from England* were the most widely read, and generated affection for Britain), of his *Gardener's Year*, of his book about his wire-terrier Dášenka and his contemporary fairy tales. He was a master of the short story, some presenting metaphysical mysteries clad in the garment of ordinary life, others using psychological insight to solve commonplace criminal problems.

The loneliness of modern man and deep psychological analysis, rather than the portrayal of society, are the main features of his three novels. *Hordubal* is about a Yugoslav farmer returning home from abroad, *Meteor* about a crashed pilot in a hospital where he has arrived from nowhere with a complete loss of memory, and *Ordinary Life* about a man who has never left his home and wife and unexciting employment but carries on four extraordinary lives in his sleepless nights.

Indeed, the remarkable lives of the ordinary Czech, a man lost at the crossroads between the farm, the factory and the small town, is the main theme of Czech literature of the first half of the twentieth century. In this respect Kafka, Hašek and Čapek were preceded by great humorists, Ignat Herrmann whose Kondelík became a Czech petit-bourgeois prototype, and Vojtěch Rakous, whose Modche and Rezi are portraits, painted with a mixture of love and ridicule, of a Jewish couple running a village shop. The grandsons of Jan Neruda's heroes and the sons of Hermann's anti-heroes are the shopkeepers, salesmen, officials, football fans and young men in the trenches, in the satirical writings of Karel Poláček.

Hašek, Čapek, Poláček – in that gradation – were past masters in manipulating the cliché, which is the petit-bourgeois's armour, sword and shield and for that reason much of their writing is difficult, almost impossible, to translate. By exposing the emptiness of the cliché these humorous and satirical writings, no less than Kafka's *Trial* and Čapek's *R.U.R.*, expose the conformist's slide into the abyss of the utilitarian society.

Art and creed

The warning of the terrors of the utilitarian society was delivered too soon and either not heard at all or misunderstood. The poor, whose numbers were swollen by unemployment, were deprived of the basic necessities of life even in the richest countries and were dying in their millions of starvation in the less fortunate parts of the world. No wonder that Communists and capitalists alike identified progress and mankind's glorious future with economic growth.

It was at this time that Lenin wrote that Communism is Soviet power plus electrification, and the Czech Communist poets took him at his word. Vitězslav Nezval, a master of the poetic language but much too conformist to be a really great poet, gained fame by a glorification of Thomas Alva Edison, the inventor of incandescent electric light; the poem pleased those intoxicated with the American dream no less than the author's Communist friends. Jiří Wolker, another, but more genuine Communist poet, died so young that only a few of his promising works transcend pubertal moods; but one which does is a ballad on the power-station stoker. S. K. Neumann, Jiří Mahen and Konstantin Biebel were other prominent members of the Communist literary group of nine called Devětsil.

In those early years Communists were fairly free to entertain all sorts of ideas and styles. *We*, by Zamiatin, a Russian Communist, whose writings are now supressed in the Soviet Union, was a utopian novel attacking Communist utilitarianism with great force and art and it was translated and widely read in the Prague of those days; nor were Communist editors shy of publishing Milena Jesenská's translations from Kafka's novels in their magazines.

Stalinist conformism and Zhdanov's literary dictatorship came only late, after the Czechoslovak Communist Party entirely lost its independence. Both Kafka and Čapek were then placed on the Communist *Index of forbidden books*. Even so some real poets, like Josef Hora, survived in the Party and Vitězslav Nezval thrived in it, always ready to be just a melodic sounding-board resounding whatever vibration reached him: the nostalgia of Manon Lescaut, the nation's grief on the death of Masaryk, revolutionary fervour. But when the time came for him to produce an adulation of Stalin, it turned out that poetry can accommodate foolishness only as long as it is sincere: Nezval, by then in an almost constant state of alcoholic intoxication, had to discard the metaphoric language of which he was such a master and turn to the method of the nursery rhyme.

The lack of a genuine social ethos in the Communist Party was even more clearly reflected by the Party's inability to influence the writings of two of its prominent members who were also great masters of Czech prose. The greater of the two is probably Ivan Olbracht, descendant of a literary family, a narrator with a supremely musical language who always remained close to reality and homeliness. His characters are of the same breed as those of Karel Čapek and Poláček, although they are often cast under the more tragic sky of Ruthenia where Jewish tailors aspire to saintliness and young robbers to revolutionary heroism. Both are no less opposed to the utilitarian society than Kafka's Mr K., Hašek's Švejk or Čapek's architect.

The other great Communist writer, Vladislav Vančura, applied his rich, intentionally jarring and archaic language to cruel medieval stories. A physician by profession, he looked back rather than forward, and in his preoccupation with the past and a more brutal society he was nearer to the Catholic Jaroslav Durich and was probably more baroque in his style than any of those who politically stood far to the right of him.

The distance between Olbracht and Vančura indicates that, in spite of what the writers themselves tended to believe, the dividing line running through the cultural life centred on Prague had little to do with the contemporary political creeds. It rather divided those who were constrained by allegiance or opposition to a creed, be it Catholicism, patriotism, Communism, from those who were inwardly free. For these it was easier to take advantage of the sadly privileged position on the European crossroads, halfway between north and south, halfway between east and west, to sense the contradictions of an industrial society which run deeper than ethnic or party-political divisions.

If Czech prose and theatre rang most true when treating the fear of lonely man in an alienated society, the painters' and poets' safest inspiration was the countryside of their childhood, the paradise lost to those who flock to cities in the pursuit of industrial growth. The Czech countryside emerges with the same painful loveliness from the canvases of painters so different as the impressionist Antonín Slavíček and the almost academic Kavan, the realistic Rabas and the surrealist Antonín Zrzavý, the lyrical Josef Kerhart and Josef Filla, rationally composing his abstract paintings, and provides the religious visions painted by Josef Konůpek with a remarkable credibility. With the power of a beloved, the landscape gets the better of the pubertal mannerism of Wolker and the political doctrines of S. K. Neumann. But it is kept out of the splendid artefacts of Vitězslav Nezval.

While Slovakia is bigotedly Catholic and Moravia sincerely so, Bohemia is Catholic only in name. In Bohemia almost everybody was Catholic but only a small minority attached any importance to it. Catholicism was on the defensive because the Roman Church was seen as an historical adversary. This feeling became much more overt after 1918 and though a *modus vivendi* was later concluded with the Vatican, the troubles caused by the Slovak Catholic Party tended to stress the antagonism. It is against this background that the religiously oriented literature must be set to understand its function of a spiritual opposition.

For this reason Durich's *Wallenstein* (Bloudění) is conceived as an historical novel in defence of the Church engaged in the post-1620 repression of the Protestants. In a country where 1620 meant loss of independence, such attitudes led to the isolation of the Catholic intellectuals and to a spiritual élitism evident in the fragile mystique of Durich's erotic prose. The same religious eroticism is more clearly evident in the poems of Rainer Maria Rilke, one of the Prague German writers – a spiritual playboy whose intense longing for God was another way of rejecting the utilitarian society. The Czech parallel to the aristocratic, refined and somewhat sickly Rilke is Otokar Březina who, isolated in the country, waved God's flag single-handed in dithyrambic and ecstatic poems of rare quality, full of baroque passions but lacking Rilke's more subtle mysticism.

Franz Werfel, another Prague German writer, had already revealed a sympathetic understanding for religion in *Forty Days on Mussa Dag*, an epic of Armenian villagers besieged by genocidal Turks after the First World War, a theme close to him through Jewish and Czech associations. Werfel's religious affinities, however, came into full blossom only in his *Song of Bernadette*, a novel of the saint of Lourdes written in thanksgiving for his salvation from the Nazis during the war.

Modern spiritual Catholicism had a great attraction for the intellectual Prague Jew to whom his own religion seemed petrified and Protestantism suspect of utilitarian rationalism. Conversions were frequent – though more often brought about by a mixed marriage than by conviction. One of the outstanding Catholic archbishops of Olomouc, elected in opposition to a Habsburg candidate, was Josef Kohn and for the best part of the 1918–38 period the intellectual leader of the Czech Catholics was a Prague Jew, Alfred Fuchs, a philosopher who enjoyed the confidence of both the Castle and the Vatican, which conferred on him the title of Papal Chamberlain.

In Bohemia and Moravia the integration of the Jews – 'assimilation' was the term used – was a natural result of their dispersal in villages and small towns. As soon as the progress of urbanization made a reversal of this trend possible, assimilation became a programme opposed first to segregation, later to assimilation into the German cultural sphere, and finally to Zionism. Provided with a political ideology by Josef Kapper, and until 1917 promoted in day-to-day politics by Mořic Steindler, farmer, chairman of the Jewish community in Benešov near Prague and member of the Regional Diet of

Bohemia for the Young Czechs, the movement soon developed a literary side with the publication of a Czech–Jewish year book. Its spiritual leader during the 1918–38 period, Jindřich Kohn, advocate and philosopher, attempted to give the movement a wider validity by claiming that Jews were neither a race, a nation nor a religious community but a multinational clan.

The literary offshoots of the movement, however, reached their highest levels of achievement in the shadow of Nazi advance which forced on many a new awareness of their Jewishness. From this Czech–Jewish background came Egon Hostovský, a promising novel-ist who in the late thirties became a leading member of a new generation more introverted than their patriotic, Communist or Catholic predecessors. It included Čep, Slavík, Hrubín and František Halas. Many of them published their first attempts in the *Student Magazine,* edited by grammar school boys and girls.

This literary generation of the late thirties eagerly absorbed new streams of European thought and poetry – Dada as well as de Bloy, the French Catholic philosopher; African folklore as well as Hof-mannsthal. Romain Rolland with his literary treatment of music and musicians was a powerful influence in musical Prague. It had a par-ticular hold on Hanuš Bonn, a young poet with the extreme sensitiv-ity of a Jew placed at the point of contact of the Czech and German worlds. The same *genius loci* which prompted Kafka and Čapek is at work in his early poem on Beethoven, opening with a confession of loneliness and fear, followed by an incantation of pain, and re-verberating in its finale with the universal declaration of love of Beethoven's Ninth Symphony.

This youthfully ecstatic poem was followed by a book of ex-tremely sparse verse in language so light that it could almost express silence and darkness. But all his small poems with the recurring theme of fear, love and homecoming proved to be only a low-keyed introduction to a great poem written when the Germans started de-porting Jews from Prague. Shortly before his execution by the Nazis, this softly-spoken poet gave voice to a clarion call against the devil-ish enemy. Hatred of evil liberates from fear and may become the only form of love left in the hour of mortal danger. This answer to the *Czech Question* probably came nearest to the message Masaryk believed the world expected from the Czechs. It was only heard by a small circle of Bonn's friends.

19 From Versailles to Munich

Introduction

The independence of Czechoslovakia, lasted only twenty years, all but a month. Its fate was sealed in Munich, on 29 September 1938 when the four major powers of Western Europe agreed that Hitler should be given the Czech border regions with most of the country's industry and all of its fortifications. This agreement is usually viewed as a diplomatic tragedy which under the guise of appeasement precipitated the Second World War. This may well have been the case, but it does not seem entirely right to put all the blame on the principal actors.

No doubt they were handicapped by a unique assortment of personal shortcomings: it took all of Daladier's weakness to leave Mussolini's ambivalence unexploited and all the arrogance of Chamberlain to under-estimate the mad determination of Hitler and the craftiness of Soviet diplomacy. This, however, should not obscure the fact that they came to Munich merely to declare the bankruptcy which had been inherent in the Versailles system ever since it was established on the unrealistic assumption that both Germany and the Soviet Union would remain powerless.

The disaster, by which the Czechs lost not only independence but also human rights and political freedoms, must be put on the account of a whole generation of statesmen. By accepting that part of Thomas Masaryk's programme which called for the disintegration of the Habsburg empire while rejecting his plea that they should make peace with the Soviet Union, by ignoring his project for a confederation which would replace the Habsburg empire and trusting they could, unaided, keep Germany on its knees for ever, the shortsighted statesmen of 1918 were swayed by Clemenceau into sowing policies that were not to be mastered.

One can speculate that much could have been repaired during the first ten years, before Hitler and Stalin were firmly established in power. Whether possible or not, this was not done; indeed Western Europe's politicians and business leaders went on rocking the boat, heedless of the approaching storm. In 1938, when the crisis could no longer be ignored, they panicked and sold their souls to the devil. The Slovak right wing and anti-semitic separatists hoped Germany would help them establish a Slovak state, as it did. Poland had its eyes fixed on the Těšín coalfields. Observing French vacillation and Britain's pressure for a reversal of policy, Romania and Yugoslavia were shy of further involvement and rejected the proposal (already made in January 1937) of a pact between the Little *Entente* and France. As a result in 1938 Czechoslovakia was the only democratic country east of the Rhine and south of Denmark, and completely friendless.

The phoney peace treaty

The small countries which succeeded the Habsburg Empire all suffered economically from the disintegration of that great common market in Central Europe. Austria and Czechoslovakia made an attempt to replace it by finding export markets for their industries. But for mainly agricultural Poland, Hungary and Romania the only hope was the German market.

Poland experienced a Soviet invasion, Hungary a Communist revolution, and Romania felt the presence of the Red Army on the Dniester as a direct threat to territories which were historically part of the Ukraine, and as an indirect threat to its government. The regimes established in these countries were of a repressive character and as they gradually turned to Germany for support their fascist features came into the open. Even in Austria the impoverishment and feeling of isolation finally led to the emergence of strong fascist and Nazi movements.

Of all the successor states only Czechoslovakia had a diversified economy in which industry and agriculture had about equal weight. Its problems of readjustment were more complex because its economy was more developed. It differed from the other successor states also in its political climate. Its leaders had done much to convince the Allies that the Austro-Hungarian Empire should be dissolved, but Czechoslovakia retained the heritage of democratic institutions and liberal and tolerant ways while the monarchic and feudal traditions of this empire were kept by the Hungarians, Romanians and, partly at least, the Poles.

Czechoslovak international traditions also differed greatly from those of the rest. The Hungarians did not like the Germans but feared the Russians – who had crushed their 1848 revolt – more. And as they ruled harshly and exploited their Slav provinces, while the Austrians ruled with moderation, conceding at least formal equality, the Hungarians felt much more deprived by the secession of subject territories. Hurt national feelings separated them much more than the Austrians from the new states, and made them turn first to Soviet Russia and then to Nazi Germany for help against them. For the Czechs, the Germans were not only the historical enemy but also, during the last fifty years of Austria–Hungary, the ever-present adversaries in the political arena.

With little inclination to make friends with the Nazis or the Soviets, the Czechs had pinned all their trust on the distant ally France, and all their hopes on Britain and the United States about whose politics and economy they entertained the most lofty illusions. These prospered not only because Masaryk was an Anglophile, and had an American wife, but also because the political part of the Czechslovak establishment inherited from Vienna the tendency to overrate the importance of intellectual achievement and view economic matters as dirty business best left to the moneylenders. It is remarkable that the Živnostenská Banka, the Skoda works and the Bata works, all enterprises with world-wide interests and possessions, contributed so little to a sober view of the international scene. Only when it was already too late to change the basic patterns did the rising Agrarian Party bring into Czech politics some of the realism and earthiness which were more at home in other successor countries where economics and politics remained more closely mixed.

If a different historical experience and a higher level of economic and social development formed a barrier between the Czechs and the nations of south-eastern Europe, and the defeats of 1918 and 1921 set the Hungarians apart, the political ambitions of the young intelligentsia, the jockeying for pensionable jobs and diplomatic and military careers, produced divergent forces in all the new states, working powerfully against any attempts to reduce national sovereignty by a higher degree of international cooperation.

The combination of forces working against the project of a confederation with which Masaryk returned in 1919 from the United States was so overwhelming that no serious attempt to realize the project was ever made. The torso of this scheme, which, on paper at least, survived till 1938, was the Little *Entente*, an alliance of Czechoslovakia, Romania and Yugoslavia. It had been called to life not so much by federalist desires as by the need to check Hungary which – whether Red or fascist – never ceased to claim the territories lost by the Treaty of Trianon.

The idea of an integrated Central Europe never caught on in Britain, which in the past had derived much of its influence on the Continent from the ability to play off the Habsburg Empire and Germany against each other. The fact that these two fought on the same side and were jointly defeated in the 1914–18 war, confused the issue for a while. In view of the role that France played in winning that war, it was impossible to resist Clemenceau's ideas of European security, and indeed the need to call in the devil of nationalism in order to drive out the Beelzebub of Communism gave some credibility to the French concept of a *cordon sanitaire* made up of small nation states.

However, the shaky nature of this defensive wall and the cracks which appeared in it as a result of internal divergences and external pressures from the Soviet Union and Germany, led France to consider an alternative solution. An agreement of the four big powers of Western Europe was attempted in Locarno in 1925. There and then the seed was planted for the Munich *fleur de mal*. The French 'solution' was formulated even more precisely in the proposal for a European Directory of Four at the end of 1933.

But these plans were halted for a few years by the expansionist moves following Hitler's takeover in Germany: the Italian invasion of Abyssinia, and German and Italian support for the Falangist uprising in Spain. It was not easy for either the French or the British openly to foster an alliance with powers which to anti-semitism and anti-marxism now added diatribes against western plutocrats and made them sound real by military action. Finally, a government of the Popular Front installed in France and led by Léon Blum could not become party to such a pact with the fascist powers.

In 1934 a series of attempts was made to create a new security system based on Franco–Soviet understanding. The first public move was the visit of Barthou, French Foreign Minister, to Prague in April 1934. Soon afterwards Czechoslovakia endorsed the Franco–Soviet proposal of an Eastern pact – opposed by Germany and Poland – and recognized the Soviet Union *de jure*.

In January 1935 the Czechoslovak Government made an attempt to win over its partners in the Little *Entente* for the conclusion of a Danube Pact proposed by France and Italy. In May Czechoslovakia concluded a treaty with the Soviet Union by which the two parties agreed to come to each other's aid if attacked, but only if France would do likewise.

The last attempt to improve Czechoslovakia's security system was made in January 1936 when President Beneš and Premier Hodža discussed the possibility of political and economic cooperation with the Austrian Chancellor Schuschnigg. These talks were followed in February by Hodža's visit to Paris, where he tried to win support for his scheme for the political and economic cooperation of Danube countries in a bloc able to negotiate with Germany from a position of equality.

But it was too late, to recreate the Habsburg Empire. On the eve of Hodža's next visit to Vienna, on 7 March 1936, Hitler's troops marched into the demilitarized zone of the Rhineland. France did not stir, and became dependent even more on British support when the civil war in Spain uncovered its southern flank and at the same time greatly increased the antagonism between Left and Right at home.

The weakness of France cast its shadow on Czechoslovakia and its attempts to strengthen the system of alliances pivoting on France. In June 1936 Beneš proposed a summit meeting of the Little *Entente* in Bucharest so that its defensive pact, directed only against Hungary, might be widened to provide cover against any aggressor – meaning Germany; and in January 1937 the French Foreign Office came up with the idea of a pact between the Little *Entente* and France. But the shadow of Germany loomed large. Yugoslavia and Romania, which had shown no enthusiasm for the Czechoslovak proposal in 1936, now in January 1937 turned down the French project. At the end of that year even France began to turn away from Czechoslovakia, adopting the British attitude of 'non-intervention'.

The occupation of Austria by Hitler spurred Léon Blum to give an assurance to Czechoslovakia on 17 March 1938 that it could count on 'immediate, effective and complete assistance' by France in the case of a German attack.

But the policy of Blum's Popular Front government was opposed not only by the British Government, which feared that through France it could be involved in a war with Germany, but also by French conservatives, who toppled him soon afterwards. Moreover French business circles, no less than French politicians depending on the agricultural vote, were not averse to the idea of a larger market for French agriculture and of a political arrangement with Germany securing respectability to the already established cooperation between the heavy industries – coal, steel and chemicals – of the two countries. The economic interest in a common market existed on both sides of the Rhine already in the thirties.

The British Foreign Office never fully accepted the idea of a European security system based on French hegemony and a *cordon sanitaire* formed by its small allies wedged between Germany and the Soviet Union. The idea seemed preposterous to men steeped in the traditions of the British Empire and inclined to think of small countries as padding to fill a frame constructed of the great powers. But as long as Germany and the Soviet Union were weak the French could be allowed their silly game.

By 1938 both Germany and the Soviet Union were again the two major powers Britain had to fear. It was unavoidable that the Foreign Office should begin to view the French system of alliances – and particularly its alliance with Czechoslovakia – no longer as an absurdity but as a positive danger: should it involve Germany in a war on its western front, who could prevent Russia turning its attention to India and China?

If, conversely, Hitler were given a free hand in Central Europe as a stepping-stone to the Balkans, conflict between Germany and the Soviet Union would become unavoidable. There was, as can be seen, good nineteenth-century method in this madness. Moreover, the British Foreign Office executed the almost suicidal manoeuvre with foreseeable swiftness and precision, as soon as this became possible through the fall of Blum's government and its replacement by the right-wing government of Bonnet and Daladier.

Anglo–French talks held in London in April 1938 added to

Blum's assurance of March 17 – that France would fulfil its treaty obligations if Czechoslovakia were attacked – the limiting condition that it would do so only in the case of unprovoked aggression. Early the next month, on 7 May, there followed the joint Anglo–French *démarche* in Prague, asking the Czechoslovak Government to give its Nazis, represented by Hitler's puppet, Konrad Henlein, what they wanted. This *démarche* started the ideological build-up for Munich: the Czechs could either give up and be lost or, if stubborn, be accused of provocation and abandoned.

Poland and Hungary, who during the crisis of 1938 advanced their own demands against Czechoslovakia, had fairly obvious reasons for doing so. The unsettled Polish claim to part of the Silesian coalfields around Těšín was of relatively small importance compared with the expectation of the Polish right-wing dictatorship that it would receive from Hitler support and protection against the Soviet Union. The weakness shown by France, and her pact with the Soviets, did not recommend her as an ally to the Poles, who had already in 1934 rejected plans for an East European pact. The Hungarian fascist regime hoped that Germany and Italy would return Slovakia to Hungary.

Thus both big and small powers had a short-term interest in the carving up of Czechoslovakia by Germany. And they all hoped that they would not be the hindmost left for the devil to take.

Hitler wins British support

For almost two years Hitler was quietly preparing the political and diplomatic ground for further action. When he finally outlined to the inner caucus of the Nazi Party his plans against Austria and Czechoslovakia, he could be fairly certain of benevolent non-intervention on the part of Britain and a paralysing reluctance to act on the part of France.

When Hitler disclosed his plans to his party on 5 November 1937, he must have already been certain that Lord Halifax, the British Foreign Secretary, would visit him in Berchtesgaden a fortnight later to confirm that Britain had no interests in Central Europe, though it would like to see German claims satisfied peacefully. Shortly afterwards, in December, the French Foreign Minister, Delbos, visiting Prague, made it clear that France, which was bound to Czechoslovakia by a treaty of alliance, was moving towards the British policy of non-intervention.

Having obtained cover in the West, Hitler started to move eastwards and in March 1938 occupied Austria. From that time on, his pressure against Czechoslovakia almost daily gathered momentum. On 28 March Konrad Henlein, the Nazi leader in Czechoslovakia, was called by Hitler to Berlin and instructed to step up his demands so as to make them unacceptable to the Czechoslovak Government. A month later Hitler agreed with Field Marshal Keitel directives for 'Fall Gruen', the code word for an invasion of Czechoslovakia.

Almost simultaneously with this start of military preparations in Germany, Henlein published his demand for full autonomy for Germans including the freedom to spread Nazi propaganda, which in the context of those days meant freedom to step up the terror against the Social Democrat, liberal, and Communist Germans in the country. A fortnight after the publication of these demands came the French and British joint *démarche* of May 7. The two Ambassadors informed the Czechoslovak Foreign Minister, Kamil Krofta, that their Governments demanded that the Czechoslovak Government should reach an agreement with the German minority.

After a further fortnight the German army began to move operational units to the Czech frontier at a time when local elections provided much opportunity for provocative incidents staged by the Nazis. Though the collusion of France and Britain with Hitler was by now obvious, the Czech Government answered by a partial mobilization, hoping to gain time and alert its friends in the West.

This move frustrated the concept formulated by Lord Halifax in Berchtesgaden in November 1937, that Hitler should satisfy his claims in Central Europe peacefully while Britain remained disinterested. The people of Czechoslovakia were kept completely in the dark about the French betrayal and British hostility, and any government which retreated before the German threat at that time would have been swept away as treacherous.

It became apparent that it would be necessary to apply much greater pressure to force Czechoslovakia into capitulation. The British Government assumed the initiative and took complete control of the diplomatic process by which Czechoslovakia was to be liquidated.

On 26 May 1938 Sir William Strang, Permanent Secretary at the Foreign Office, arrived in Prague to inform himself about the Czechoslovak Government's attitude to a plebiscite in the German districts and to a neutralization of the country. Four days later Hitler approved detailed directives for an attack on Czechoslovakia.

However, in June there was still the possibility that the Czechs might fight, probably with some support from the Soviet Union. The General Staffs of continental armies in those times were most reluctant to begin operations before the harvest was over, hence there was a need to mark time and keep the tension high by political and diplomatic games.

Accordingly, June began with demonstrations for Slovak autonomy, organized by Andrei Hlinka, leader of the Slovak Catholic extreme right-wing, while Henlein's party submitted to the Government a new memorandum reiterating demands which in April had been rejected as unacceptable. The Czechoslovak Government was thus being squeezed in Hitler's political pincers – one arm of which was Henlein's Nazi Germans and the other Hlinka's Slovaks – in order to soften them sufficiently and make them accept the British Government's proposal that Lord Runciman, a shipping magnate, should conduct an 'independent inquiry and mediation'.

Lord Runciman arrived in Prague on 3 August as the figurehead of a mission whose real leader was Ashton-Gwatkin, of the Foreign Office. Diplomatic missions of this type decide nothing and should be spared the blame (or praise) for results attributed to them by governments. However, by adding insult to injury the Runciman mission succeeded in making itself more hated than the powers hiding behind it. The Czech press restricted itself to publishing, mostly without comment, 'court circulars' issued daily by the mission's press officer, and the Czechs – whether workers or bankers – only gasped when they read about Lord Runciman's tour of castles and his 'talks' with people whose ancestors may have had some importance in the seventeenth century when they arrived as Catholic mercenaries to suppress the Protestants, but about whom little – and nothing favourable – had been heard during the preceding twenty years.

But Lord Runciman also managed to meet Henlein and send him to Hitler with word that Chamberlain would welcome the opportunity of discussing world problems, and the Czech problem, with

Hitler in person. Hitler, as transpired later, was interested only in the second subject.

The meeting between Henlein and Runciman took place on 18 August. On 12 September, after Hitler's inflammatory speech at the Nuremberg rally, the Henlein party staged a putsch which the Czech army suppressed in two days. The putsch was over on 14 September and Henlein and other leading Nazis fled to Germany. On 15 September Chamberlain paid his first visit to Hitler in Berchtesgaden. He voiced no objections to the dismemberment of Czechoslovakia but only asked for time to consult with the French and Lord Runciman on the practical aspects of the deal. The basic agreement between Hitler and Chamberlain thus came into the open and deprived Lord Runciman of further justification for visits to the country houses of former aristocrats. He returned to London the day after Chamberlain's visit to Berchtesgaden. In fact he returned much too late, and could recommend only what Chamberlain had already conceded: that Czechoslovakia's border territories, including the triple chain of fortifications and most of her industry, should be ceded to Germany.

From now on events moved with a speed unprecedented in diplomatic history. The understanding reached between Hitler and Chamberlain in Berchtesgaden on 15 September found expression in a joint Anglo–French note of 19 September proposing to the Czechoslovak Government that it should cede to Germany all border regions in which more than half the population was German. This was rejected by the Czechoslovak Government on the following day, when Beneš also received a promise of help from Moscow.

From this point onwards Britain and France dropped all pretence of respect for Czechoslovakia's sovereignty or for the solemn and explicit treaty of mutual assistance which Czechoslovakia had with France. At 2.00 a.m. on 21 September the British and French ambassadors called on Beneš and presented him with an ultimatum to accept the Anglo–French plan within forty-eight hours. If he did not, the two powers would take the view that Czechoslovakia had provoked the war which Germany could be expected to start.

President Beneš and the Government of Milan Hodža gave up and accepted the Anglo–French plan. Hitler had the foothold he wanted: once he had occupied the fortified zone which the plan handed over to him he was in a position to take the rest without asking. He had therefore no need to step up his demands and it has never been explained why he did so during the two further days which Chamberlain spent with him in Godesberg. It has also remained unexplained why France and Britain temporarily withdrew their pressure on Czechoslovakia and agreed to the mobilization of the Czech army. Like Hitler, they must have known that even after the carrying out of the Anglo–French plan already accepted by Czechoslovakia there would be nothing left to defend and that the country was lost in its entirety. No further demands by Hitler could have made things worse.

The only possible explanation is that the western powers needed this intermission because of a Soviet diplomatic intervention and because events within Czechoslovakia threatened to get out of hand. A further dramatization of the situation could also help Chamberlain and Daladier to overcome the opposition to appeasement with Hitler that existed within their own parties.

On the day the Czechs accepted the Anglo–French ultimatum the Soviet Commissar for Foreign Affairs – Litvinov – stood up in support of Czechoslovakia in the Assembly of the League of Nations; and at the same time the Communist Party of Czechoslovakia started to agitate feverishly against the surrender. A big protest meeting, organized mainly by the Communists but in which non-Communist patriots also took part, assembled on the Old Town Square in Prague and marched to the Castle, demanding a new government which would fight. The Communists proposed a 'government of the popular front'.

The right-wing elements of the establishment, especially the Agrarians and the influential caucus of the Živnostenská Bank, were frightened at the possibility of popular rising against the government that had surrendered. On 21 and 22 September many leading personalities panicked and scattered to the country, fearing that 'the mob would take over' in Prague.

In fact, there was not the slightest reason for such an assumption, and there is little doubt that the Agrarians and the Živnostenská Bank exaggerated rumours to push Beneš into preventive action. The first step was the replacement on 22 September of Hodža's Government by an administration composed of top civil servants and led by the one-eyed General Jan Syrový, hero of the Czech legions of 1914–18. This move was accompanied by vague statements designed to make the people believe that the new Government would defend the country.

On the following day, 23 September, the Government ordered a general mobilization of the army, having received word from the British and French Governments 'that they no longer could stand by their formerly given advice not to mobilize'.

The mobilization was completed during the night of 23–4 September with a speed surprising to outside observers, who did not anticipate the keenness of both the Czech and the many German reservists to get to their posts. Henlein's call to sabotage the mobilization failed, revealing much about the nature of Nazi support in Czechoslovakia. Of the 3.5 million Germans living in that country, about one million were Social Democrats and liberals who felt even more immediately endangered by Nazis than the Czechs. As Henlein's call for sabotage of the mobilization had no great effect even in the purely German regions bordering on Germany, the conclusion has been drawn that many of those who were known as Nazis in fact only posed as such out of fear and would have wished for Czech victory.

All such observations, however, are of only academic interest. Having encouraged the Czechs to mobilize on the 23rd, Chamberlain and Daladier met in London on the 25th to consult how best to continue negotiations with Hitler. These consultations continued on the 26th, when Chamberlain sent Sir Horace Wilson to Hitler with a letter assuring him that the 'problems of the Sudeten Germans can be solved speedily'. In this way Chamberlain removed any possible deterrent effect out of the Czech mobilization and accordingly Hitler promptly uttered a new blast of threats in his speech at the Nuremberg Party rally on the evening of that same day.

Having encouraged the Czechs to mobilize on the 23rd, Chamberlain answered them by a letter of 28 September assuring him 'that he could get all essentials without war and without delay'. The only meaning this could have was that Hitler should ignore the mobilization that Chamberlain had encouraged the Czechs to carry out only five days earlier.

This, then, was the tortuous but premeditated road to the Munich meeting which the British Prime Minister proposed to Mussolini on the same day and which took place the next, 29 September. Represented by Heads of Government, the four powers disposed of 27,000 square kilometres of Czechoslovak territory and 4.5 million of its inhabitants. This was half the territory of Bohemia, over a third of the country's population. What remained was a defenceless and economically non-viable trunk. Czechoslovak representatives were not admitted to the conference, and it has been recorded that Chamberlain was yawning when he came out to tell them the results.

Was at least President Beneš serious when he ordered the general mobilization? Hardly, if one is to believe what he said in his memoirs, that his final decision not to fight alone, or only with Soviet support, was taken on 21 September.

Looking over the eight long days from 21 to 28 September, the impression cannot be escaped that the British and French at no point departed from their resolve to give Hitler a free hand in Central Europe – a policy based on a double hope that German economic and military aggression could be deflected from the West towards Eastern Europe and the Balkans, and that this – on the pattern of 1914 – would make conflict between Germany and the Soviet Union unavoidable.

One explanation, current at the time, of the encouragement the British and French gave on 23 September to the Czechs by declaring that they no longer could advise against mobilization was that they intended to bluff Hitler into granting better conditions to the ally France was selling down the river. This charitable explanation, however, has been disproved by the publication of documents revealing the character of the mission on which Chamberlain sent Wilson to Nuremberg on the eve of the Nazi rally.

The only other explanation, which agrees with the political climate of those days both in Czechoslovakia and in Western Europe and which is not contradicted by anything revealed subsequently, is that the Czechoslovak mobilization was intended to be not a bargaining expedient but rather a preventive measure against a Communist-inspired popular uprising in Czechoslovakia and a lever against Chamberlain's and Daladier's own opposition at home. The anti-appeasers, and all the people of Britain and France, were to be made to believe that the alternative was an immediate war for which they were not prepared.

It was revealed only much later that while Chamberlain and Daladier were doing their best to frighten their countries into accepting 'appeasement', Hitler's main problem was to reassure his frightened generals that 'Fall Gruen' would not lead to a war for which they too did not feel prepared. Indeed, well-informed observers believed at the time that the German army was not issued with live ammunition – perhaps Hitler feared that the Generals might turn against him to avoid war. The Generals felt more confident in another year's time when the Munich agreement enabled them to use Czechoslovak arms and armament industry and to conclude an armistice with Stalin.

At a time of a great international crisis, like that of September 1938, one can observe a general tendency to personalize events and attribute responsibility for them to the leading statesmen of the day. This tendency is even stronger in Britain, where the press reports developments on a day-to-day basis, than on the European continent where historical perspectives are ever present. For this reason the drama of the Munich agreement overshadowed for some time more fundamental factors which ultimately led to the Second World War. True, had the four powers which concluded the Munich deal chosen their leaders better, instead of allowing themselves to be led by Hitler, Mussolini, Daladier and Chamberlain, the worst consequences of the Versailles blunder could perhaps have been averted. As things were, the four who met in Munich did much to aggravate the situation and made a war almost unavoidable. But it is wrong to think that their responsibility was complete and that they could reverse the forces which were let loose in Europe in 1918 and the subsequent developments.

Postscript

It reveals an ironic sense of history that the decision not to defend the country against a coalition of Britain, France, Germany, Italy, Poland and Hungary, and to submit to the dictate of the four powers, was announced by President Edward Beneš to the commanders of the fully mobilized Czechoslovak army in the room which Masaryk used as his study in the Royal Castle of Prague. It is a room offering a magnificeent view of the town spread in the deep valley of the River Vltava and on the hills enclosing it on all sides. To a Czech, the view is full of the landmarks of history.

In the south, on the eastern bank of the river, is Vyšehrad, the seat of the Premyslid rulers, who often succeeded in gaining greater security by linking Bohemia and Moravia to Poland, Hungary and Austria. On the rising ground facing the Castle on the other side of the river are the towers of the New Town founded by Charles IV of Luxembourg, who by marriage and diplomacy extended his realm as far north as Berlin, secured for his son the throne of Hungary, concluded a dynastic treaty with the Habsburgs, and made the thus strengthened Czech kingdom the centre of the Holy Roman Empire.

North of the New Town is the hill bearing the name and equestrian statue of Jan Žižka who led the Czech peasant armies against the invading crusaders of Rome and of the Emperor, only to be succeeded by the Hussite king, George, whose prime concern was to re-establish, by new dynastic links with Poland and Hungary, the security of the kingdom – and indeed of a Europe threatened by the Turks. Looking nearer, one can count the baroque churches and palaces, conceived as monuments of a Catholic victory over the defeated, decimated and exiled Czech Protestants; they are no longer seen as such and are now an essential part of this most beautiful city, which for a longer time than Vienna was also the metropolis of the Danube empire. Looking closer still, and leaning out a little from Masaryk's window, one can rest the eyes on a simple, neglected terrace, extending from the square below but above the deeper lying bizarre growth of red roofs on the western side of the river: this is where the newly crowned kings swore that they would defend and uphold the freedoms of Prague.

It was in this room on 29 September 1938 – about the time when Chamberlain, Daladier and Mussolini were converging on Munich – that General Jan Syrový, newly appointed Premier, General Ludvik Krejčí, C.-in-C. of the armed forces, and the three regional commanders of Bohemia, Moravia and Slovakia tried to persuade Beneš that the country should be defended. If Czechoslovakia went to war alone, they argued, the Western powers would have to join her later to protect their own security.

For Beneš, according to his memoirs, the matter had been decided nine days earlier when, on 21 September, the British and French presented him with an ultimatum that they would treat Czechoslovakia as having provoked the war if she resisted Hitler alone.

From that day he refused to be guided by the feelings of the country or the reasoning of the generals.

He agreed with them that a European war would be the next act of the tragedy and that the Western powers would then have to fight Hitler under worse conditions, without the help of the best equipped, probably best trained, and certainly most determined army opposing the Nazi regime in the heart of Europe. But he did not think that France and Britain were bluffing and told the generals that it would be irresponsible to lead the nation to slaughter in an isolated war. Even in the unlikely event of effective help from the Soviet Union, France and Britain would, so he believed, in the end link hands with Germany, to establish in Central and Eastern Europe a 'barrier against Bolshevism', leaving the Czechs under Nazi domination for a very long time indeed.

A few days later Beneš abdicated and on 22 October left the country for Britain. The Munich agreement stripped Czechoslovakia of its defences and industry. On 15 March 1939 the rest was dismembered: Slovakia was transformed into a German satellite and Bohemia and Moravia occupied by Hitler.

This was the last step in the disintegration of the Central European power system, a sophisticated and always precarious construction, but which in one way or another for a thousand years had served as a barrier against invaders from west and east alike. The process of disintegration became manifest only after 1914, but its cause can be traced back to the eighteenth century when Britain switched its European alliances and gave support to rising Prussia. Taking this longer view, Versailles can be seen as an unsuccessful French attempt to acquire a Danubian empire – consisting of Czechoslovakia and the other successor states – and Munich as a reaffirmation of the British link with Prussia forged in the second half of the eighteenth century. However, eighteenth-century precepts failed to solve a twentieth-century problem. The political immaturity of the French and British establishments, their clinging to obsolete political concepts in the hope that these would keep the ruling class protected against the vulgarities of the advancing industrial society, led ultimately to the decline of Europe into the shadow of the rising superpowers. Munich was the last major decision taken by the former 'big four' of Western Europe without either the U.S. or the Soviet Union.

1939–1945

Though in Central Europe most people realized that the country's total occupation by Hitler would follow quickly, Western public opinion grasped the full implications of the Munich agreement only when Nazi occupation took place on 15 March 1939. In much the same way, the agreement concluded between the Allies at Yalta in 1944 led unavoidably to the Communist takeover in Czechoslovakia in 1948. Though it would hardly do justice to the statesmen who sat round the table at Munich and Yalta to assume that they were so naive, or that they indulged in so much wishful thinking as not to see the consequences of the agreements they signed, most people in the West seemed genuinely surprised when the unavoidable happened.

The Czechs felt they could hardly have had a worse deal had they fought the Allies instead of being on their side in two world wars. They lost not only their statehood and independence but also basic human freedoms, and as a result it is hardly possible to speak of a Czech political history from 1939 to 1969. With the brief interludes of 1945–8 and the revolutionary year 1968, they were at all times during this period under complete foreign domination, either German or Soviet.

The economic and administrative changes and the succession of puppet governments were throughout these years prompted by the controlling power whose decisions were sometimes delayed but rarely modified by local resistance. Both as individuals and as a nation the Czechs were concerned more with the question of survival, knowing that there is hope as long as there is life and learning at great cost that there is no life without hope. This struggle for survival was not always heroically beautiful; indeed it had some very ugly aspects.

But as Richard Davy, the *Times* correspondent, reported from Prague in 1970, the Czechs developed the ability to survive into a fine art.

Let me briefly recall the sequence of the main events. The occupation of what remained of the western part of Czechoslovakia after Munich was completed by the German army in the course of twenty-four hours on March 15. On the following day Hitler proclaimed Bohemia and Moravia an integral part of the German Reich to be governed as a protectorate by a Reichs Protector. Two days earlier, on March 14, the Slovaks succumbed to German pressure and declared an independent Slovak state which Hitler promised to guarantee against the threat of Hungarian occupation. On the same day the Hungarian army occupied Ruthenia.

The first period of occupation was marked by a residual resistance, both within the Government of Bohemia and Moravia and in the mood of the population. Drastic measures taken by the occupying power soon put an end to that. The last mass demonstration took place in Prague on Independence Day (28 October) of 1939, and afterwards the resistance movement, apart from small-scale sabotage action, mainly provided intelligence services for the Czech resistance movement abroad in London and Moscow.

The Germans stepped up their pressure considerably after the recognition of the provisional Czechoslovak government in London by Britain on 21 July 1940. Edward Beneš, who abdicated the presidential office after Munich in 1938, and was given asylum in London started to represent the occupied country as its President in exile. A week later the Slovaks were obliged to subscribe fully to German policy and allow a free rein to Nazi ideology in Slovakia.

The future designed for the Czechs was outlined in a memorandum submitted to Hitler by Konstantin von Neurath, the Reichs Protector, and Karl Hermann Frank, leader of the Sudeten–German Nazis, on 31 August 1940. They proposed that the Czechs should be eliminated as a nation, primarily by systematic germanization of the population and by the settlement of Germans.

Towards the end of 1941 von Neurath, a career diplomat, was replaced as Reichs Protector by Reinhard Heydrich, a leading S.S. officer and head of Soviet-aimed espionage. His appointment marked the stepping up of repressive measures against real and potential resistors. There were many executions and deportations in

Bohemia and Moravia, while the Slovaks were made to declare war, first on the Soviet Union and then on Britain and France.

At about this time also began the first deportation of Jews to a special ghetto established in Terezin and from there to the extermination camps in Poland. Similar transports of Jews from Slovakia began in March 1942. Only about 5,000 out of 150,000 Jews living in Czechoslovakia in 1938 survived.

On 27 May 1942 five Czech parachutists dropped from British aircraft ambushed Heydrich's car in Prague and killed him. The Germans answered with random arrests in which over 2,300 Czechs were executed. Two mining villages, Lidice and Ležáky, were burned down and their male inhabitants shot, while women and children were deported. The population of Bohemia and Moravia never recovered from the shock of this mass terror, and it contributed much to their intransigent attitude towards the Germans after the war.

Things were different in Slovakia where the local government provided at least an illusion of independence. Compared with the thoroughly bureaucratic organization of Bohemia and Moravia, Slovakia was more easy-going. Family and village community provided protection against the Germans and their Slovak helpers, and where this did not reach, bribery mostly did. Mountains made large areas of Slovakia impenetrable to tanks and highly suited to partisan warfare.

Preparations for partisan activities in Slovakia proceeded during the second half of 1943 simultaneously with a *rapprochement* between Beneš's Government in London and the Soviet Union. In December 1943 this government in exile signed a treaty of friendship with the Soviet Union, which in May 1944 was followed by an agreement concerning the relationship between the Czechoslovak authorities and the Soviet Army in the event of its occupation of the country. The pact between Beneš's Government and the Soviet Union also sealed the outward unity of the Czechoslovak resistance movement at home and abroad.

The first Czechoslovak political organization of refugees, the Czechoslovak National Committee, had been formed in France around the Ambassador, Osuský, who was more acceptable to the French than Beneš. This committee, financed from assets the Brno Armaments Works had in the West and which were abroad controlled by its chairman, Edward Outrata, organized the first Czechoslovak army unit of about 9,000 men plus about 1,000 airmen.

After the fall of France 3,780 Czech soldiers and airmen – and the National Committee – were evacuated to Britain where they formed the nucleus of a unit which served with the British Army. Once in Britain, the Communists in the Czechoslovak army unit declared – in correspondence with Soviet policy as manifested by the Ribbentrop–Molotov pact – that, as Stalin had declared, the war between the Western Allies and Germany was an imperialist conflict and consequently they did not wish to have any part in it. Most served for some time in the British Pioneer Corps but all rejoined the Czechoslovak Army in Britain after Hitler's attack on the Soviet Union.

Beneš appointed as Premier František Šrámek, a leading Catholic politician; and as Foreign Minister, the former Ambassador in London Jan Masaryk, son of the late President. They were about the only men of independent views – most of the rest of Beneš's entourage were sadly sycophantic. The two important Slovak personalities in the West, Milan Hodža, the last Premier before Munich, and Štefan Osuský, did not see eye to eye with Beneš and spent the war in the United States, where the Slovaks form a strong ethnic group. The establishment in London was mainly made up of former embassy staffs from countries at war with Germany and some neutral countries, mostly men who had been picked by Beneš during his long tenure of the Foreign Ministry in Prague. They were not in the habit of thinking independently, and if they were no hindrance they were no help either.

The professional officer corps of the Czechoslovak Army in Britain was different, and more independent of Beneš; indeed, the Czech airmen, 560 of whom lost their lives in the Battle of Britain, helped him to establish British recognition of the government in exile in July 1940. The Czech Army established a special unit working for British military intelligence and in this way gained a status of its own in Britain.

All this added up to a certain splendid isolation of Beneš in his house in Putney in south-west London, and reinforced his tendency to continue along the track that had once already brought his country to disaster.

His career had started during the First World War in France and after the war he had become Foreign Minister. It is only natural that he was always mainly concerned with securing international support rather than support at the grassroots as would a partisan leader – and as Tito did in Yugoslavia. In contrast to Masaryk, who claimed that his successes were more often due to the failure of his plans than to his foresight, and who kept revising his concepts until old age, Beneš kept trying to prove that he was always right.

In 1914–18 he had convinced the French that Austria–Hungary should be divided into nation states, and he was not the man to accept now the British view that it was a mistake. He failed to establish any real links with the Yugoslav partisans, and the talks initiated between the Poles and the Czechs in London in 1942 were allowed to break down, before they had really begun, on the question of Tešin, the coalmining district disputed between the two countries. The British Foreign Office favoured at that time the idea of a Central European federation and was encouraging the Czechs and Poles to come to an understanding. Unfortunately the Tešin question was not the really important cause of disagreement. The real divergence between the two exile governments was in their attitude to the Soviet Union. The Poles felt that Stalin and Hitler who had divided their country between them in 1940 were both enemies and that they were at war with both. The Czechs, however, were seeking Soviet support.

During the second decade of Czechoslovak independence Beneš had tried to secure the country against Gemany by a tripartite pact with France and the Soviet Union. He now hoped to repeat the exercise, replacing France by Britain in the triangle, quite ignoring the Munich experience. He also tried to keep up good relations with Stalin through Fierlinger, the Czech Ambassador in Moscow and a crypto-Communist, Colonel (later General) Pika, a gifted intelligence officer and the London communists. But more important than this was the alliance treaty he signed with Stalin on 12 December 1943. This was at a time when the Czechs who had escaped to Poland were being extremely harshly treated in Soviet concentration camps. These Czechs, mainly Jews escaping from Hitler, were later allowed to form a Czechoslovak brigade under General Svoboda (elected President in 1968) and suffered severe losses on the Kiev front and – quite unnecessarily – in the Dukla Pass in 1945. The patriotic General Pika was executed in the early fifties on Soviet orders because he knew too much about Soviet policy towards Czechoslovakia and its plans in the West. Fierlinger who knew hardly less became the first Premier after 1945 and in Soviet service survived all purges and changes.

Although the Slovak partisan movement recognized the authority of the Czechoslovak Government in London, it was in fact organized and armed from the Soviet Union. In July 1944 the Soviet Union despatched to Slovakia twenty-six units totalling 448 partisan organizers and large-scale activities began within a month. The German military mission was taken prisoner by partisan units and shot on 28 August; on the following day the German army began to occupy Slovakia. On 30 August the partisans established an independent administration in the territory they controlled in central Slovakia.

On 6 October 1944 Czechoslovak units moving as a vanguard of the Soviet Army crossed the frontier from Poland into Czechoslovakia – only one day after the Czech tank brigade in the West started the siege of Dunkirk. A day later Minister F. Němec, a Social Democratic Trade Unionist who was a member of the London government, arrived in Slovakia with full powers from London, but his authority was rejected by the Slovak National Council. He later retreated to Ruthenia, then already under Soviet occupation, but was asked to leave within three days. The Soviet Army was preparing to annex the territory.

1945–1968

On 3 April 1945 President Beneš, with a group of politicians made up of members of the freedom movement both in London and Moscow, arrived in Košice and formed there the first government on the liberated territory. The government, in which Communists arrived from Moscow had the leading part, agreed the so-called 'Programme of Košice' which provided for nationalization of large-scale business and industry.

A month later, on 5 May, when the American Army was already in occupation of the western part of Bohemia, the Communist Party organized a 'revolution' in Prague obliging the German units moving out to fight small rearguard skirmishes. Prague Radio called for help but the American Army, fifty miles away in Plzeň, was prevented from moving by the Yalta agreement. The 'liberation' of Prague was left to a token Soviet unit sent over for the purpose from East Germany.

The circumstances in which liberation took place made it more than clear what sort of independence would follow. Even so, many people in Czechoslovakia were confused by the reappearance of Beneš as President, and by the formation of a government in which all the political parties were represented. Real power, however, was in the hands of the Communists, who held the office of Prime Minister, the Ministry of Defence and the Ministry of the Interior, and who also controlled a newly formed revolutionary trade-union movement.

The Communists quickly enlarged their power-base by organizing National Committees, particularly in the region from which the German population was being transferred according to the agreement concluded by the four powers at Potsdam. This transfer of the German population, proposed by Beneš during the war, while satisfying the clamour for revenge and the Czechs' craving for greater security at home, also fitted into the Soviet grand design. It denuded Czechoslovakia of its considerable consumer goods industries and thus made it ready for a further expansion of its engineering industries in the service of the Soviet Union. The other objective pursued by the Soviet Union in this transfer was fortification of the barrier of mistrust and hatred between the Czechs and Germans.

The expropriation of German property was the first step towards nationalization of industry and collectivization of agriculture. The next step in this direction was the systematic resistance of the Communist Party to restitution of Jewish and some other property confiscated by the Germans. Finally, on 28 October 1947, the first nationalization decrees were signed by the President.

At the beginning of 1948 the Communist Minister of the Interior began to purge the police and replace its officers by reliable Communists in preparation for a total takeover. The rather clumsy resistance to this move by President Beneš and the non-Communist members of the Government speeded up the takeover, which took place on 28 February 1948 under the direction of Soviet Ambassador Zorin, while units of the Soviet Army were being moved in an undisguised threat from Poland across Slovakia to Hungary.

President Beneš abdicated, following the pattern he had already established after the Munich agreement. Soon afterwards the Foreign Minister, Jan Masaryk, a liberal who enjoyed great popularity in the country, was assassinated by Communist agents. The official version of this third (but not last) defenestration of Prague was that he committed suicide by jumping out of his bedroom window, and he was given a state funeral.

Immediately after the takeover the Communist Party formed Action Committees in enterprises as well as in localities but the idea that these committees should take over the administration of the country was soon given up and they were disbanded after they had purged all institutions and enterprises of persons not considered reliable by the Communists. The next steps to consolidate power in the hands of the small group of men who returned after the war from Moscow proceeded in fast succession.

In the first few months after the takeover the Communist Party exerted pressure on all employees to sign membership applications. The aims of 'mass membership' were greater control, indoctrination and the forestalling of opposition. Soon, however, most of the new probationer members were again expelled, leaving in the Party only those who could be easily controlled because of ambition, greed or stains on their past record. At the same time the new, Communist-appointed leaderships of the non-Communist parties were admitted, together with the government-controlled trade unions and other mass organizations, into the 'National Front'. Members of the Social Democratic Party and a few of its leftist leaders were integrated into the Communist Party.

The progress of nationalization was immediately accelerated and carried beyond the limits of the laws passed before the takeover. In a few years Slánský and Gottwald could claim that they alone in Eastern Europe had succeeded in total nationalization of industry and trade and total collectivization of agriculture. This was achieved by a variety of devices, ranging from declaring entrepreneurs anti-social and fiddling the tax laws, to sending shopkeepers and small traders to labour camps without trial and phony trials of farmers who could not meet requisitions after they had been deprived of machinery, labour and traction animals and refused supplies of seeds and fertilizers.

Towards the end of 1949 the political trials began. Liberal, centrist and Social Democratic politicians and others suspected of right-wing sympathies were tried and sentenced to long terms in prison; some were executed. Simultaneously old-time Communists and executives in the nationalized industries and foreign trade, particularly those who had spent the war years in England, including the author, began to be rounded up. Trials organized and supervised by Soviet experts started with 'Slovak nationalists' and culminated in the trial of the entire leadership of the Communist Party headed by its Secretary-General, Rudolf Slánský, who was accused of Titoism, revisionism and zionism. He and ten other leading members of the party were executed in 1952. President Klement Gottwald, who signed the death warrant of his life-long friend Slánský, died in the course of the same year, a few days after his return from Stalin's funeral in Moscow.

In ordering the removal of pre-war Communists who were in control of the national parties, like Slánský, or at least enjoyed a certain popular support, Stalin aimed at substituting party bureaucrats, wholly dependent on Moscow for leaderships capable of resisting the further stepping up of Soviet exploitation. The trials staged in those years in all satellite countries, including Northern Korea, were characterized by the same composition of the 'anti-state centre', by the same 'confessions' and by the same methods of torture, physical and mental, employed to make the prisoners 'confess' in the hope that the executioner would take them out of the hands of their torturers.

In 1953 Klement Gottwald was succeeded as President by Antonin Zapotocký, who had played a big role in the 1948 takeover as chairman of the national trade-union organization and who was of a somewhat more humane character than his predecessor. By this time, however, the personality of the President was hardly of any importance, since all government departments, in particular the Secret Police and the Army, were firmly in the hands of Soviet advisers.

The new First Secretary of the Party, Antonín Novotný, and the new Prime Minister, Viliam Široký, a Slovak of Hungarian origin, played a more active role than Zapotocký. Both Novotný and Široký used the purges and political trials to get rid of their political opponents and were personally very much involved in them. This explains why the process of de-Stalinization, started in the Soviet Union by Khruschev in 1956, was so much delayed in Czechoslovakia. Not only Novotný and Široký but almost the entire party leadership and many leading officials were afraid that they would have to face the consequences of their implication once the Party admitted in public that the trials were staged under the guidance of Soviet experts who provided the scripts of confessions. The report of the Party committee which established this as far back as 1956 was never published in Czechoslovakia, but was published in Italy after 1968, by Jiří Pelikán.

It has been estimated that about 100,000 political prisoners passed through the labour camps on the Soviet-owned uranium mines in Czechoslovakia during this period. There was remarkably little resistance to this reign of terror, and not much help for the families of those who were imprisoned. Only the monetary reform of May 1953, which by a stroke deprived workers of all their savings, led to protest demonstrations and even strikes, particularly in the Skoda Works in Plzen and the C.K.D. works in Prague.

While, in Poland, Gomulka returned from prison to power in 1956, in Czechoslovakia most political prisoners remained confined until 1960, and some for even longer. Hesitant admissions that the trials had been staged and the accused, by sophisticated torture, forced to learn 'confessions' by heart, were the final blow to the prestige of the Communist Party, which had already lost all credibility in the economic field.

Economic policies and methods originally developed in the Soviet Union, rich in raw materials and with a low density of industry, could not but fail when blindly transplanted to a country poor in raw materials and with a highly developed industry. The series of calamities caused by this sort of planning was aggravated by large-scale unemployment when China, after its rift with the Soviet Union, cancelled all its Czechoslovak orders. A series of further losses in developing countries and in the Soviet Union made recovery impossible. The Czechoslovak economic crisis reached its nadir in 1962, and from that time on it has been generally recognized, though not officially admitted, that the system of central economic planning and bureaucratic control over the econony as exercised by the central and regional party hierarchy completely failed.

The Stalinist leadership survived the 1956 events when de-Stalinization started in the Soviet Union, in Poland and Hungary. In the following years, however, the Czech Stalinists were obliged to compromise by relaxing censorship and travel restrictions. The police no longer dared to use torture and fabricated trials, and this led to greater activity on the part of the intellectuals and allowed men in charge of the nationalized industries to express more openly their criticism of the management of the economy. Life in general became more vocal: in particular the Party College, which educated the higher ranks of party officials, became a centre of highly critical social and political studies.

During 1967 Western observers became aware that President Novotný could no longer silence the students, writers, scientists and economists calling for reform, though he continued to try by all means short of arrests. Not this, however, but his failure to stop the economic decay and supply the goods required by the Soviet Union, combined with his reluctance to admit Soviet troops, brought about the end of his political career. This was sealed when Leonid Brezhnev, the Soviet Party chief, withdrew his support during the Party congress held in Prague in January 1968.

1968–1971

A combination of Czech economic reformers and Slovak federalists in the January 1968 Party congress toppled Novotný from his post of the Party's First Secretary, and, failing to agree on any of the stronger candidates, elected in his place Alexander Dubček.

Dubček had an open argument with Novotný whom he had accused in 1967 of taking an anti-Slovak line. He was little known outside Slovakia where he held the post of First Secretary in the Slovak Communist Party, and was believed to be a safe and docile Party byrocrat.

The general public took this to be no more than the replacement of a disgraced Communist leader by one who had a clean record, and a fundamental change in policy was not expected. The greater was the surprise when, contrary to custom, Dubček chose as the audience for his first public speech as First Secretary of the Communist Party not an assembly of workers but the national congress of collective farmers.

Dubček haltingly read a speech which was a bombshell, proposing nothing less than that in future the farmers should themselves decide what crops they wanted to cultivate and acknowledging that they knew more about such things than the central office of the Party. This humility and reasonableness was immediately recognized as an abdication of the 'leading role of the Party'. The speech, though ostensibly about agricultural policy, heralded a major change in the relationship between the Party and the rest of the population – in other words a change in the regime of the country.

During the following two months the Communist Party's change of heart enabled the country to return to sanity from the schizophrenic state in which it was generally accepted that people's private and public opinions were diametrically opposed. However, nothing irreversible was done and the liberal speeches could be, and indeed were, taken by many as a temporary expedient designed to restore the credibility of the Communist Party and enable it to disclaim responsibility for the economic disasters, purges, phoney trials, persecutions and executions of the past. Past experience of changes in the Party line justified the expectation that, after blowing off some steam, Dubček would gradually return things to the normality expected of a Soviet satellite.

But things went quite the opposite way, and very fast. Censorship was abolished and the past mistakes and crimes of the Communist Party were freely discussed and reported in detail. General Pavel, who had been kept in prison by Novotný for many years and had subsequently cultivated strawberries for years, was made Minister of the Interior. Members of the state police lived in fear of retribution.

Novotný, still clinging to the presidency after being deposed from the chief party office, was made to abdicate. Work on economic reform was speeded up with the aim of establishing a socialist market economy. At the same time the recognition grew that economic reforms could not be carried out without a major change in the political structure, that no economic levers could be really effective as long as the District Party Secretary remained supreme. The most revolutionary thing that could now be said aloud was that the economy of the country could not be regenerated as long as it was a subservient appendix of the Soviet economy. Contrary to views already spread at the time by Walter Ulbricht, the East German Party leader, there was not the slightest intention in Prague of leaning to West Germany. The unattainable ideal in everyone's mind, though never officially admitted for fear of Russian reaction, was for Czechoslovakia to have neutral status, perhaps as a socialist parallel to capitalist Austria.

By April it became abundantly clear that the events associated with Dubček were not a mere manoeuvre to gain popularity for the Communist Party in order to continue in the old policies. It is quite possible that some of those who endorsed the movement in January had nothing more than that in mind, and it is certain that this was the reason why Brezhnev allowed Novotný to fall. As the spring arrived, however, the politicians were faced with a national movement to rescue socialism from its deep rot and make it viable by bringing it into line with the democratic traditions of the country and with the freedom of initiative required for the running of a sophisticated industrial society.

For a while it appeared that the Soviet Union would accept these changes and profit from them in its relations with Communists and socialists in Western Europe. There was the vague possibility that because of Chinese revolutionary competition in the developing countries the Soviet Union might welcome the new permissive image it could gain by adopting a magnanimous attitude towards the Czech experiment.

Before April was out it was quite clear that the Soviet Union would not take up this option: on the contrary, Soviet pressure on the Czech party leadership increased dramatically. At the Communist summit meeting in Dresden, the Czechs were still able to ward off the holding of Soviet military exercises on Czech soil. In May the Russians massed their tanks on the Polish side of the Czechoslovak frontier. The Czechs answered by staging military exercises on the other side of the frontier, in Slovakia. This was their last defiant move.

Soviet army chiefs, Marshal Grechko, the Defence Minister and General Yepichev, started to work in parallel with Brezhnev and Kosygin, making use of their Warsaw Pact links with Czechoslovak army leaders and other key officers. It was at one of such meetings with Czech officers that Yepichev spelt out Soviet plans for an armed intervention. His statement, denied later by the Soviet news agency, started in the Czechoslovak army command a process of differentiation: the realists began to count the risks of associating themselves too clearly with a government which was opposing the Soviet Union with words but which hesitated to take any real measures of defence. They were confirmed in their doubts when in July, at a meeting with Soviet leaders in Čierná-nad-Tisou, on the Czechoslovak–Soviet frontier, Dubček dropped General Prchlik who demanded that the Warsaw Pact command should not be composed exclusively of Soviet officers. These initial vacillations made it quite impossible for Dubček to act decisively in the later stages. The Czechs made the Russians angry but did not convince them that they were ready to defend themselves.

In June the Party leadership yielded to Soviet threats and agreed to Warsaw Pact military exercises on Czech soil. They were nothing less than a preparatory operation for the invasion, to test roads for heavy tanks, select quarters for troops, and deploy Soviet signal units which then remained in the country.

The Prague reformists tried to gain time and mobilize support within the Warsaw Pact countries and in Yugoslavia. There were frequent meetings between Dubček and Kadar, the Hungarian Party chief, on the frontier separating Slovakia and Hungary. Tito visited Prague and so at the last minute did Romania's President Nicholae Ceausescu.

The Soviet Party leaders avoided as much as possible appearing in public as the initiators of ideological warfare against Czechoslovakia. This role was assigned to the East Germans and discharged by them with vigour but without much originality. The Party propagandists in Berlin, of whom many had made the grade serving Goebbels, reached for the old scripts of 1938 : in 1938 they invented stories about Soviet airports in Czechoslovakia; in 1968 the same people reported in *Neues Deutschland*, the Party newspaper, that American tanks were stationed near Prague. They even produced a picture – it was taken on the set of a war film being shot at that time in Zbraslav, south of Prague.

The Italian Communists, who had rebelled against Moscow before, were wishing well, and their leader, Lunghi, visited Prague and assured the reformists of moral support. The French Communists were of a divided mind, being financially dependent on Moscow but realizing how odious it would be to side openly against the Czechs. As a result *Humanité*, the French Communist newspaper, had in Prague during the summer of 1968 two correspondents, one presenting the Soviet view and the other reporting what was really happening in Czechoslovakia (see page 287).

It is not without significance that the strongest support for the reform movement came from Austria, northern Italy (where the Italian Communist Party was based), Yugoslavia, Hungary and Romania; that is from the former Habsburg Empire.

The situation offered great possibilities for improving Europe's security. Pressed by China, the Soviet Union was bound to attempt an improvement in its relations with the West. It was certainly in no mood to risk a war in Europe. The situation created by the Czechoslovak reformists opened up the possibility of extending the neutral zone northwards from Yugoslavia and Austria so that it could one day join in the north with the Scandinavian countries after a relaxation of the regime in East Germany. But even leaving East Germany out of the picture, there was the possibility of forming in Central and South-Eastern Europe a large bloc of countries committed to the preservation of peace and of the balance of power between the Soviet Union and Western Europe.

The neutralization of Czechoslovakia would not have affected any vital interests of the Soviet Union, though Russia was interested in preserving and strengthening its control of Central Europe so that it could start negotiations with the West from a position of greatest advantage, with sufficient reserves for the making of some concessions. In the absence of military resistance to the occupation of Czechoslovakia, the only argument against a hard line was regard for the feelings and future of Communist Parties in the West, particularly in Italy and France. But this had no great weight, because the Italian party was seen from Moscow as undisciplined and unreliable and the French party could probably be controlled by economic means whatever happened. Finally, Russian experience gained over centuries of oppressive rule led them to rely more on advancing the line of their own armies than on help from a fifth column behind the enemy lines.

The Soviet Union had also good reason to fear that the economic reforms proposed in Czechoslovakia would make it much more difficult to extort the tribute from that country. Reforms carried out earlier in East Germany, Poland and Hungary, and the proposals discussed in the Soviet Union consisted only of small improvements in the procedures and routines by which the economy responded to a multitude of political commands emanating from all levels of the Party hierarchy. The Czech reform proposals, however, were based on the recognition that there was little sense in introducing economic incentives as long as their effects could be overruled by political commands at every stage. As foreshadowed in Dubček's first public speech, the Czechs were indeed proposing to give up this type of leading role of the Party. This party control, however, provided the Soviet Union with massive supplies *à fond perdu*. The marshals of the Soviet Army command were directly concerned as the Czechs contributed so much to Soviet armaments and the military establishment.

The motives of Czechoslovakia in moving from total dependence on the Soviet Union to a somewhat neutral position, possibly reinforced by cooperation with Austria, Hungary, Romania and Yugoslavia, were evident. So were Soviet motives opposing this development. As for Western Europe, it is not known whether or not Western leaders saw the benefits for peace in Europe which could be derived from the success of the Czech reformists. They observed a guarded silence in public, and diplomatic archives will remain closed for some time yet. The domestic considerations of Western governments spoke against siding with the Czech reformists. Any open action in favour of Czechoslovakia would have met with opposition not only from the sectors allied to the Soviet Union by politics, ideology or business interests but from the right-wing sectors of European and American politics which did not wish the Czech reformists to succeed because this would have given impetus to a new socialist or Communist movement more acceptable and therefore politically more effective in advanced industrial countries with similar liberal traditions to those of Czechoslovakia.

Western countries were therefore of a divided mind about Czechoslovakia in more than one sense, while the Soviet Union had a single mind, recognizing that it was necessary to put a quick end to the experiment both for reasons of international politics and to remove a challenge to the supremacy of Party and Army. Above all, it wanted to move its army further west.

Though they were quite clear about what they wanted, the Russians proceeded with circumspection. They delivered warnings of impending action to Britain, France, the United States and West Germany and waited for indications that these warnings were accepted without protest. The Foreign Ministers of Britain, France and Germany, obliged with declarations that the Western powers had no intention of interfering in the affairs of the Warsaw Pact. This was all the Soviet Government needed to give Marshal Grechko the green light.

By a surprise attack on the night of 20–21 August, the Soviet Air Force obtained control of Prague Airport. During the same night a Soviet unit abducted to Moscow the four key men of Czechoslovakia: Alexander Dubček, First Secretary of the Party, Oldřich Černík, Prime Minister, Josef Smrkovský, chairman of the Parliament, and František Kriegl, chairman of the National Front. President Svoboda was at first interned in Prague Castle in the hope that he would appoint a Soviet-nominated government, which he refused to do, and so he too was taken to Moscow.

During the same night Soviet tanks moved swiftly from East Germany and Poland into Czechoslovakia so that in the morning hours the entire country was occupied and heavy tanks were fanning out towards the Western frontier. To make it clear that they wished to avoid friction with the Western powers the Soviets stopped their tanks fifty kilometres short of the frontier.

There was much speculation about what would have happened had the Czechs defended themselves. The extreme care the Soviet Union took not to arouse Western fears and to avoid all frontier incidents indicates that they were anxious to preserve normal relations with the West. The Czech leaders did not play on this Soviet scruple. Protracted fighting on Czech soil could have had unpredictable international consequences: the creation of a Central European Vietnam was not in the Soviet interest. In the case of a speedy defeat the Czechoslovak army, well equipped and extremely hostile to the Soviet Union, would have attempted to retreat to West Germany or Austria, or both – and N.A.T.O. powers could hardly have opened fire to keep them out. The presence of such an army in West Germany would have delayed more the East–West settlement so much desired by the Soviet Union.

Why, then, did not the Czechs resist, and above all, why did they make it so clear from the early spring that they never would? The people forming Dubček's brains trust were too much at home in the field of ideology and too little in the field of power politics – after all, like Dubček himself, these were men of a generation which knew no other political activity than the application of rules and directives received from above, be it a provincial capital, Prague, or Moscow. Primarily propagandists, they were much too quick in broadcasting their plans and much too slow in purging the army and police of Soviet agents. This was the ultimate reason for their failure. Having failed, the reformists further disgraced themselves by accepting Soviet terms and setting the country on the way 'back to normalcy', that is on the way back to subservience.

For some time, the reformists were allowed to talk. In a couple of years, however, they were removed and replaced by Soviet puppets, and not only were all the reforms given up but the country was brought to a course so strict and orthodox that by comparison the former Stalinist President, Novotný, appeared almost as a liberal.

The leading role in this process was assumed by Gustav Husák, a clever small-town lawyer and petty provincial politican who joined the Czech reformists because he hoped they would help him to accomplish the Slovak autonomists' programme in the framework of a federalized Czechoslovakia. Indeed the federalization of the country was completed only after occupation of the country by the Soviet Army and for some time this part of the reform continued to be official policy.

But by 1971 the last practical vestiges of federalization had been quietly buried. Husák himself lost interest in it when he discovered that in Soviet service he could be Number One in the whole of Czechoslovakia and no longer had any need of Slovak autonomy to fulfil his personal ambitions. He should not be judged too harshly. He is the kind of man whose personal ambitions make him believe that he serves his country by giving the occupying forces less power than the other man, kept by the Soviet as a permanent threat in reserve would give them if allowed to take his seat.

The tragic aspect of this for the Czechs and Slovaks is that the difference between *all* that the 'ultras' would give and *less than all* which the 'centrists' are giving grows always smaller.

Echoes in the West

The Munich agreement led to protests by those factions of the conservative parties in the West who did not believe that the dictators could be appeased. However, the public debate of the issue did not last long: the war came within a year and there was nothing more to discuss. If in 1938 the Left asked the searching questions and prodded conservative consciences on the Continent, in 1968 the whip was in the other hand: the suppression of the Communist reformation by the Soviet Union obliged the Communist parties to take a stand in the full view of those who maintained that, though claiming democratic privileges while in opposition, these parties would establish dictatorships once in power.

The questions asked by western Communists go beyond the rights and wrongs of the Czech events and touch on a problem more fundamental than that of Stalinism. Philosophers as well as many simple Party members are back to the basic question: can socialism and communism be really achieved and if so, then where and how? A man who joined the Communist Party in Germany almost fifty years ago, at the time when Lenin still expected that country to become the springboard of world revolution, told the author: 'It is wrong to blame Stalin. Socialism and communism can be achieved only by an advanced industrial society. An underdeveloped country could produce only an oriental despotism.'

This man, a highly successful executive who, true to his convictions, keeps for himself only what he consumes, leading a frugal and ascetic life, would probably be considered a 'leftist deviationist' by the professional Party bosses of today. But they too grapple with the same fundamental question. In Italy and France, Communist parties look to Czechoslovakia as the only country with an advanced industry and democratic traditions where Communists were in power. In 1968 both the Italian and French parties protested against the Soviet-led invasion, but their leaders differed about the subsequent 'normalization' of Czechoslovakia. The Italians rejected it while the French condoned it. By 1970 both were faced with breakaway groups which held contrary views.

The differences of opinion of course went back much earlier. A good while before the name of Dubček had been heard of outside his country, the Prague correspondent of the Italian Communist Party newspaper *Unita* was expelled for siding with the Czech 'progressive' reformist faction. And long before Roger Garaudy, formerly the Party's most orthodox philosopher, openly revolted, the split was apparent in the ranks of the French Party and in the minds of its members.

This split within the French Party was reflected by the difficulties *Humanité* the Party newspaper, had with its coverage of the 'Prague Spring'. Philippa Hentches, an Englishwoman, herself perhaps not entirely out of sympathy with the 'progressive', was closely linked through her husband to the pro-Soviet hard core of the French Party. Her despatches from Prague reflected the Soviet line so faithfully that *Humanité* felt obliged to send another man there to work with her and to secure a more balanced opinion.

During that time both Waldeck Rochet and Luigi Longo, then the French and the Italian Party leaders, visited Dubček in Prague, the Frenchman to dissuade him from his line of action, the Italian as I heard him saying at the time in Prague, to assure the Czechs of his Party's support.

The French Party later provided the Soviet-imposed Prague leadership with a record of Rochet's conversation and this caused a big stir in the Communist world in May 1970. The fact that it was used as 'evidence' against Dubček became the main point of a passionate indictment of the French Party's leadership by Garaudy. As a result – after 36 years of militant membership, 25 years in its Central Committee, the last 14 years spent in its steering body, the Politbureau – Garaudy was expelled from the Party.

There was, of course, more to the affair than the sending to Prague of a document which could convict Dubček of no more than what he repeatedly expressed in public speeches. More relevant to French politics was that Waldeck Rochet told Dubček on that occasion that political enemies must not be given freedom of expression and thus confirmed what anti-communists all the time have said about the Party: that once in power, it would forget all about freedom. Those who were worried by the Communist danger gave a sigh of relief: led by the mellowed Garaudy and professing a 'communism with a human face' the Party would have been a much more formidable enemy. The pro-Soviet stand assured the French Party apparatus of continued subsidies from Moscow but weakened its electoral appeal.

The Italian Party remains a formidable political force in its own country. Though this is due primarily to the much sharper social conflicts there and the need to counter a militant Catholic Church, the consistent rejection of despotic methods by the Party leadership is also a contributory factor. The Italian Party refused to rewrite history or to help to hunt down Dubček, but it has agreed to be silent, 'to preserve cooperation with the French Party in spite of different opinions'. At the French Party congress of February 1970 Giorgio Napolitano submitted to the humiliation of being called to speak only fourteenth, after representatives of smaller and less significant national parties, and to the cuts which eliminated from his speech any reference to Czechoslovakia.

The essence of the dispute, after all, is not the fate of Dubček, but that in the highly productive Western World, communism would hardly appear attractive if only promising increased output, even if such a promise were to be taken seriously. It could be attractive, it is argued, only if it offered the broad mass of workers not less but more freedom, a greater outlet for individual initiative and higher moral standards in a more humane society. This argument of Garaudy and the Italian Communists has been recently reinforced by the voice of a dead man, claiming that without this moral element communism cannot be achieved even where a Communist regime does succeed in increasing productivity.

The voice is that of Eugene Varga, who after the 1921 defeat of the Hungarian Soviet Republic, in which he was Commissar of Finance, lived in Moscow as a member of the Soviet Academy of Sciences and gained fame as economic adviser to the Kremlin. In essays written before his death in 1964, and published in Paris, he wrote, 'Communism is not only an increase in productive forces.' In his view the Soviet Union can never achieve communism without first giving up the use of despotic methods, which can only lead to a 'parody of communism'. The western Communists are now torn between allegiance to the Soviet Union, and the growing conviction that Varga's conclusions apply with an even greater force to the prospects of Communist parties in the West.

The economy of exploitation

In 1938 the German armament industry could not be expected to sustain great armies unless the workers drafted into them were replaced by others. Czechoslovakia, which was exporting armaments all over the world, had all the skills needed by the German war lords. Even before the occupation of the country, German banks were buying up Jewish industry with the help of the Živnobanka. After the occupation, the large armament and metalworking industry, Skoda, Brno Armament Works, Vitkovice, the electrical engineering factories of C.K.D. and Križík, and others were integrated into the German economic system, and largely became part of the Hermann Göring Werke. The formal independence of Slovakia did not stop the Hermann Göring Werke at the Slovak frontier. The new Skoda armament factories, built in Slovakia to be at a safer distance from the Germans, were also acquired for the German war machine.

By 1939 Germany could make use of Czechoslovakia to produce armaments for its armies for the Czechoslovaks were not to be drafted. Moreover for geographical and political reasons Czechoslovakia was never seriously bombed by the Allied air forces – the Slovakian factories were particularly valuable because they were completely out of reach of the British-based bomber fleets.

The Germans soon proceded to include the industry of Bohemia and Moravia in the network controlled by a system of horizontal over to Germans except for very small enterprises 'aryanized' by 'armament commissions'. Small and medium industry was left in Czech hands, unless it was Jewish-owned in which case it was turned over to Germans except for very small enterprises 'aryanized' by Czechs.

Agriculture was subjected to a strict procurement system and illicit sales were often punished by death. But a black market did exist and traffic between town and country relied on family ties – most town dwellers in Bohemia and Moravia have close relations on farms.

Towards the end of the war two economies existed in parallel: in one goods changed hands according to rules, quotas and rations at official prices; in the other there was a free circulation of goods and services at black-market prices among people who could trust each other. The black-market prices seemed staggering. But so were the incomes of some families, composed of 'official' earnings on farms and in factories feeding the German armies – plus payments obtained for underhand products and services at black-market prices.

The German war machine stripped the country of all reserves of raw materials, products and even household effects, including clothing, which was difficult to replace during the war. By 1945 the people were shabby, short of cigarettes, reduced to an inferior diet but not starving. Buildings, roads and public transport were in ill repair. Consumer-goods industries were obsolete and agriculture ran out of machinery. But the country was left with a greatly increased iron and steel industry, expanded metalworking industries and a new large chemical combine producing combustion engine fuel from alcohol supplied by the numerous distilleries.

This shift in the pattern of industry was continued further, in a negative way, after the war when the transfer of German population decimated the textile, glass, ceramics and domestic appliances industries. The larger companies were stripped of their labour force and many were run down, though some gradually reached their previous output. A very large number of medium and small enterprises, including many cottage industries, disappeared with the expelled German families on whom they completely depended.

The death of this small-scale industry and of the West Bohemian spas – which used to be great earners of hard currency – was further speeded up by the looting tolerated by the Government after the expulsion of the Germans. Every weekend, in 1946, one could observe streams of people carrying heavy bags and suitcases from the Prague railway stations. They were returning from an outing in the frontier regions. The more enterprising, if ready to leave home for some weeks or months, moved into the frontier areas, got appointed as 'national administrators' and sent home not suitcases but truck-loads of machinery, products, stocks and equipment from the factories and shops they were to administer, and stripped bare the hotels and restaurants of which they assumed temporary control.

The Communist-dominated National Committees which assumed power in those parts were composed of the same sort of scavengers and tried to justify the looting by an ideology produced for the purpose out of a real desire for national revenge and a pretended hostility to private ownership.

In 1949 fires started to break out each night, burning down the empty shells of houses and small factories. The official explanation was that this was the work of foreign agents. But these were never caught, though the fires burned with heartbreaking regularity every night. The obvious motive for the arson was to remove the evidence of the looting; the less obvious motive, private as well as political, was to make the expelled Germans less interested in returning. After a few years the fires ceased. Those who remained in the frontier districts, or had recently arrived, were there not to loot but to work and start new careers. The crofters' houses which survived were bought by towns people and turned with loving care into week-end cottages.

The destruction of small-scale industry, which was an accidental consequence of the Nazi occupation and war economy as well as of the subsequent transfer of the German population, was continued after the Communist takeover in 1948 as a matter of policy. The Soviet Union wanted from Czechoslovakia more and more steel and steel products. The systematic scrapping of perfectly useful machinery from small factories seemed to solve several problems: it increased the supply of scrap to the steel-works – badly needed to supplement poor Soviet ore, which moreover was slow in arriving; the elimination of small production units, often closely linked with small-town communities, made political control of workers and police control of managers easier; and, absurd as it sounds, the loss of the ability to continue exports to Western Europe and the United States, where many of the small, specialized enterprises had established business connections, was in the early fifties considered of great political advantage. The so-called dollar-offensive, an export drive designed to alleviate the foreign-exchange plight of the country, which the author proposed in a naive ignorance of Soviet economic aims in Czechoslovakia, was one of the counts on which Eugen Löbl, the

Communist head of the Ministry of Foreign Trade, was in 1952 sentenced to life imprisonment.

Unfortunately, human skills – the only economic resource of which Czechoslovakia had enough – were not harnessed for the new large steel mills and mammoth engineering factories that began mushrooming in the fifties. Instead, in 1949, the versatile and enterprising men and women, who previously had run small-scale industry as working owners or managers, began to be rounded up and sent to labour camps on the Bohemian uranium mines, which had been given to the Soviet Union in 'exchange' for the industry 'owned' by the Germans and which the Soviet Union claimed as its war booty. After two to four years they returned, and though they had never been tried or sentenced they remained branded as 'bourgeois elements'. They were rarely allowed to rise to positions where they could employ their inventiveness, skills and experience, and most of them were too embittered even to try.

On the higher level of management in industry, trade and finance, the first purge was carried out immediately after the liberation when many had to leave because they either had collaborated with the Germans or were accused of it. The second purge followed in 1948 when many old hands had to go, to be replaced by Communists or camp followers, and also some Jews who had survived the Nazi death camps or spent the war years in Britain or with the British Army in the Middle East and Africa, or served in the Czechoslovak unit of the Soviet Army.

Most of these fell victims to the third purge – in the early fifties. Not only those named in the 'trials of general managers' but scores of lesser people too were sent to prison where most remained until 1961. Some were rehabilitated but in most cases they were let out on a conditional remission of their sentence after having served ten years. Most of these last had joined the Communist Party during the war or immediately after, regarding it as a bulwark against the Fascists and Nazis who had decimated their friends and sent their families to death camps. The reason why men devoted to Communism had to be purged was their expertise and business sense. The economic policies which the Soviet Union planned for Czechoslovakia were a poor testimony to the ability of Soviet planners to grasp their own country's long-term interests. They were a blatant assassination of the advanced Czechoslovak economy.

Just as the Government of Klement Gottwald was ordered by Stalin to withdraw its application for economic aid under the Marshall Plan, the general managers received orders which they viewed as economically suicidal or quite impossible to carry out. Nor was it possible to replace these men by workers who knew something about their particular industry and had qualities of leadership. They would have only added to the 'obstinacy' of the experts a 'false solidarity' with their fellow workers whose lives and experiences they shared. Old Communists who could claim that the future of socialism was as near to their heart as to that of the Soviet experts were also not suitable.

In this situation the 'cadre department' of the Secretariat of the Party's Central Committee reached for people who could be trusted under all circumstances to carry out orders regardless of their own opinions and of the interests of workers under them.

It has been estimated that in the years 1949 to 1956 about a hundred thousand people were sent to prison camps for 'political reasons'. The Soviet experts, who displayed a genius for making one policy serve more than one purpose, did not want them in industry or agriculture but could make excellent use of them as forced labour in the uranium mines. There the Soviet Union not only exploited the greatest European uranium deposits without paying any compensation, royalties or taxes, but it also demanded and obtained priority supplies of mining equipment and building materials. And it turned the most skilled of the population into slaves.

Drastic as this aspect of Soviet economic policy in Czechoslovakia sounds, it was far from the most detrimental to that country's economic future. The greatest disaster was brought about by forcing the country to expand basic industries far in excess of its material and human resources. While any new industry was likely to increase the wealth of the semi-feudal Balkan countries, the problem was not so simple in Czechoslovakia. There industrial density was high, raw materials scarce and economic growth could be profitable only by making better use of the skill of the workers and by greater participation of the country in the world's trade.

This basic proposition was totally ignored by the planners, who insisted on pursuing policies which would make Czechoslovakia into an appendix of the Soviet economy: first, by forcing the country to develop its steel and heavy engineering industry out of all proportion to its resources and needs: and secondly, by imposing the curious system of economic management developed under Stalin to serve the rapid industrialization of the underdeveloped Soviet empire and maintain the power of the party bureaucratic pyramid of which he was the head. The combined effect of such distortions of the pattern of industry and management made Czechoslovakia into a machine shop processing Soviet raw materials on a cost-minus basis.

The disastrous results of this became apparent in the early 1960s, when the national income increment crashed to zero. In spite of various attempts to redress the balance by improving details, no improvement was made: the situation only became worse. Most capital resources had been invested in new steel works and heavy engineering factories and none remained for replacing obsolete machinery in the established industries or for building houses and roads and developing new science-based industries.

Life was becoming more difficult until ultimately the Czech worker had to work about four times as long as a British worker to buy a suit of clothing, five times as long to buy a sewing machine, and about six times as long to buy a motor-car, for which, moreover, he had to wait four to five years. Of far greater consequence, however, was the fact that no man could support a family alone: his wife also had to work. This, together with difficult shopping, absence of services, and an extreme housing shortage, has led to a severe depression of the birth rate. There were over 800,000 legal abortions in 1959–68, in a country which has a population of only 14 million. In the late sixties, in Prague, for example, the death rate exceeded the birth rate.

The need for restructuring the economy and for an improvement in its management was felt in Czechoslovakia all the more acutely because a gradual relaxation of foreign-travel restrictions enabled people to make comparisons with the West.

The system of central economic planning, which inspired many convinced socialists with great hopes prior to 1948, was in practice revealed to be a hopeless race of the planners to catch up with economic reality. Development did not take place according to plans but in day-to-day response – within the limits set by the availability of resources – to Soviet demands.

The annual economic plans are usually approved only belatedly in the spring, and none of the first four Five-Year Economic Plans could be completed because of changes in the international situation. The first was reversed in 1951 in favour of armament production and abandoned in 1953 when the Korean war ended. The second was completely revised in 1956 to fit Khrushchev's new Soviet economic policy. The third was shattered in its first year – 1960–61 – by the break with China. The fourth, up to the end of 1970, did not survive the combined effect of Soviet occupation in 1968, and of the new wind in East–West relations, which enabled the Soviet Union to switch many contracts to West Germany.

By 1967 the realization that without a radical change in economic targets, patterns of industry and methods of directing the economy, Czechoslovakia would sink to the level of a developing country penetrated all ranks of the Communist Party. Even ministers and members of the praesidium of the Central Committee saw the need of a reform, though not all were fully aware of the political and international consequences.

It is widely assumed that the Soviet Union opposed the proposals for economic reform associated with the name of Ota Šik because these could not be realized without emancipating managers from the day-to-day tutelage of Party officials and because this would have been a dangerous precedent for the entire Soviet bloc. But the Soviet Union had another, equally important reason for opposing the reform: it could not be combined with continued subsidies to the Soviet economy. The 'price scissors', the terms of trade with the Soviet Union not only worked against Czechoslovakia but, by Soviet design, Czechoslovak exports were constantly in surplus of imports from the Soviet Union. The proceeds of this surplus were not convertible and could not be used for purchases in other countries of the Soviet bloc. Every few years the balance accumulated on the Czechoslovak clearing account in Moscow was converted into 'investment' in Soviet industrial development – of non-ferrous metallurgy, or the Tjuman oil fields, for example – so that by 1967 Czechoslovak export proceeds frozen in the Soviet Union amounted to some $800 million.

The economic reform as proposed would have made this sort of trading impossible and this was one of the main reasons why the Soviet Union opposed it. Nothing can illustrate this clearer than the fact that one of the principal points of the capitulation signed by the kidnapped Czechoslovak leaders in Moscow in August 1968 was the promise that Czechoslovakia would participate in the development of Soviet gas fields and construction of pipe-lines by the supply of lorries, tubes and compressors and that it would construct at its own cost a peletization plant for the concentration of iron ore in Krivoi Rog, the Soviet iron-ore mining centre. Both these Soviet demands had been put off by Czech industry since 1967 with the argument that it could not further increase its financial contributions without collapsing into uncontrollable inflation at home and without incurring unrepayable debts in the West.

It is one of the ironies of history that after having occupied Czechoslovakia in 1968 the Soviet Union had to concede a temporary relaxation of its demands: the economic collapse was made worse by the presence of the Soviet army. The last interest in work disappeared with the consumer goods bought up by the Soviet Army commissariat wholesale and mopped up in retail stores by individual Soviet soldiers. This was perhaps what has triggered off a new Soviet appreciation of the potentialities of consumer-goods production in Czechoslovakia. Between 1938 and 1968 the occupying power's attitude seems to have travelled full circle.

Collaboration and intellectual genocide

A prisoner who begins to see himself with the eyes of his jailers and adopts their view of himself will sooner or later suffer a disintegration of his personality. Though one must be careful in drawing parallels between an individual and a nation, the same sort of identification with the occupying power can lead to the spiritual breakdown of a people.

On all three occasions in recent history when the Czechs fell under foreign domination, in 1938, in 1948 and again in 1968, the spiritual shock which they suffered was always composed of two elements: first, the feeling of having been betrayed by their allies; and second, the gnawing doubt whether the nation had not lost, or, at least, mortgaged its future, by giving up without an armed resistance. The two factors were not present always with the same intensity. The feeling of betrayal was most justified and also most intense at the time of Munich, when the country was kept in total ignorance of the gradual fading of the French involvement in Central Europe and relied, until the last minute, on the treaty of alliance with France and, on condition of its being honoured by France, also with the Soviet Union.

In 1948 this feeling of betrayal was much less intense, though not entirely absent. The liberal politicians pushed out were those who had spent the war with Beneš in Britain and who, in their outlook and politics, were clearly allied to the western-European concept of democratic government. Czech soldiers had fought in France and Czech airmen had played an important role in the Battle of Britain and, after all, the Potsdam treaty and other Allied agreements re-establishing an independent Czechoslovakia bore the signature of these powers.

In 1968 the West could not be reproached for anything. The Yalta division of Europe into an Eastern and a Western zone had been accepted. The Western powers neither initiated nor encouraged the reform movement in Czechoslovakia. Such feeling of 'betrayal' as there was could be only explained by an unrealistic expectation that the Western powers would do what the Czechs believed to be in their own interest.

As the element of betrayal gradually diminished in importance from the first to the third occasion, so the element of doubt, whether after all it would not have been better to die with arms in hand than to lead the life of a prisoner, steadily gained. If there was such a feeling after Munich, it was washed out by subsequent events and the policy of waiting for the great conflagration, chosen by Beneš, was fully vindicated by the results of the Second World War.

No such subsequent justification was available after 1948 and on this occasion the tactical weakness – even foolishness – of the liberal politicians, and the lack of resistance to the Communists as they took over on the factory floor and in offices was most evident – no doubt because most people were dispirited by the Nazi terror during the war.

In 1968 the feeling that much could have been saved by more resolute action and by taking to arms has even gained greater intensity after the events – partly because it became only later generally known how hard pressed were the Russians in the Far East, how eager they were to avoid conflict with the West, and also because

Romania, far from undergoing the same fate, succeeded in upholding a relatively independent policy.

The feeling of guilt and cowardice was all the more heightened by the unprecedented feeling of unity which the country achieved in 1968 and which survived long after the invasion. In 1938 the country was divided, some fearing the Communists more than the Germans; in 1948 the overwhelming majority wished to preserve a democratic way of life and had a good reason to fear a powerful Communist fifth column, by that time in control of the Army and of the police. In 1968 there was no such inner opposition which could have weakened or threatened a national resistance or even serve as an excuse for its absence after the event.

The absence of armed defence against the invader is primarily a collective failure and the resulting feeling is therefore much easier to bear than guilt resulting from collaboration with the enemy, for this is essentially composed of individual failures, misjudgements and misdeeds. Because individual guilt in this sphere can be detected with such uncomfortable ease, theories of a 'collective guilt' abound. Such a theory helps the collaborator to submerge his own individual feeling of guilt – to get 'lost' in the collective. When applied by one nation to another it serves very much the same purpose: when all Gemans are guilty, whatever their individual performance, it follows somehow in the muddled logic of the subconscious mind that all Czechs are innocent, whatever they did. Or all Englishmen, or all Frenchmen for that matter.

However, the fact that such theories serve a purpose does not exclude the possibility that they are sometimes genuinely believed. After 1945, few Czechs believed Germans who lived in the proximity of concentration camps when they asserted that they knew nothing about the horrors perpetrated on their doorsteps. When 1968 brought to light the methods of torture and the fabrication of trials, the executions and the suffering of the innocent and manipulation of the population and the mismanagement of the economy by governments in the service of a foreign power, and people learned about these things that had been happening at their own doorsteps, they recalled 1945 and began to doubt whether, after all, it was right to speak about a collective guilt of the Germans. Instead they became intensely preoccupied with the mechanics of collaboration. The problem was not so much of evil and asocial people, of the ambitious and greedy who try to better themselves by pushing their neighbour down, but rather about good and decent people who become accomplices in evil deeds.

The anatomy of collaboration shows that it is willed and urged by fanatics, that is by people who have no moral stand of their own and have to replace conscience by adherence to a creed, a club, a power. They have to cling to an outside concept in order to fulfil ambitions which they cannot satisfy in the ordinary way. Such hard-liners are always a small, easily detected group. The second much larger group of collaborators are 'good' men, in charge of operations, choosing at each step the path of the lesser evil – but still evil. If they are turning against their own countrymen it is because they know better what is good for their country. Finally there is the silent majority, who collaborate because they serve and obey. It is here that the rules of civilized society play havoc by identifying law with morals and by putting bureaucracy above human rights. Not only is an official order considered a sufficient exculpation for any deed but obedience to law can even become a perverted virtue in itself, supressing and overshadowing all other moral values. It represents the most favoured method for rationalization of collective aggressiveness, be it manifested by sending people to concentration camps or by self-sacrifice and suicidal devotion to duty.

In recent Czech history it is possible to establish a close parallel between the manipulation of the puppet regimes by the Germans and by the Soviet Union. In 1939 the Protectorate Government started by trying to resist the most outrageous demands of the occupying power. The same was attempted by Dubček after his release from temporary Soviet imprisonment and even by Husák later on. In each case the occupying power successfully manipulated the moderates into harsh actions by threatening to place the hard-liners in their place. This kind of bluff is, of course, rarely called. The occupying powers fears few things more than having to rely on a small group of hard-liners who they know would get very little cooperation from the population.

On the other hand, if the 'centrists' are left in charge, there is no end to the crimes they can make their compatriots perpetrate. Thus the Nazis made not only Czechs cooperate in the rounding up of Jews – even the elders of the Jewish communities were enlisted to ensure that the transports to the extermination camps proceeded in an orderly fashion. During the Communist period, many 'good' men helped the purges. This was achieved by a simple device: a factory, a local Government department, a professional organization was given a quota of people to be weeded out, which might mean sacking, sending to the mines or handing over to the security police as class enemies under the accusation of whatever happened to be the fashionable crime. The steering committee of the organization, or the man responsible for personnel matters knew that if they did not comply they would themselves be the victims. So they did comply, telling everybody that they saved ninety-eight good people by selecting two sacrificial lambs who were anyhow 'not much good', were spoiling things for everybody by working too hard, drinking too much or too little, were odd because they refused to sleep with the right person, or simply, and this was always a safe argument, were Jews.

However, there is also a hard core of men and women who save the nation from insanity by rejecting the occupying power's view of what it is or should be, the dissenters, and these are being perpetually bred in the intellectual stratum of the nation, and if the first generation living under occupation is too terrified, their children will not be and will lift their heads. For this reason the occupying power's first measure was to close the universities, in 1939 as in 1969, and to terrorize the intellectuals. After Hitler and Stalin the memory of concentration camps, torture and phoney trials makes it possible to operate with dismissals and threats alone. Even these can amount to intellectual genocide in a country so poor in raw materials and other resources that it depends for survival on its brains and skills.

Jan Palach's suicide by fire: the redemption of a Czech guilt-complex

On 16 January 1969 Jan Palach, student of history and political science at the Charles University, aged twenty-one, poured petrol over himself and set himself alight in Wenceslas Square in Prague.

The suicide, followed by at least twenty others in Czechoslovakia and elsewhere in Central Europe, received world-wide publicity as a political protest and as an indication of the despair of the young generation over the post-invasion developments. This overt meaning of the event can hardly explain the tidal wave of mass emotion which it released in the country and which at one point threatened to lead to a great popular outburst which could not have but ended tragically. It was felt by many at the time that something had snapped in the Czechs, and that never again would they be the same placid and restrained people that they were in the past. This cathartic effect of Palach's suicide suggests that there were forces at play which did not spring from the immediate political situation but from the deeper layers of national and social consciousness.

Let us first examine the immediate psychological climate preceeding the suicide. The defiant mood in which the country united to demand the return of its political leaders kidnapped by the Soviet Army in August 1968, was followed by a nation-wide depression as the rescued leadership started to sell to the population the promises it had made to the Soviet overlords and their further demands. The discarding of the liberal programme was not admitted, but everyone knew that it would never be put into effect. The economic situation deteriorated and, more important still, hope of its improvement vanished. No one was arrested by the Czech authorities but the Soviet Army started to make terror arrests, usually releasing the detainees fairly quickly but in a condition often requiring hospital treatment. There was a fear that such things would get worse with time. The almost complete freedom of travel achieved during the first half of 1968 was restricted severely and the Czechs had the feeling of being locked in with an armed and ruthless intruder.

In the first half of January there were rumours that the formerly progressive leadership had made important concessions to the Soviets at a meeting held in Kiev and that these would be enforced against the will of the population after the Central Committee meeting convened for 17 January. It was on the eve of this meeting that Palach committed his public suicide by fire. To attract the greatest possible attention, he was running to and fro in the shadow of the statue of St Václav. This statue had become the resistance shrine after the Soviet invasion though, ironically, Václav bought his peace from the German emperor by agreeing to pay him a yearly tribute – for which he was assassinated by his more independence-minded brother in 935.

A letter found on Palach's body stated that he was a member of a group of fifteen who had pledged to burn themselves, one every three days, as long as press censorship was not removed and no action was taken against a clandestine anti-reformist news-sheet purporting to be speaking for Czech Communists but in fact published by the Soviet Army. Several people have testified that Palach was a gifted and successful student, with a balanced personality and with no other but a political motive for his action. Yet the choice of the demands made under the threat of further suicides sounds irrational. True, at Soviet insistence the Government had introduced a sort of censorship, but at that time the newspapers, though restrained in form and avoiding any open criticism of the Soviet Union, still managed to express the opinions, feelings and demands of the population. Indeed the press was then much freer that it had been under President Novotný in 1967, when no voice was lifted in protest. As to the demands for the suppression of the Soviet propaganda sheet, this was hardly a matter of great importance. As the publisher was known, it could not influence anyone, and if it was read at all, then one could only laugh at its absurdities.

It seems therefore that Palach's demands were only of symbolic significance and that the Government was not the real addressee of his protest. Like other young people at the time, he feared that the country was slipping into indifference and his suicide was in order to generate the counter-pressure which would enable the Government to resist the mounting Soviet demands.

The motives of the young people who decided to protest in such a horrible and heart-rending way sprang, no doubt, out of helplessness, unwillingness to live without freedom, a passionate desire to do a great deed, a feeling perhaps, nourished by fashionable existentialist philosophy, that suicide is the only real action. Much more difficult to explain is the immediate reaction of the population, young and old, and the power of the spell which emanated from the event far beyond the country's frontiers – to Hungary and Italy, where Jan Palach found followers.

If we take a close look at contemporary reports we can see that the doctor who was called immediately after the event was still un-affected by the mass psychosis which followed. He said (and this was broadcast over Prague radio): 'It was a pathological act'. But already during the same radio-report a student, though not yet denying the pathology of the act, had made the first attempt to give it a general significance. He said, 'By a distorted act Palach presented a distorted mirror to a distorted time.'

In the course of a few hours it became clear that the horror evoked by the act had a very strong ingredient of self-identification, and made people demonstrate their feelings in a strongly compulsive way. The Government knew that it could not dismiss the event as the regrettable act of an unbalanced mind. This would have outraged not only students but also workers, and a national congress of the trade-union movement was about to take place at that time.

In this situation a remarkable sequence of events could be observed. A Government completely dependent on Soviet tolerance and approval paid homage to an act which was manifestly a protest against the Soviet presence in Czechoslovakia. The head of state, the head of government, the First Secretary of the Communist Party, all sent condolences to the unhappy mother and were followed by the establishment and by all organizations, social and economic, as well as thousands of individuals. The decision that Palach should be buried at the Slavin cemetery, reserved for the great men of the country, was cancelled under Soviet pressure only at the last minute. Even so, he was given a national funeral, with the Týn bells tolling and all public transport in Prague ordered to stand still. It was attended by half a million people and became a solemn, silent demonstration of grief such as the country had not expressed since the death of its founder-president, Tomáš Masaryk in 1937.

The body lay in state in the Charles University courtyard under the statue of Jan Huss, the dissenter whose burning at the stake in 1415 was the signal for an uprising and a bloody war the Czechs fought for eighteen years against the Catholic powers in Europe. The connection between Jan Huss and Jan Palach was stressed loudly, as are protestations designed to conceal the real truth. For there is a very important difference between Huss and Palach. The first was a fighter who had a great academic and political career behind him and who did not want to die. He was condemned to be burnt because he did not recant his convictions as the Catholic Church demanded. Jan Palach, on the other hand, was a man who never had a chance of fighting for anything, who had not yet done much in his life and from whom no one had demanded that he should give up his convictions. It might seem more natural that a young man, ready to give up his life for a cause, would want to give it up fighting and make the adversary pay dearly for it.

If Palach and those who followed him did not fight, this has perhaps something to do with the national experience of reprisals after the assassination of the German Protector Heydrich. The Germans felt insufficiently revenged by the death of the young boys and began mass arrests, shooting every tenth person and selecting the villages of Lidice and Ležáky for burning down and a complete massacre of its male population. Palach and the students who joined him must have had in their minds the possibility that their acts could release a similar wave of terror against people whom they did not and could not consult. If this was indeed their line of thought one can understand that they saw public self-sacrifice as the only means of stirring the masses into more active resistance and of instilling more courage into the Government.

The assumption that the act was directed more against cowardice in the Czech ranks than against the enemy – an explanation so painful as to be unmentionable – seems to be also supported by a well-known historical precedent, the subject of a play by Josef Medek, that used to be staged frequently up to 1945. This studiously ignored precedent was the suicide of Colonel Švec, the commander of an armoured train of the Czech legions who fought their way through Communist-controlled Siberia to Vladivostok in 1917 and 1918. Faced with the demoralization of his men under the influence of Communist sympathizers, Colonel Švec shot himself, leaving a letter which helped to restore fighting spirit to the Army spread along the many thousands of miles of the trans-Siberian railway. However, this historical resonance, though important enough to be suppressed, cannot explain sufficiently the lightning speed with which the entire country identified itself with the young man and the fact that no one dared to condemn the suicide on religious, rational or political grounds.

A better clue is provided by the strong emphasis placed by the Czechs on the sacrificial–salvationist aspect of the event. 'Jan Palach gave his life for us – we must live up to his sacrifice' was the recurrent theme of all writers and public speakers, meaning the familiar: he gave his life so that we can live and have our salvation if we remain true to his spirit. This is, of course, poor logic, but a time-honoured one.

To understand this salvationist mass-explosion triggered by the sacrificial death of the young man one has to know the basic trauma of the Czechs, who since the religious wars of the fifteenth century have never really taken up arms in defence of their own freedom. The Protestant towns made a slight attempt in 1547 to join hands with the German Protestants in their fight against the Catholic Church and the Habsburgs, but they came too late and were betrayed by the barons. In 1618 the barons revolted but the towns no longer trusted them and the war was lost in a single skirmish lasting two hours. There followed 300 years of foreign rule. Though Czechs and Slovaks crossed the lines and fought on the side of the Allies, those at home did not revolt and were given their independence in 1918, when the victorious Allies approved the disintegration of Austro–Hungary.

President Beneš refused to lead the country into national suicide in 1938, and to fight Hitler alone after the four Western powers reached an agreement in Munich. The Czechs remained largely impassive and some of them even helped when first Hitler and then Stalin drove their compatriots to concentration camps and death. The Dubček leadership also feared a suicidal war when the Soviet Army marched in on 21 August 1968, it was the second army of occupation admitted without armed resistance. Both in 1938 and again in 1968 the Czechs were left with a bitter taste in their mouths, an irrational feeling of guilt for having given preference to reason over a deeper-seated instinct that when attacked one must fight back.

The subconscious significance of Jan Palach's death for the Czechs seems to be that of a human sacrifice. By his suicide he seems to have redeemed the guilt-feeling of a nation which preferred humiliation and survival to heroism and death twice in its recent history. By appeasing the feeling of humiliation, Jan Palach's suicide had, no doubt, a restraining, conservative effect. But as in every drama, so here, though the tragic outcome appeases remorse, the example stirs. Few Czechs will in future feel the daily discomforts, disadvantages and dangers resulting from passive resistance to be quite as important as they seemed to them before they could be compared with the self-sacrifice of an innocent, noble-minded young man.

Only the future will show whether the cathartic effect of the drama enacted by Jan Palach, and of all the tragic events of 1968 and after, will last and influence the course of history.

Index

Index

ek, Master, mathematician, 51

Karl of Habsburg, see Charles I

'Karlín Boys', 183, 187, 188, 189; i.e. Klement Gottwald, Rudolf Slánský, Václav Kopecký

Karoly, Count, Hungarian Prime Minister, 157

Kaunitz, Prince (Kounic, Václav Antonín), 79, 80

Keitel, Wilhelm, Field Marshal, 259

Kelsen, Professor Hans, jurist, 164

Keppler, Johannes, astronomer, 51

Kerensky, Russian Prime Minister, 132

Khruschev, Nikita, 277, 295

Kisch, Egon Ervin, journalist, 244

Kladsko, Duchy of, 81

Klofáč, Václav Jaroslav, politician, 108, 129, 145, 147

Kohn, Jindřich, philosopher and lawyer, 251

Kollár, Jan, poet, 93, 94, 112, 197

Koltchak, Russian Admiral, 152

Komenský, Jan Ámos – see Comenius

Kompaktata, 41, 44

Koniáš, Antonín, inquisitor, 69, 72

Kopecký, Václav, Communist leader, 183, 187, 189

Korean War, 295

Kosmas, chronicler, 28

Kozina, Jan, leader of the Chods, 75

Kralická Bible, 43, 69, 88, 196

Královec (Konigsberg), 18

Kramář, Karel, Prime Minister, 106, 123, 124, 127, 129, 145, 147, 148, 151–154, 168, 172, 240

Kramerius, Václav M., publisher and journalist, 93

Kreibich, Karl, Communist politician, 179, 183

Krejčí, Ludvík, General (C-in-C), 266

Kriegl, František, politician, 284

Krivoi Rog, 296

Krofta, Kamil, Foreign Minister, 259

Krosnár, Josef, Communist politician, 189

Kun, Bela, Hungarian Communist, 145, 158, 187

Kuunsinen, Otto, Finnish Communist, 187

1